Information Age Economy

Information Age Economy

F. Rose
The Economics, Concept, and Design
of Information Intermediaries
1999, ISBN 3-7908-1168-8

S. Weber
Information Technology in Supplier Network
2001, ISBN 3-7908-1395-8

K. Geihs, W. König and F. von Westarp (Eds.)
Networks
2002, ISBN 3-7908-1449-0

F. von Westarp
Modeling Software Markets
2003, ISBN 3-7908-0009-0

D. Kundisch
New Strategies for Financial Services Firms
2003, ISBN 3-7908-0066-X

Tim Weitzel

Economics of Standards in Information Networks

With 110 Figures
and 70 Tables

Physica-Verlag
A Springer-Verlag Company

Dr. Tim Weitzel
University of Frankfurt
Institute of Information Systems
Mertonstraße 17
60054 Frankfurt (Main), Germany

ISBN 3-7908-0076-7 Physica-Verlag Heidelberg New York

Cataloging-in-Publication Data applied for
A catalog record for this book is available from the Library of Congress.

Bibliographic information published by Die Deutsche Bibliothek
Die Deutsche Bibliothek lists this publication in the Deutsche Nationalbibliografie; detailed
bibliographic data is available in the Internet at *http://dnb.ddb.de.*

Physica-Verlag Heidelberg New York
a member of BertelsmannSpringer Science + Business Media GmbH

http://www.springer.de
© Physica-Verlag Heidelberg 2004
Printed in Germany

Cover design: Erich Kirchner, Heidelberg

SPIN 10932117   88/3130-5 4 3 2 1 0 – Printed on acid-free paper

Felix qui potuit rerum cognoscere causas
Vergil (70-19 BC), Georgica: 2, 490

Happy the one who is able to know the underlying cause of things

„No theory in economics is ever exactly true.
The important question is not whether or not a theory is true
but whether it offers a useful insight in explaining an economic phenomenon"
Hal Varian (1989)

Foreword

Compatibility and thereby the associated role of standards are a core Information Systems research domain. Since standards constitute networks, standardization is a predominant issue in IS and economic research as well as in corporate reality that too often suffers from a lack of understanding and sophistication. Network as a widespread metaphor describes structures of interrelated elements as e.g. in corporate Intranets, supply chains, economies or other social systems. Expected network benefits result from improved coordination designs and generally include - depending on the particular problem domain - optimized business processes, more advantageous allocations, enhanced availability of information and other resources as well as decreased information costs or increased revenues.

But even when focusing on information and communication (ICT) networks, the dynamics governing these networks are not yet sufficiently understood. Inherent in networks, the commonality property of network agents deriving from the need for compatibility implies coordination problems. From a theoretical perspective, the existence of network effects as a form of externality renders efficient neoclassical solutions improbable. The externality property deriving from network effects (and thus the multifaceted dynamics behind diffusion processes in networks) challenges traditional economic theories. Examples include monopoly and policy issues, societal infrastructures and market efficiency. From a practical perspective, a virulent lack of theoretically sound and yet applicable methods for controlling networks leaves substantial efficiency potentials unused. Examples include software vendor strategies as well as integration and standardization problems in business networks. Accordingly, a key challenge is to propose a theoretical foundation for ICT network analysis. Since there is literally no area in the social and economic world unaffected by the recent advancements of ICT, a relevant network theory needs to pursue an interdisciplinary research approach.

The thesis of Tim Weitzel aims at exactly this. Extending a research framework originally rooted in economic equilibrium analysis by interdisciplinary elements and the research paradigm of agent-based computational economics, in this work an important building block to a theory of networks is developed that addresses the complex mutual feedback between microstructure and macrostructure that has long been discussed in economics, e.g. 1948 by F. A. v. Hayek (Individualism and Economic Order).

In this work, Tim Weitzel develops a standardization framework that incorporates many singular network determinants and findings from network effects theory into a single research approach. The framework is rooted in a game theoretical network equilibrium analysis. To cope with the massive complexity of the standardization problem given raise to by the evolving information sets and decisions sequences of the network agents, the author employs computer simulations to enable the creation of a virtual laboratory. Using this joint approach, many findings from traditional network effect theory can be described as special cases of the model at particular parameter constellations. Based upon this, solution strategies for standardization problems are developed, and a methodological path towards a unified theory of networks is proposed.

The author builds his work on a critique of traditional network effect theory, focusing on decentralized solutions to standardization problems which have found only slight attention in most parts of the literature so far. A game theoretic equilibrium analysis, which is the foundation for the standardization framework, reveals the implications of standardization decisions not only on the extent to which compatibility can be achieved but also on the informational environment of all agents.

This book is an impressive contribution to the theory of standardization. The research results of Tim Weitzel presented here provide an important building block to a more sophisticated theory of standards and networks and offer valuable solution concepts to this important research domain.

The dispersion of information networks makes the topic of this work predominantly important, touching many aspects of our individual, corporate and social life. There are many examples of standardization problems, ranging from document management systems and corporate directories to supply chains, and generally any kind of communication. There is almost always the trade-off between centrally and decentrally selecting and implementing standards. The challenge results from the reciprocity of local and global phenomena: local efficiency cannot sufficiently be analyzed independent of macro-effects like especially network effects. Hence, as provided in the book, decision support models have to incorporate not only the local determinants of standardization processes but also the global diffusion effects and their dynamics. Also, conditions for equilibria and standardization paths need to be considered to explain system behaviour under network effects and to eventually contribute to a methodological foundation for a future theory of networks as proposed in section 6 of this book.

The research work is rooted in economic and game theory and extends important findings in the literature towards a standardization and network theory in a fundamental and original way. The research strategy as well as the methodological scope and the systematic interpretations are exceptionally sophisticated. Hopefully, this book will contribute to the growing and significantly important research domain. Or, as the First Governor General of India, Shri C. Rajagopalachari, started his inaugural address at the Conference on Standardization and Quality Control in Calcutta in 1948: "standards are to the industry as culture is to society".

Prof. Dr. Wolfgang König

Preface

In 1997, scientists from disciplines as diverse as Computer Science, Economics, Geography, Information Systems, Labor Sciences, Law and Legal Sciences, Political Sciences and Sociology set out to lay the foundation for a common theory of networks. The research project "Networks as a competitive advantage and the example of the Rhine-Main-Region" (SFB 403) at J. W. Goethe-University was funded by the German National Science Foundation (DFG) from 1997 until 2000.

In these three and a half years, we faced the challenge of interdisciplinarity, i. e. the striving for a common goal amongst most diverse individuals and scientific disciplines. The objective was to gain a deeper understanding of the mechanisms behind social, economic, technical and other kinds of networks. Based upon a mutual understanding of both the diversity of the network metaphor(s) as well as their common properties, a unified theory of networks should guide public and private decisions concerning the planning, operations and controlling of different kinds of networks and contribute to a responsible and efficient development of state-of-the-art networks.

The enormous impetus of new technologies pointing to a "network society" made us agree on pursuing an interdisciplinary research approach as an adequate means of incorporating the expectation that there is literally no area in the social and economic world unaffected by the recent advancements of information and communication technologies and their application to real world problems.

While on an abstract level the project's pace was driven by the common belief in the necessity of a common (even unified) theory of networks, it was slowed down by the need to identify mutually agreed starting points as well as particular homogeneous research goals. Research approaches turned out to be substantially different between the participating disciplines. Fundamental positions on the transferability of utility, the possibility of micro-models or the extent to which individual decision making is (solely?) dependent upon the institutional embeddedness of the deciding agents slowed down the process.

One of eleven subprojects was called B3 "*Economics of Standards in Information Networks*". From 1997 until 2000, the main focus of the research project was

  ▸ to find theoretical contributions explaining standardization processes in networks and supporting corporate standardization decisions,

  ▸ to identify the drawbacks of traditional theories about network effects,

  ▸ to gather empirical data about the use of IT standards such as EDI, office software or standard software and

  ▸ to develop simulation models describing the decision behavior of actors (users as well as vendors) when network effects exist as a foundation for deriving and evaluating internalization strategies.

X

The results of this project are the core of two dissertation theses, one of them being this book, the other Westarp (2003). A summary of the results and many articles covering the topic can be found at http://www.vernetzung.de/eng/b3/. Particular results from all the different disciplines are documented in many articles (www.vernetzung.de/eng). As a whole, they ought to provide a broad platform of a variety of views about networks and define a methodological path for further research.

Among the main outcomes of our subproject are two simulation models: one describing the way *technology users* decide which standard to use and providing a first-best standardization solution for any given network (developed in this work); the other describing the diffusion of technological innovations from a *vendor's viewpoint* and providing a basis for deriving pricing strategies in software markets [Westarp 2003]. In this work, based upon an analysis of network effect theory and some of its deficiencies for both the theory and practice of standardization, a standardization framework is developed, and these two models are merged, combining the consideration of anticipatory decision behavior in our standardization model with a consideration of the topological properties of networks as described in our diffusion model.

The author's sincerest thanks are due to many friends and colleagues at the Institute of Information Systems. Particular mention must, however, be made of the assistance given by Daniel Beimborn for his sophisticated contributions and nightlong work on programming some of the simulations, and of the endless discussions and writing papers with Dr. Falk v. Westarp and Dr. Oliver Wendt that proved to be both highly instructive and valuable as well as great fun. I am also very grateful to Professor Dr. Wolfgang König for providing an extraordinary research environment and for stimulating discussions and to Prof. Dr. Müller for his very instructive support.

The author is indebted to the German National Science Foundation for funding the project and also for funding the follow-up project "IT standards and networks" that emerged from it as proposed in section 7.

Dr. Tim Weitzel

Table of contents

1 Introduction

"The good thing about standards is
that there are so many to choose from"
(A. Tanenbaum)

The good thing about standards is that there are so many to choose from. But which one should one adopt?

Standards play a prominent role in many systems that are characterized by interaction or interrelatedness. In information systems such as software environments or Intranets standards provide for compatibility and are a prerequisite for collaboration benefits [Besen/Farrell 1994, 117; Gabel 1987, 94]. More generally speaking, standards can constitute networks. *"Network"* is increasingly used as a metaphor to describe a set of means of cooperation designs between agents aiming at exploiting common synergies or more precisely network effects. The semantics of networks are very vague and even limiting the scope to "information networks" still includes supply chains, the "network" of users of certain software products, corporate intra- and extranets or more generally information infrastructures. Expected benefits result from improved coordination designs and generally include - depending on the particular problem domain - optimized business processes, more advantageous allocations, enhanced availability of information and other resources as well as decreased information costs or increased revenues [Braunstein/White 1995; Kleinemeyer 1998, 63; Picot/Neuburger/Niggl 1993]. Since networks are based upon standards, decisions about standards are a key factor in building information infrastructures (networks).

Inherent in standards, the commonality property deriving from the need for compatibility implies coordination problems. From a theoretical perspective, the existence of network effects as a form of externality that is often associated with communication standards renders efficient neo-classical solutions improbable. The externality property deriving from network effects (and thus the multifaceted dynamics behind the diffusion processes of standards) makes standardization problems somewhat complex and interesting to solve.

In this work, a standardization framework based on an analysis of deficiencies of network effect theory and a game theoretic network equilibrium analysis is developed, identifying fundamental determinants of diffusion processes in networks (e.g. price, network topology and density, number of alternative technologies, agent size and choice sequence, installed base effects) and incorporating them into a computer-based simulation model showing different possible system behaviors (e.g. particular diffusion paths) for standards in networks. The framework tries to contribute to the ongoing discussion about the implications of increasing returns industries and to discuss possible theoretical, policy and managerial implications.

1.1   Standards in Information Systems

"The good thing about standards is that there are so many of them,
every one can have one of their own"
http://www.chipcenter.com/circuitcellar/august99/c89r6.htm

Networks rely on network agents' capability to work together in the sense of exchanging information. The use of common standards generally makes possible or simplifies transactions carried out between actors or eases the exchange of information between them [Braunstein/White 1985]. Examples are DNA, natural languages and currency or metric standards as well as communication protocols (IP, TCP, HTTP) and syntactic and semantic standards such as XML and EDI. In the context of information and communication systems *compatibility* is important [Gabel 1987, 94]: many different computer networks, operating systems, user surfaces, and application systems have evolved in companies over a number of years. One of the major drawbacks of this heterogeneous legacy is the fact that there is no seamless integration of different data and applications. Recently, this has been discussed in the context of Electronic Business and Enterprise Application Integration (EAI) focusing on the integration of all actors in a value chain. Prominent examples are the various incompatible Electronic Data Interchange (EDI, see section 5.1.4) standards and efforts aimed at the introduction of Web-based EDI or XML/EDI. While the (opportunity) costs of a lack of integration are hard to approximate, OAG estimates that IT companies spend at least 40% of their IT budgets on integration [OAG 1999, 4] or, in a broader sense, on network engineering.

As a consequence, corporate information management is increasingly occupied with coordinating standardization decisions as a basis for information and communication infrastructures. These decisions have to deal with numerous problems. First, of course, the existence of network effects makes decisions by otherwise possibly autonomous agents interdependent. The ultimate decision quality is thereby not only the result of individual decisions but is strongly determined by the decisions of others. Hence a major uncertainty to be dealt with concerns the standardization behavior of communication partners. Second, there might be additional uncertainty about the costs and benefits associated with the implementation of standards or future application flexibility. In this work, the focus is on the first kind of uncertainty. The second kind is discussed in section 5 and the literature review in section 2.

Depending on the institutional settings of the deciding agents, standardization decisions can, principally, be centrally coordinated or they can be decentralized as, for example, in sovereign business units with autonomous IT budgets. Besides incomplete information about others' behavior, the source of the coordination problem associated with standardization decisions is an asymmetry between the costs and benefits resulting from standardization. This constellation (together with the frequent underestimation of potential savings) is often regarded as being responsible for a very (s)low propensity to standardize. In corporate reality, this *aggressive awaiting* is an often-witnessed strategy of agents trying to avoid the risk of being the first - and possibly only - adopter of a new technology that then does not offer enough benefits to compensate for the costs.

Thus there are possible conflicts and coordination problems when deciding about standards. An important finding is the existence of a standardization gap: although there are considerable potential savings from standardization these are not achieved [Buxmann/Weitzel/König 1999]. In other words, there are situations when, although there are advantages from an aggregate (even decentralized) perspective, no common information infrastructure will emerge in a decentralized network. A prominent example is the failure of EDI to cover more than small parts of value chains leading to significant efficiency potentials in supply chains that remain unrealized, others are the many corporate and (partly) redundant but incompatible directories (section 5.3), document and knowledge management systems, security infrastructures or office software [Westarp 2003].

The prevalent role of network effects in modern high-tech industries makes standardization a relevant topic of research. At the same time, the influence of those technologies on basically all areas of economic, public, and private life makes an interdisciplinary perspective inevitable. The externality property associated with network effects disturbs the automatic transmission from local to global efficiency implying welfare questions. Still, dynamics in networks result from many different influences. Since network problems often comprise coordination problems of information infrastructures and allocation and require state-of-the-art methods of copying with complex system dynamics, developing contributions to a network effect theory is within the purview of the discipline of information systems. Recent trends of trying to bridge theoretical gaps or blind spots by integrating the findings of other scientific disciplines contribute to the role of IS in establishing a sound theory of (social, economic) networks.

1.2 Motivation and research questions

> "The good thing about standards:
> There are so many of them"
> *http://www.advisor.com/Articles.nsf/aid/MEB0011NW*

The theoretical relevance of the standardization problem is fundamental in that it addresses the general coordination problem behind systems subject to demand side positive externalities. Examples from numerous industries have been presented [Westarp/Weitzel/Buxmann/König 2000].

Although the implications of the existence of network effects (of which the standardization problem is a perfect problem instance) might be vast, they have only attracted moderate attention so far. It was only in 1985 that contributions to what will be called a theory of positive networks effects started to systematically analyze phenomena in information networks.

While the traditional models contributed greatly to the understanding of a wide variety of particular problems associated with the diffusion of standards, they failed to explain the diversity of diffusion courses in today's dynamic information and communication technology markets [Westarp 2003]. Additionally, almost all contributions deal with standardization problems from a technology vendor's perspective, and there are only a few contributions which aim at supporting standardization decisions on the individual user's level. The examination of network effects is made in a rather general way, which does not cover the heterogeneous properties of the markets with products such as office software, Internet browsers, or EDI-solutions. Furthermore, the specific interaction of potential adopters within their personal socio-economical environment and the potential decentralized coordination of network efficiency are neglected. As a result, important phenomena of modern network effect markets such as the coexistence of different products despite strong network effects, the appearance of small but stable clusters of users of a certain solution despite the fact that the competition dominates the rest of the market or the fact that strong players in communication networks force other participants to use a certain solution cannot be sufficiently explained by the existing approaches.

Apart from the economic importance of markets said to be subject to network effects (e.g. the software market: $114 billion [WITSA 1998] to $300 billion dollars [Gröhn 1999, 23] in 1997) the methodological deficiencies of the neo-classical paradigm make standardization a relevant research domain. The externality property of network effects still needs to find adequate consideration in models trying to reap network benefits.

In contrast to focusing on macroeconomic public policy implications as in large parts of the literature, the goal in this work is to use and extend already elaborated theoretical findings to support individual decision processes associated with the diffusion of standards while incorporating the mutual dependencies of micro- and macroeffects characteristic of networks. We propose the hypothesis that assumptions and simplifications implicitly and uncritically used for modeling standardization problems inevitably lead to the described results such as market failure under network effects and that the analysis of the diffusion of standards needs to be extended in order to capture real world phenomena descriptively and be actionable.

The **overall goal** of this research work is thus to get a more subtle understanding of standardization processes in information networks, analyze individual as well as overall efficiency and welfare implications and derive solution proposals.

The main **theoretical goal** is to congregate existing theoretical approaches towards standardization problems, identify deficiencies in terms of their explanatory power and their applicability to real world problems, and develop a catalogue of requirements, proposing how future research methodology and practice in this area might advance. It will be shown that many traditional findings are special cases of the proposed standardization framework that is used to learn about network behavior and its determinates.

The main **practical goal** is to develop a framework that will be applicable and provide some guidance in deciding on corporate standardization problems.

In particular, the following research questions form the scope of the work:

- ▸ What are the determinants of standardization processes in information networks?

- ▸ What are the typical phenomena of technology diffusion in networks and how can they be explained (section 2)?

- ▸ What are possible equilibria in standardization processes (sections 3 and 4)?

- ▸ What are the diffusion patterns of standards and what are the determinants of their paths (section 4)?

- ▸ How can corporate and governmental standardization decisions be supported (section 5)?

- ▸ What are theoretical requirements for understanding systems subject to increasing returns as a methodological foundation for a future theory of networks (sections 2 and 6)?

1.3   Structure of the thesis

"The computer industry loves standards;
it has a million of them."
http://www.nap.edu/html/whitepapers/ch-56.html

The structure of this thesis is as follows: Section 2 offers a brief overview of the history (and theories) of standards. We show that the theory of network effects has been developed and used to explain important aspects of diffusion processes of standards. To get a subtle understanding of systems subject to network effects and to identify requirements for the standardization framework in sections 3 and 4, we show how this work is based on previous work on the way markets select network goods such as technology innovations or especially communication standards. The general findings of traditional approaches concerning network effects are identified (2.2). Section 2.3 identifies drawbacks of traditional approaches to network effects and recognizes areas requiring improvement. These are a foundation for the standardization model presented in sections 3 and 4 and for solution proposals and discussing managerial, policy, and theory implications in sections 5 and 6.

Based upon the findings and requirements of section 2, in section 3 a model for standardization decisions is developed and used to understand determinants of diffusion processes of standards in centrally and decentrally coordinated networks (3.1). Different possible equilibria for the alternative institutional settings are compared and discussed using basic game theory (3.2 and 3.3).

6

Next, in section 4, a computer-based simulation model of agents deciding on the use of standards is developed (4.1). First, fundamental phenomena are analyzed using a basic model with a simple standardization yes/no decision situation (4.2). For different standardization costs, the existence and efficiency of possible equilibria are analyzed with respect to the number of periods, the agents' decision sequence, network size, network structure and density, installed bases, and agent size. In section 4.3. the model is extended to capture multi-standard decisions as well, i.e. the selection between different standards. Again, diffusion patterns are analyzed as in the previous basic model. These sections are organized correspondingly, for example agent size for the basic and extended model are analyzed in sections 4.2.5 and 4.3.5 or installed base effects in sections 4.2.7 and 4.3.7. In section 4.4 the implications of using a different decision calculus are investigated, and in section 4.5 the standardization model is fully integrated with the relational diffusion model of Westarp/Wendt that has also been developed within the research project "Economics of Standards".

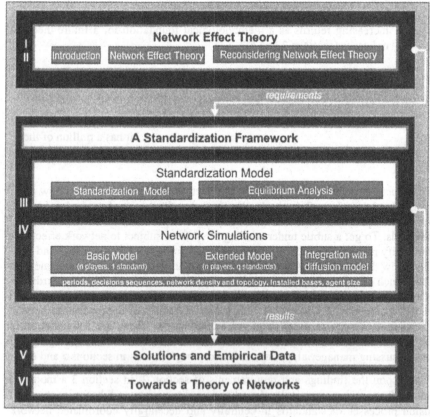

Figure 1: Structure of the thesis

In section 5, empirical data about standardization problems focusing on EDI networks is presented (5.1) and solution strategies are developed (5.2 - 5.6). The model and the simulation results are used to discuss managerial and policy implications as a basis for further research (section 5.6).

Eventually, in section 6, a possible methodological path towards a general theory of networks is proposed. Promising extensions to the framework, further research requirements focusing especially on providing building blocks for an interdisciplinary theory of networks, and possible generalizations linked to other standards and application domains are discussed. Finally, section 7 provides a brief summary of the main findings

Figure 1 visualizes the structure of the thesis.

1.4   Methodology and definitions

1.4.1   Methodology

This work is theoretical and uses a computer-based simulation model to understand the complex dynamics of diffusion processes in information networks. It draws on network effect theory. A theoretical discourse on the applicability of traditional theoretical approaches, i.e. the neo-classical paradigm, provides the methodological scope.

Based on an analysis of deficiencies of network effect theory and a game theoretic network equilibrium analysis, a standardization framework is developed. A possible methodological path for further research is proposed. Empirical data and case experiences are used to support the derivation of policy implications.

Due to the complexity of the standardization problem resulting from interdependencies associated with network effects, and in order to capture the dynamics of the diffusion processes, computer-based simulations are used throughout chapter 4 and parts of chapter 5. All simulation results were generated using JAVA 1.2 applications. For data analysis SPSS 9.0 was used. The paradigm of computational economics is introduced in section 6.2; the complexity problem is described in 5.2.2.2.

1.4.2   Standard semantics

"There are nearly as many definitions for the term "standard"
as there are standards available"
[Cargill 1997, 169]

"Ironically, standards have not been completely standardized" [Hemenway 1975]. This famous quote describes the Babylonian variety of approaches trying to categorize and define standard semantics. Standardization activities cover a wide range of application domains, as can be seen by the numerous initiatives by standardization organizations such as ISO, ANSI or DIN [Farrel/Saloner 1988]. Early proposals to give standardization research and practice a name include industrial standardization or standards engineering [Verman 1973, XII] highlighting the industrial and vendor focus still found in many contributions. A rare exception is Coles (1949) taking a consumer's perspective (but focusing on brands of 'typical' consumer goods). However, there is a general consensus that standards enable and facilitate the interaction between at least two system elements.

Every interaction and all coordination in economic processes is based upon communication. The exchange of information necessarily requires both the sender and receiver of a message to use a mutual language or set of communications standards. Communications standards can be generally defined as rules which provide the basis for interaction between actors (man, as well as machine). If n actors bilaterally agree to a set of communications standards, then $n \cdot (n-1)/2$ rules must be defined. The uniqueness of communications standards lies in their solely bilateral functionality; they work only when both the sender and the receiver of a message use identical or at least compatible standards.

In this work, we use the term *standard* to refer to any technology or product (software, hardware) incorporating technological specifications that provide for *compatibility*: Many authors emphasize the importance of compatibility [e.g. Gabel 1987, 94]. Products are said to be compatible "when their design is coordinated in some way, enabling them to work together" [Farrell/Saloner 1987, 1-2]. Compatibility is a technological property of system components [Pfeiffer 1989, 17] enabling two products to "...somehow go together" [Gabel 1991, 1] and that makes them subject to a network effect. Communication between system elements is characterized by the output of one system becoming the input of another while this sending and receiving of content requires a connection between compatible system elements that is provided for by interfaces [Niggl 1994, 31; Kleinaltenkamp 1993, 16].

Compatibility standards hence enable users "to participate in networks that allow them to share databases, have access to large selections of compatible software, exchange documents (...) or simply communicate directly" [Besen/Farrell 1994, 117]. Thus, "technology", "IT standard" etc. are used synonymously unless otherwise noted. David/Greenstein (1990, 4) define standard as a set of technical specifications. "In certain countries standardization authorities have issued standards dealing even with 'good government'" [Verman 1973, XII]. Verman (1973, 14-31) gives an extensive early overview of semantics concerning standards. Other definitions are proposed by Meffert (1994), Kleinaltenkamp (1990), Glanz (1993), BitschMartini/Schmitt (1995), DIN (1991).

Standardization, according to the user perspective taken in this work, is defined as the implementation of a standard or technology consistent with (interface) specifications in such a way as to provide for compatibility with a communication partner (and yielding network benefits as described in section 3.1) from the perspective of an individual technology user, and is not to be mistaken for the many different interpretations of the term, especially when taking a software producer's perspective with standardization largely being discussed as a decision concerning the design of product properties.

Similar approaches define standardization as a process of unification [Kleine-meyer 1998, 52]. Thum (1995) presents different definitions of the term *standard*. Generally, the concepts of standards and compatibility are vaguely defined throughout the economic literature, most of the time using examples [David/Bunn 1988, 171] and including security standards, quality standards, product standards etc. [Hemenway 1975]. David/Greenstein (1990, 4) distinguish between reference and minimum quality standards reducing transaction costs of user evaluation on the one side and interface or compatibility standards on the other.

An *information system* or *communications network* consists of a set of system elements and their information relations. Elements can be human as well as machine actors and usually represent technology users (individual agents, business units, enterprises). Alstyne (1997) distinguishes between the network as computer, economy, and society.

"Interoperability is the ability of two or more systems (computers, communications devices, databases, networks or other information technologies) to interact with one another and exchange data according to a prescribed method in order to achieve predictable results" [Perine 1995].

1.4.3 Empirical data from Fortune 1,000 study

Examining questions of managing IT standards in enterprises, as part of the research project B3 we conducted a survey in the summer of 1998 which will be referred to in this work as *Fortune 1,000 study*. A questionnaire containing about 30 questions on 8 pages was sent to 1,000 of the largest companies both in Germany and the United States (for an online-version of the questionnaire see http://caladan.wiwi.uni-frankfurt.de/IWI/projectb3/eng/survey). Prior to mailing the questionnaire, each company was contacted by telephone to identify the head of the MIS department to whom the questionnaire was then directly addressed. 250 completed questionnaires were returned in Germany (25%), and 102 in the US (10.2%). The goal of this study was to gain empirical data about the corporate adoption and use of various IT standards. On the one hand, the study was designed to provide an insight into the determinants of strategic standardization issues like the diversity of software solutions, compatibility problems, and the centralization of decision structure. On the other hand, more detailed questions, e.g. about benefits and costs, were asked for the selected categories *Internet* and *electronic commerce standards, business software* and *EDI*. Full results are presented in Westarp/Buxmann/Weitzel/König (1999). For the empirical relevance of the standardization problem and corporate decision-making see Westarp/Weitzel/Buxmann/König (1999).

Other empirical data and case studies retrieved in the course of our projects are presented in section 5.1.6. The EDI data for SME in section 5.1.6 was collected

10

with the help of Roman Beck using a written questionnaire. The X.500 data used in section 5.3.1. was collected together with Sertac Son using a questionaire and expert interviews.

2 Standardization problems

> "Standards are to the industry as culture is to society"
> *Shri C. Rajagopalachari, First Governor General of India,*
> *after Independence in 1949 [Rajagopalachari 1949, 11]*

In this section, a short outline of historic standardization cases is used to close in on communication standards by illustrating the paradigmatic shift of standardization efforts from production side to demand side economies of scale. In section 2.2, the main findings of network effect theory(ies) are presented and critically discussed (section 2.3).

2.1 A brief history of standardization

2.1.1 From DNA to railways

> "Natural selection is a process of standardization"
> *[Perry 1955, 271]*

One might easily consider the history of standardization to begin as early as in the first moments of our universe: "The discreteness of elements and indeed their fundamental particles constituting the elements, their individual characteristics, their well defined tendency to act and react with each other, amply illustrate what is ordinarily understood to be a well organized standardized pattern of behavior" [Verman 1973, 1]. The whole genesis of life, too, heavily depends on standards.

Among the first consciously set standards, language plays an important role. The development from the spoken language of monosyllabic grunts and growls used by hunters and cave-dwellers through symbols and pictograms to what we now understand as written language is a perfect standardization process. The path of business documents, for example, can easily be traced back some 20,000 years when humans carved pictures on rocks. 15,000 years later with the appearance of the first abstract languages a new chapter of human development dawned. While early graphic expressions had a restricted ability to convey content, the beginnings of writing as we know it are supposed to originate from about 1,000 B.C. [Weitzel/Harder/Buxmann 2001, 12-13]. On the Indian sub-continent, in the Indus valley, decimally subdivided length scales of the ancient Mohenjo-daro or Harappa civilization dating back as far as 3500 B.C. have been unearthed [Verman 1973, 4]. Kindleberger (1983) describes the evolution of monetary standards.

The French Revolution is considered to be an important step in the history of man's conscious evolution of standardization, with the responsibility for standardization given to scientists by the state, as is the advent of mass production that brought the necessity of interchangeable parts [Verman 1973, 8]. Here, one can also find interesting cases of failed standardization efforts. When changing the weights and measures of the Ancien Régime to a metric system, some changes were successful, like money. But the decimalization of time widely failed. Year one of decimal time began on September 22, 1794. It consisted of 12 months of 30 days each, a week was 10 days, and a day had 10 hours of 100 minutes. While the decimal year system lasted between 10 or 12 years, decimal days did not survive even two years [Kindleberger 1983, 389-390; Carrigan 1978].

A very often cited example of historic standardization problems is the standard railway gauge of 4 feet and 8 ½ inches which is believed to be the "width of a hind end of a Norfolk mule used to pull coal wagons on wooden rails" and was set by the British Parliament as a standard for all railroads in the Gauge Act of 1846 [Kindleberger 1983, 384]. Companies using other widths, like Great Western, of course opposed and said that five feet between the rails provides smoother and more stable rides; they used different locomotive axles and transshipped cargo at certain stations before finally adopting the standard gauge in the 1890s. Railway gauge problems are also known between Germany and Russia: "...the Germans for a time shifted one track inward on sleepers as they conquered Russian territory in World Wars I and II, and then adopted locomotive and wagon axles with an extra wheel to fit the wider size to make transfers possible without relaying track. In Australia each state kept to its own gauge until after the middle of the (20th) century, forcing most interstate cargo to be carried by sea between settlements along the coast, and interstate shipments by rail to be reloaded from one system to the other" [Kindleberger 1983, 384-385]. In World War I, Britain is reported to have had 24 different voltages and 10 different frequencies produced by electricity generating companies [Plummer 1937, 21].

Another well-known historic (non) standardization case is a fire in Baltimore on February 7, 1904. Firefighters from Washington could not help extinguish the huge fire because their hoses wouldn't fit the Baltimore hydrants. This sad incident resulted in over 1,000 burnt houses and damage to the value of $ 125 million [Warren/Warren 1983, 125; Hemenway 1975, 3].

2.1.2   From production side to demand side economies of scale

> "The earliest deliberate efforts on organized scale can be traced back
> only to the early part of the twentieth century"
> *[Verman 1973, XIII]*

In practically every country of the world, there are organizations responsible for the development and use of standards. Most of these organizations were established in the late 19th and early 20th century with World War I being a substantial driving force. Then the focus was improving national productivity with standardization as a means of reducing the heterogeneity of products and processes in order to obtain production side economies of scale. A prominent example of early standardization efforts to reap compatibility benefits is the U.S. and the U.K. harmonizing the pitch of the screw thread between them during World War II to make screws exchangeable [Kindleberger 1983, 392]. After the Second World War the standardizers' goals slowly started to change giving way to compatibility standards. This new dynamic first peaked with the release of the papers of McGowan and Fisher [Fisher/McGowan/Greenwood 1993] concerning the antitrust lawsuits versus IBM in the 1970s. Building on this, the influential works of Farrell/Saloner and Katz/Shapiro can be said to have opened standardization as an area of research of its own. We will refer to this research field as the *theory of positive network effects*.

Arthur (1996) calls this the transition from "Alfred Marshall's World" to the "Increasing-Returns World": from bulk production (of metal ores, pig iron etc. associated with the law of diminishing returns; "commodities heavy on resources, light on know-how") with market prices (equaling average costs of production) of goods in perfect competition making way for perfectly orderly Victorian equilibria to the reverse situation characterized by increasing returns and therefore market instability, multiple potential outcomes, possibly huge profits, and unpredictability. Unlike John Hicks who warned that admitting increasing returns to enter economics would lead to "the wreckage of the greater part of economic theory", Arthur is known for saying it rather complements it.

The general problem associated with standards is their commonality property, which gives rise to a coordination problem since standardization decisions therefore exhibit externalities. While it is common in many markets that the buying decision of one consumer influences the decisions of others (e.g. *bandwagon, snob,* and *Veblen effect* are broadly discussed in economic literature [e.g. Leibenstein 1950, Ceci/Kain 1982]) a discussion emerged about whether some markets are determined by strong demand-sided economies of scale which are often called positive network effects deriving from the need of product compatibility as for example in software markets. The network effects in these markets mainly originate from two different areas, the need for compatibility to exchange information or data and the need for complementary products and services.

Leibenstein (1950) anticipated parts of the phenomenon, stating that demand curves are more elastic when consumers derive positive value from increases in market size. Parallel with the growth of the telecommunication and information technology markets in recent years the discussion has gained considerable momentum. Especially in terms of the implications of demand-side returns to scale on market coordination and overall efficiency, it became obvious that these effects needed some more attention.

2.2 Network effect theory as theoretical foundation

2.2.1 Basics

> "The benefits from compatibility create demand-side economies of scale:
> there are benefits to doing what others do. These benefits make stan-
> dardization a central issue in many important industries"
> *[Farrell/Saloner 1986, 940]*

Network effects have been defined as "the change in the benefit, or surplus, that an agent derives from a good when the number of other agents consuming the same kind of good changes" [Liebowitz/Margolis 1995a; see Thum 1995, 5-12 for different sources of network effects].

The externality property implies coordination problems in markets subject to network effects, which are said to be endemic in high tech industries in particular "and that such industries experience problems that are different in character from the problems that have, for more ordinary commodities, been solved by markets" [Liebowitz/Margolis 1995a]. Network effects are primarily discussed in the literature on standards, in which a primary concern is the choice of a correct standard, and in the literature concerning path dependencies, in which patterns of diffusion, i.e. standards adoption processes, are a focus.

Thus, discussions about the use of standards or the diffusion of technological innovations are often based upon the theory of positive network effects, which describes a positive correlation between the number of users of a network good and its utility [Katz/Shapiro 1985; Farrel/Saloner 1985].

Therefore, network effects imply demand-side economies of scale in the adoption of technology and make otherwise possibly autonomous decisions of agents (about the use of technologies subject to network effects) interdependent, creating a coordination problem that is often called *the standardization problem* [Wiese 1990, 1; Besen/Farrell 1994, 118; Buxmann 1996]. As will be shown, the problems associated with standardization processes are quite complex. That is the reason for many simplifications in the literature and in this work alike, among them reduction to quite particular problems (e.g. standardization decisions instead of general analysis of "networks") and scenarios. Additionally, as throughout the entire literature, the term network effect essentially always describes *positive* effects. Of course, there are negative externalities, too [Roever 1996]. But they are not within the focus of the pure standardization problem, see sections 3.3.1 and 7.2 for a discussion of considering negative network effects. For the differentiation between network effect and network externality see section 2.3.1 and for a proposed generalization towards a universal theory of network effects see section 6 .

2.2.1.1   General findings of network effect theory

The first groundbreaking contributions to this relatively young research field stem from the early 80s. Of course, there are earlier contributions in the field of standards [e.g. Gaillard 1934; Rohlfs 1974 or Hemenway 1975]; but it was not until about 20 years ago that standards emerged as a separate topic of research. A common finding is the existence of network effects, i.e. the increasing value of a standard as the number of its users increases (demand side economies of scale) leading in many cases to Pareto-inferior results of standardization processes. Katz/Shapiro differentiate between *direct network effects* in terms of direct "physical effects" [Katz/Shapiro 1985, 424] of being able to exchange information (as in the case of telephones) and *indirect network effects* arising from interdependencies in the consumption of complementary goods [Braunstein/White 1985; Chou/Shy 1990; Church/Gandal 1992; Teece 1987]. Examples are computer operating systems and available application software, or video cassette recorder systems and the format of the tapes. This relation is sometimes called the "hardware-software-paradigm" [Katz/Shapiro 1985, 424]. Other sources of indirect network effects can be the availability of after sales services (support: automobile makes that are often sold will probably have a higher availability of different services than rare models [Katz/Shapiro 1985, 425; Katz/Shapiro 1986, 823]), learning effects, uncertainties about future technology availability or the existence of a market for used goods [Thum 1995, 8-12; Glanz 1993, 31]. Complementarity can formally be described by negative cross-price elasticity ($\frac{\partial x_1}{\partial p_2} < 0$) (the existence of a demand curve for network effect goods is discussed in Wiese (1990, 26-46)). Habermeier (1989, 1294) identifies four sources of increasing returns from adoption: network externalities ("joining a well-established network" as IBM PC or telephone users), informational economies of scale (better known properties of products, e.g. brands), technological interrelatedness (complementary effects) and dynamic learning processes. Cabral (1987) states that processes subject to positive feedbacks (due to network effects or learning by doing) are analytically similar to learning processes. Arthur (1989, 116) emphasizes "learning by using" effects [Rosenberg 1982; Habermeier 1989] and describes the phenomenon "*in a context where increasing returns arise naturally: agents choosing between technologies competing for adoption. Modern, complex technologies often display increasing returns to adoption in that the more they are adopted, the more experience is gained with them, and the more they are improved*".

According to Braunstein/White (1985, 339), the more intense the network effects, the higher the converting and standard switching costs, the more long-lived the good and the higher the stack of complementary goods (e.g. data files in a certain format) the more a common standard is important.

Kindleberger (1983) describes free-rider problems due to the public good properties of standards. Arthur (1983, 1989) shows that technologies subject to increasing returns (in contrast to constant and decreasing returns) exhibit multiple equilibria and will finally lock-in to a monopoly with one standard cornering the entire market. Since this standardization process is non-ergodic (or path dependent) the ultimate outcome is not predictable. Analogously, Besen/Farrell (1994) show that tippiness is a typical characteristic found in networks describing the fact that multiple incompatible technologies are rarely able to coexist and that the switch to a single, leading standard can occur suddenly.

An important distinction is to be made between sponsored and unsponsored networks: in sponsored networks, there are agents in possession of property rights concerning the standard at choice. Particularly, the possession of those rights enables internalization strategies by means of pricing, for example. In contrast, unsponsored technologies are not subject to proprietary means of control and accordingly might suffer more strongly from the externality property associated with standards. Some contributions distinguish between *unsponsored de facto* standardization processes and diffusion in *sponsored networks*: a quite commonly adopted terminology differentiates between the market-mediated diffusion processes of compatibility standards (leading to de facto standards [Saloner 1990]) and de jure standards resulting from either political ("committee") or administrative procedures. De facto standards can either be sponsored (with certain actors holding property rights and the capability of restraining the use of the standard) or unsponsored (no actors with proprietary interests) [David/Greenstein 1990, 4; Arthur 1983]. The pattern of argument for standardization processes is always the same: the discrepancy between private and collective gains in networks under increasing returns leads to possibly Pareto-inferior results. With incomplete information about other actors' preferences, *excess inertia* can occur, as no actor is willing to bear the disproportionate risk of being the first adopter of a standard and then becoming stranded in a small network if all others eventually decide in favor of another technology. This start-up problem prevents any adoption at all of the particular technology, even if it is preferred by everyone. On the other hand, *excess momentum* can occur, e.g. if a sponsoring firm uses low prices during early periods of diffusion to attract a critical mass of adopters [Farrell/Saloner 1986]. In the case of complete information on the part of all actors concerning their symmetric preferences for a certain standard, a *bandwagon* process will overcome the coordination problem, with actors who stand to gain relatively high stand-alone utility or private benefits from adoption (as compared to network effects) starting the adoption process. Nevertheless, in the case of heterogeneous preferences, Farrell/Saloner (1986) show that due to strategic behavior even perfect communication might not be able to overcome excess inertia or momentum. In the case of sponsored technologies the situation is somewhat different. Here there is a possibility of internalizing the network gains, which would otherwise be more or less lost, by strategic intertemporal pricing, for example [Katz/Shapiro 1986]. There are private incentives to providing networks that can overcome inertia problems; however, they do not guarantee social optimality per se.

Due to the importance of these results, the most common findings - phenomena, fundamentals, and results - of traditional network effect theory are described in some more detail below in sections 2.2.2 - 2.2.8. They will be identified again within the examination of different diffusion processes in networks in sections 3 and 4.

2.2.1.2   Related literature

The primary goal of most traditional approaches to standards and network effects is an analysis of particular properties of modern information and communication technologies, i.e. increasing returns to marginal adopters, or network effects [e.g. Farrell/Saloner 1985; Katz/Shapiro 1985; Besen/Farrell 1994]. Thus, the particularity of network effects lies in the fact that they are considered to be characteristic of IT products and standards that are therefore different in character from more traditional commodities and subject to different problems which cannot be solved as smoothly by markets [Katz/Shapiro 1985; Farrell/Saloner 1985; Arthur 1996]. Various perspectives can be distinguished in the literature [Kleinemeyer 1998; Yang 1997; David/Greenstein 1990]. The authors using *empirical approaches* mainly try to prove the existence of network effects and estimate their values by using regression analysis to estimate the hedonic price function of network effect goods [Hartmann/Teece 1990; Gandal 1994; Economides/Himmelberg 1995; Moch 1995; Gröhn 1999]. *Theoretical approaches* mostly use equilibrium analysis to explain phenomena such as the start-up problem [Rohlfs 1974; Oren/Smith 1981; Katz/Shapiro 1985; 1994; Wiese 1990; Besen/Farell 1994; Economides/Himmelberg 1995], market failure [Farrell/Saloner 1985; 1986; Katz/Shapiro 1986; 1992; 1994; Gröhn 1999], instability (also called "tippiness") of network effect markets [Arthur 1989; 1996; Besen/Farell 1994; Farrell/Saloner 1985; Katz/Shapiro 1994; Shapiro/Varian 1998], and path dependency [David 1985; Arthur 1989; Besen/Farell 1994; Katz/Shapiro 1994; Liebowitz/Margolis 1995b]. A rich online bibliography is provided by Economides (2000) and Agre (1998).

Many contributions focus on the **infrastructure** side of standards. The multitude of standards are interpreted as components of a society's infrastructure by Tassey (1995). Hanseth/Monteiro/Hatling (1996) argue that flexibility is a major success factor for infrastructure standards in terms of positively being able to react to future changes and unpredicted innovations.

An important issue for standard vendors is the consideration of markets that offer various standards that might contain compatible components so that users can compose their systems from different **components**. This phenomenon is called a mix and match market in network economics [Matutes/Regibeau 1988; Einhorn 1992]. Also, between vertically integrated markets there is the typical strategic vendor's question whether to provide components compatible with those of other firms [Economides/White 1993] thus deciding between competing within or between standards [Besen/Farrell 1994, 117-118]. Modularity in various markets is analyzed in Langlois/Robertson (1992). A systematic overview of standard producers' **incentives** for or against standardization in terms of providing compatibility to rival standards is provided by Besen/Farrell (1994). Different individual interests and their influence on participation in standardization processes is analyzed in Jakobs/Procter/Williams (1996).

As noted above, there is a vast literature on software **producer/vendor strategies**. For software vendors, many competitive strategies have been proposed: versioning (or market segmentation) to make basically the same product appealing to different user groups [Varian 1999; 2001], bundling to closer fit consumers' valuation on average [Bakos/Brynjolfsson 1999], increase switching costs to enhance lock-in, strategic pricing or second sourcing. Notably, Wiese (1990) proposes pricing, product, and communication strategies for network effect goods vendors using elaborate simulations. He analyses problems indicative of the three stages of market development: market creation (start-up problem in a not-yet-existing market), market entry (installed base) and oligopoly battle. Westarp (2003) identifies the relevant determinants of modern software markets and incorporates these in a simulation model as the basis for managerial directions for software vendors. The influence of different topologies, in particular, leads to interesting results. This interdisciplinary approach is based on the consideration of geographic and sociological proximity measures and their impacts like group membership, intra-group pressure, and opinion leadership through power and structural position on standardization decisions. The model is introduced and integrated with the standardization model in section 4.5.

Actor network theory [Callon 1991] sees innovation as the recombination of interdependent (networked) entities such as people, organizations, etc. and therefore standards as social constructions [Timmermans/Berg 1997]. Many technological innovations do not follow an individual path but are instead influenced by spillovers from various industries in quite different areas [Rosenberg 1982]. A more general approach is presented by Giddens (1988) trying to close the gap between systems theory and the analysis of social systems (and institutions). See section 6.2 for the relevance of institutional theories for network effect problems and related literature and EMSS (1999) for an online bibliography focusing on computational and institutional economics.

A well-discussed example of important standardization processes is the emergence of the **Internet**. Drake (1993) discusses whether the process was an anomaly or rather typical of state of the art standardization processes while David/Steinmueller (1996) find the Internet's architecture and institutional structure to be not sustainable. Lehr (1995) draws lessons from the Internet's (or more precisely the IETF's) success.

Berg (1989) develops a mathematical model to derive the optimal degree of compatibility in an economy. Liebowitz/Margolis (1995a) show under what conditions the profit maximizing network size is also socially optimal.

Many authors have been concerned with **policy issues** deriving from standardization problems. Branscomb/Kahin (1995) provide an overview of competing models for the standards process, the emergence of standards consortia, intellectual property, and the several potential roles of government. The institutional processes associated with standard setting are analyzed by David (1995). Lemley (1996) considers antitrust laws incapable of regulating standards-driven industries with phenomena like lock-in. As elaborated in section 2.3, there are scholars who are less pessimistic about antitrust issues than David in finding that decentralized markets provide sufficient incentives for market participants to exploit all inefficiencies, leading to the best standards winning and therefore making government intervention obsolete (e.g. Liebowitz/Margolis 1996). Trebing (1994) offers a view of failing telecommunication markets, while Carlton/Klamer (1983) show that for infrastructural industries such as railroads and electronic funds transfers, social welfare requires cooperation (even among competitors). Braunstein/White (1985) look at vertical integration from an anti-trust point of view in the light of the efficiency potentials of a standards-driven market. Krislov (1997) compares standardization policies as part of national economic strategies. Farrell (1989) sees that to a quite limited extent copyrights (or more generally property rights) are useful in standards markets if compatibility is a goal.

Standard setting itself is facing changes as privately organized **consortia** like W3C or OASIS take over standardization from governmental organizations more and more. For typical processes in standardization consortia see Jakobs (2000, 101-168), for their structure see Haitz (1994, 181-185), Jakobs (2000, 54-68), Kleinemeyer (1998, 85-124). David/Shurmer (1996) discuss reforms of standards bodies to address the growing complexity of cross-industry and international goals. Sirbu/Zwimpfer (1985) demonstrate consensus conditions within consortia. Farrell/Saloner (1988) compare the efficiency of three coordination processes (consortium vs. market vs. a hybrid of both) for agreeing on a standard (see section 5.6.3).

Problems of **intertemporal coordination** when there are network effects are analyzed by Thum (1995).

Decentralized coordination processes that it might be instructive to study especially in the context of the model developed in section 3 are found in the literature on mathematical physics about dynamic Ising models of ferromagnetism [David/Greenstein 1990, 7].

In the following, the primary findings of network effect literature are elaborated in more detail. In contrast to most existing contributions, the following sections are not organized by authors but rather by the findings of their contributions, so that they can be used more easily within the analysis of sections 3 and 4.

2.2.2 Path dependency, lock-in and multiple equilibria

Demand-sided positive network effects exhibit multiple equilibria and the market will finally lock-in to a monopoly with one standard gaining total market share.

Among the first and most influential contributions to the literature on the economics of standards are the works of Brian Arthur (1983; 1989; 1996) who showed important general phenomena associated with network effects and that systems subject to increasing returns exhibit multiple equilibria. In a model in which two new (unsponsored) technologies compete he shows under what conditions network markets will eventually lock-in to a monopoly. As will become clear later,

Arthur's model is quite similar to the (user side) model developed in sections 3 and 4 in terms of the scenarios described.

He argues that insignificant events in early diffusion periods might give small initial advantages to an (increasing returns) technology and that this technology might then be more improved as it is adopted more often. "Thus a technology that by chance gains an early lead in adoption may eventually 'corner the market' of potential adopters, with the other technologies becoming locked out" [Arthur 1989, 116].

This possible dependence of diffusion results on early random historic events is usually called path dependency. "A path-dependent sequence of economic changes is one of which important influences upon the eventual outcome can be exerted by temporally remote events, including happenings dominated by chance elements rather than systematic forces" [David 1985, 332]. The interesting question of course is the implication for market efficiency: "It is well known that allocation problems with increasing returns tend to exhibit multiple equilibria, and so it is not surprising that multiple outcomes should appear here" [Arthur 1989, 116]. If multiple equilibria exist, the wrong ones might be selected as an instance of market failure. Since static analysis can identify those equilibria but not predict the ones eventually selected, Arthur proposes a dynamic model for decisions when increasing returns exist, a model that considers early random events and shows other properties associated with network effects: **non-predictability** (agents' ex ante knowledge is insufficient for predicting diffusion results) and potential **inefficiency** (the (in the long-run) inferior technology is adopted). A diffusion process is said to be path-efficient if at all times equal adoption of the technology that is behind in terms of adoption would not have paid off better. In addition, he shows that increasing returns diffusion processes can be **inflexible** (progressive lock-in, a subsidy or tax adjustment can not always influence market choice) and **non-ergodic** (path-dependent, small events are not averaged away).

Table 1: Payoff matrix (returns to choosing A or B,
previous adoptions) [Arthur 1989, 118]

	technology A	technology B
R-agent	$a_N + rn_A$	$b_N + rn_B$
S-agent	$a_S + sn_A$	$b_S + sn_B$

In his "simple model", unsponsored technologies A and B preferred by agents i of type R and S (with equal numbers) compete for adoption. Agents' payoffs are determined by past adoption of their chosen technology (n_A and n_B) with increasing, diminishing, or constant returns to adoption given by r and s simultaneously positive, negative or zero (while $a_R > b_R$ and $a_S < b_S$, i.e. R-agents have a natural preference for A) as depicted in Table 1. This is also the setting of many other models [e.g. Farrell/Saloner 1988].

The potential indeterminacy of the outcome, i.e. the consequences of random events, result from conditions outside the ex ante knowledge of the agents or an implicit observer, in this case the agents' decision sequence (the set of events that determines the time of entry and choice of the agents). This is analogous to the sequential choice scenario developed later in section 4.2.3.2 (with the exception that Arthur's agents do not try to anticipate other's decisions, of course). A path in this context is a sequence of A and B adoptions.

Arthur shows the general dynamics of increasing returns systems for homogeneous agents. Here, choice sequence is of no relevance. If returns rise at the same rate, the technology chosen first will corner the market while the other doesn't get started. The outcome is predictable and path-efficient. In his famous example, he shows that if returns increase at different rates as shown in the table, the adoption process can be path-inefficient. Arthur states that *"In this case after thirty choices in the adoption process, all of which are A, equivalent adoption of B would have delivered higher returns. But if the process has gone far enough, a given subsidy adjustment to B can no longer close the gap between the returns to A and the returns to B at the starting point. Flexibility is not present here; the market becomes increasingly 'locked-in' to an inferior choice"* [Arthur 1989, 119].

Table 2: Adoption payoff for homogeneous agents [Arthur 1989, 119]

number of previous adoptions	0	10	20	30	40	50	60	70	80	90	100
Technology A	10	11	12	13	14	15	16	17	18	19	20
Technology B	4	7	10	13	16	19	22	25	28	31	34

If agents of the two types decide in an unknown choice sequence, interesting system properties become evident. $n_A(n)$ and $n_B(n)$ are the number of choices of A and B respectively after n choices in total. With difference in adoption $d_n = n_A(n) - n_B(n)$, market share of A (x_n) is described by $x_n = 0.5 + \dfrac{d_n}{2n}$.

▸ **Under constant returns,** regardless of previous adopters R-agents always choose A and S-agents always choose B. Ergodicity of the diffusion process is obvious, d_n follows a coin-toss gambler's random walk with each move's probability 0.5. The market will be shared.

▸ **Under increasing returns** R-agents choose B if its adoption is suffi-

$$d_n = n_A(n) - n_B(n) < \Delta_R = \frac{b_R - a_R}{r}$$

ciently ahead of A (if) and vice versa. This critical mass of adopters is called absorbing barrier in the model: "under increasing returns then, the adoption process becomes a random walk with absorbing barriers"; see Arthur (1989, 117-122) for a formal deduction. The market share of A will finally be 0 or 1, technol-

ogy coexistence is impossible. Small early events determine the final outcome in a non-ergodic process.

▶ **Under diminishing returns** the adoption process becomes a random
walk with reflecting barriers. The market will be shared.

Table 3: Properties of the three regimes [Arthur 1989, 121]

	predictable	flexible	ergodic	necessarily path-efficient
constant returns	yes	no	yes	yes
diminishing returns	yes	yes	yes	yes
increasing returns	no	no	no	no

Comparable results are presented by Cowan (1991), David (1987). Habermeier
(1989) shows that rational expectations from future intertemporal spillovers may
eliminate the path-dependent property of the diffusion process, at the same time
reducing the time taken to lock-in. Other authors also find that if agents' expectations are taken into account, the lock-in period might appear even earlier [Arthur
1989, 123; Katz/Shapiro 1985; Katz/Shapiro 1986].

For sponsored technologies, penetration pricing can be expected to lead to analogous results [Hanson 1985] although strong discounting might bring forward the
possibility of market sharing again [Arthur 1989, 123; Fudenberg/Tirole 1983].

Liebowitz/Margolis (1998) note similarities between the theory of path dependence and related ideas in physics and mathematics that come from chaos theory.
Here, too, "history matters" in that there is sensitive dependence on early conditions (or in biology "contingency", i.e. the irreversibility of natural selection
[Gleick 1987], although in software diffusion, processes seem to be more easily
reversible than in biology). One important difference, though, lies in the fact that
although small events or perturbations can make systems evolve in different ways,
there is no settling down of the system towards some fixed equilibrium. The development in chaos theory may appear chaotic but actually have a determinate
structure but "the never ending 'disequilibrium' that seems the essence of chaos
theory is thus missing from the economic analysis of path dependence" [Lie-
bowitz/Margolis 1998]. See Mokyr (1991) for the relation between biological contingency and economic path-dependence (and for warnings of misapplying biological evolution to social systems).

It is interesting to note that the famous example used by Arthur (for a visualization
see also Figure 2, right) can also be used to demonstrate parts of the critique presented in section 2.3: first, the example only works if the payoffs for one technol-

ogy increase more strongly than for the other, i.e. if network effects grow at different rates. Second, it only works if there is no information or consideration as to the ultimate size of the network. Third, there is no possibility of internalization. Were the information regarding future network effect development and potential network size known, agents would certainly behave in a different manner but that would make the notion of inefficiency problematic, see section 2.3.3. And if future network effect development were known, there would be a serious start-up problem. Liebowitz/Margolis (1998) propose an internalization strategy if one of the technologies is sponsored: the network owner could simply lease applications to adopters and give them a cancellation option. This could clear the inefficiencies out as easily as implying penetration pricing strategies. The point made here is that the inefficiency proposition only holds (at least undisputedly) subject to a set of conditions that one needs to be aware of and that have not been explained in the Arthur model. This also allows for different interpretations of the table: if the numbers are ultimate payoffs (given the ultimate number of adopters, regardless of the time of decision) B is superior in case of more than 30 adopters. If the numbers are payoffs to the marginal adopter, B becomes superior if more than 50 adopt. See Liebowitz/Margolis (1995b) for different interpretations and the results of correspondence with B. Arthur.

Path dependencies are sometimes seen as a modern perspective on network effects. In some respects, the underlying concepts (and the critique of the neo-classical paradigm outlined in section 6.2) mirror some revolutionary changes in physics in the past centuries: the Newtonian view of the 1900s of the world as a deterministic machine (principal predictability of outcomes given knowledge on initial states of the world) can be compared to a neo-classical equilibrium with perfectly rational agents. Then, in physics, relativity theory and quantum electro-dynamics 'stochasticized' the world: among others, the world is seen as statistical (and observing the system can also change its behavior). Accordingly, the focus shifted to interpreting the world as a non-linear dynamic system capable of "chaotic" behavior even though the (deterministic) laws governing the system may be fully understood. This shift is quite comparable to using path dependencies for describing social systems: "Positive feedback loops occur when a given divergence from any state of the system is magnified rather than damped. A normal competitive market is a negative feedback system. If price diverges from equilibrium, market forces push price back towards the equilibrium" [Lipsey 1989, 772-773]. Matching the discussion about bounded rationality of individual agents (section 6.1.2), system behavior in non-linear systems might in principal be unpredictable even for the most sophisticated analytical models.

2.2.3   Instability ("tippy networks")

Instability is a typical property describing the fact that multiple, incompatible technologies are rarely able to coexist and that the switch to a single, leading standard can occur suddenly.

Network markets are generally considered to be *tippy*: "When two or more firms compete for a market where there is strong positive feedback, only one may emerge as a winner. Economists say that such a market is tippy, meaning that it can tip in favor of one player or another. It is unlikely that all will survive" [Shapiro/Varian 1998, 176]. Hence, the coexistence of incompatible products may be unstable, with a single winning standard dominating the market [Besen/Farrell 1994, 118]. An often cited example is VHS videocassette recorder technology and its elimination of Beta. See section 2.3.7.2 for a critical look at that example. Other examples of lock-in into inferior products are presented by Walpuski (1996) (Teletex and Telex).

Besen/Farrell (1994, 118) emphasize the role of expectations about ultimate network size for rapid tipping. Especially from the perspective of firms producing products subject to network effects like software, compatibility is an important action variable for if the market 'tips' into the firms direction it will have a most favorable monopolistic market position, sometimes called an "architectural franchise" [Ferguson/Morris 1993]. On the other hand, stern competition (before tipping) might be costly, and competitors could agree on standardization exchanging inter- for intratechnological competition. See section 3.3.1 for basic strategic situations of technology vendors.

Closely related to tipping is the observation of a critical mass of users (due to high fixed upfront costs and positive network effects) that determines when markets tip [Oren/Smith 1982, 467-468]. A very early contribution identifying critical mass phenomena as part of a formal analysis of the observation that the value of telecommunications services to a user largely depends on the number of other subscribers is Rohlfs (1974), sometimes cited as the origin of network economics. This is often called the chicken and egg paradox: "...many consumers are not interested in purchasing the good because the installed base is too small, and the installed base is too small because an insufficiently small number of consumers have purchased the good" [Economides/Himmelberg 1995, 5].

An interesting historical example of a tipping network is Sweden's decision between left-hand or right-hand car driving. Although Swedes originally drove on the left side of the road (i.e. right-hand drive cars) Royal Commissions examined that question in the 1930s and again in 1946 and decided against switching to the right side of the road; a national referendum in the 1950s voted overwhelmingly against change, and Sweden eventually changed only in the late 1960s. In the early decisions, switching (or standardization) costs (transitional heterogeneity and the necessity to discharge bus and tram passengers on the street instead of the sidewalk) were considered to be higher than benefits (cheaper cars (at least moderately) and a common standard with neighbors). Over time, increased internationalization of the car market and cross border traffic can be said to have finally tipped the decisions [Kindleberger 1983, 388-389].

2.2.4   Excess inertia: The start-up problem

The start-up problem prevents the adoption even of superior products; excess inertia can occur as no actor is willing to bear the disproportionate risk of being the first adopter of a standard.

In contrast to the models of Arthur, Farrell/Saloner (1986) investigate the battle between an existing and a new technology; see Farrell/Saloner (1985) for an earlier, static model with two new technologies. In a deterministic model they identify installed base effects and their relations to possible equilibria. An analogous stochastic model is presented by Arthur (1983).

The general coordination problem associated with the existence of network effects is that a technology or standard will be commonly adopted if a majority of the network benefits from it because it pays to bear the private costs of adoption. If, however, only a fraction of the market adopts a technology, for most users the gains will be below the private costs, hence leading to two possible outcomes with the coordination problem being reaching the right one [David/Greenstein 1990, 9]. This binary assumption of system behavior will be critically discussed in the next chapter. Farrell/Saloner (1986) analyze the underlying coordination problem. They show that if a new technology is competing with an established one and if everyone is better off switching to the new technology, where there is complete information (section 3) the network will switch in a so-called bandwagon process. The idea is that that in anticipation of others' behavior every agent will change his technology starting from those with the highest private gains. Especially when compared to situations with incomplete information and heterogeneous preferences, they emphasize the influence of early standards adopters on the decision of later adopters. This phenomenon will become most evident in the simulations of section 4.3. A key finding is that uncertainty about other agents' preferences can result in excess inertia for early adopters bear a disproportionate share of "transient incompatibility costs" [Farrell/Saloner 1986, 940; 1985]. Regardless of others' preferences there is no incentive to any individual agent to get the bandwagon rolling first (inertia). This phenomenon is also called the penguin effect: "Penguins who must enter the water to find food often delay doing so because they fear the presence of predators. Each would prefer some other penguin to test the waters first" [Farrell/Saloner 1986, 943].

And strategic pricing can lead to technology changes which are too fast or extensive (momentum, see 2.2.5). When preferences are heterogeneous, communication aiming at solving the coordination problem can reinforce coordination failure tendencies (inertia and momentum) rather than overcome it due to strategic behavior on the part of the agents [David/Greenstein 1990, 10].

The original model of Katz/Shapiro (1985) also shows lock-in effects when expectations are important because there is a tendency to self-fulfillment.

Excess inertia can occur if there is an installed base even though there may be complete information [Farrell/Saloner 1986]. Generally, the excess inertia property of network effect goods is emphasized by authors stressing the public goods character of standards, which implies that user groups are too small compared to the collective use of the standard [e.g. Dybvig/Spatt 1983; Kindleberger 1983].

For the critical mass phenomenon see Meffert (1994, 24), Picot (2000) provides a critical mass example in the Internet economy.

Another problem throughout the network effect literature is the concept of superior technologies. Apart from difficulties in qualifying objective criteria for complex technology comparisons, the relative benefits of a technology cannot be defined independently of the state of knowledge that itself depends on the technological path taken. This predicament is partly responsible for the diverse views on fundamental issues such as market efficiency and path dependency, see also sections 2.3 and 6.

2.2.5 Excess momentum: Too much standardization

Excess momentum can occur, if for example a sponsoring firm uses low prices in early periods of diffusion to attract a critical mass of adopters.

Since an installed base is stranded if a new technology is adopted, there is an incentive to jump on a bandwagon even though the old technology might be preferred individually [Farrell/Saloner 1986]. While in their earlier model [Farrell/Saloner 1985] an adoption decision was only associated with the externality in terms of affecting the options available to later adopters, the installed base externality (on those stranding) also becomes evident in their 1986 model. In this context, they identify an often used vendor strategy beneath penetration pricing: predatory preannouncements [Farrell/Saloner 1986, 942-43]. For optimal dynamic pricing from the perspective of a monopolist see Dhebar/Oren (1985; 1986).

2.2.6 Internalizing network effects in sponsored networks

In the case of sponsored technologies there is a possibility of internalizing the network gains which would otherwise be more or less lost by strategic intertemporal pricing. There are private incentives to provide networks that can overcome inertia problems; still they do not guarantee social optimality per se.

Since most of the literature on standards focuses on the producer or *vendor side*, sponsored standardization processes form the majority of theoretical contributions. The influence of the ownership of assets, i.e. the possibility of using proprietary control, makes sponsored standardization processes different in character from the use decision elaborated in this work: for analyzing decision behavior and deriving strategies for standards *users*, unsponsored diffusion processes are more interesting because for the deciders in focus the extent to which different available technologies are compatible is not a variable they can influence. Still, some of the internalizing mechanisms might be transferable to the unsponsored case. The case described in section 5.3 can be interpreted as an approach to emulating network behavior between autonomous agents as though they were controlled by a central authority holding property rights of the technology to be decided upon. Generally, coordination efforts in decentralized networks are structurally analogous to the internalization strategies of sponsoring firms or the efforts of standards bodies such as the ANSI, W3C or OASIS. This will be elaborated in more detail in sections 3 to 5.

David/Greenstein (1990, 12-24) give an extensive overview of findings in sponsored standardization processes. Interesting phenomena include partial compatibility, gateways [Braunstein/White 1985] or mix and match markets [Matutes/Regibeau 1988]. Sponsored technologies are in a particularly strong position when competing with an unsponsored technology, since the former is capable of being strategically priced.

2.2.7 Pareto-inferior market results and monopolies

In many cases, the existence of network effects leads to Pareto-inferior market results.

As became clear in the previous discussions, if there are no bounds to increasing returns, standardization processes "eventually must 'lock in' to a monopoly of the market by one technology; a point is reached after which every agent, regardless of inherent preferences, will select the same technology" [David/Greenstein 1990, 6]. In consequence, standardization processes (that are non-ergodic, see 2.2.2) may result in equilibria viewed as Pareto-inferior to others that had been available *ex post*. In contrast to neo-classical economics, there is no stopping rule like marginal costs equal marginal benefits under increasing returns [Arthur 1996].

As will become clearer later in sections 3 and 4, when discussing social optimality of standards selection there are problems as to what optimality criterion is sensible. Especially "in self-reinforcing processes (i.e. dynamical systems characterized by increasing returns (...)) social optimality is problematic" [David/Greenstein 1990, 11] and it proves helpful to distinguish between ex ante optimality of diffusion results and ex post social optimality. If decision strategies are optimal, path dependencies can imply standardization outcomes that are regrettable later. But the externality property adhering to network effects can make the process inefficient ex ante for agents might not consider the consequences of their choices on others. By chance, results might turn out to be globally efficient ex post, but the system dynamics do not guarantee this. Additionally, intertemporal dependencies can pose further problems. Beyond the problem of considering the choice of future generations [Thum 1995] there are timing problems that can make standardization inefficient in an ex ante as well as an ex post sense. David/Greenstein (1990, 12) for example note that early standardization may encourage the development of (improved) complementary products and increase the technology's value. At the same time, this might close off the exploration of alternative technologies, narrowing the range of technological options. In this context, due to compatibility standardization can lower barriers to market entry but can at the same time intensify price competition which in turn reduces profits which lessens the industry's power to sustain investments in improving the technology.

Yet Thum (1995, 19-21) argues that standards do not inhibit innovation, another finding of some contributions, but rather pose a risk of excess innovation and incompatible products. For an overview of the literature on converters and technological diversity see Thum (1995, 25-32).

2.2.8   Laissez-faire vs. dirigisme

The question arises whether the laissez-faire of decentralized markets should be replaced by centralized state control to ensure favorable diffusion of technologies subject to network effects.

Due to the suggested ubiquity of market failure under network effects there are discussions as to whether government interventions could solve some of the problems stated before. In the early (neo-classical) literature on standardization, technical choices between competing standards or technologies (in contrast to incentives for investing in their development) were largely considered unproblematic until Hemenway (1975) noted their public goods character. "Here was ground for public intervention if it could be presumed that the public authority was at least as technically well-informed as a private monopolist" [David/Greenstein 1990, 33]. In the 1980s the focus shifted to the question of whether markets provide timely technological standards in sufficient numbers [David/Greenstein 1990, 33].

Recently, there seems to be a growing consensus between researchers in the field of economics of standards and here especially the branch of welfare economics that the government suffers from significant informational deficits compared to industry groups. It especially appears that only at early stages can the diffusion dynamics for technologies subject to network effects be directed by governmental intervention (at reasonable costs and with reasonable chance of success). But especially in this small policy window of opportunity the government is most likely to be incapable of meaningfully determining "the best" technology among different alternatives, especially as compared to the technology providers. See also Thum (1995, 146-153). See Konrad/Thum (1993) for a principle impossibility of governmental regulation of long term standards.

There are different reasons beneath trying to internalize otherwise unexploited (technological) network effects for government regulatory bodies to intervene in standards diffusion processes. Prevalent among them are national goals like protecting domestic employment, influencing market structures from an anti-trust point of view and the public good aspects of standards [David/Greenstein 1990, 29-32; Dybvig/Spatt 1983]. Gabel (1991) describes governmental standardization policies. A widely adopted systematic is to distinguish standardization between market, government, and consortia [Thum 1995, 32-37]. In a broader sense, those resemble the centralized and decentralized standardization model developed in sections 3 and 4 and some of the general solution proposals in section 5.

2.3   Reconsidering network effect theory

"I don't know the key to success,
but the key to failure is to try to please everyone."
Bill Cosby

It was shown that the basic idea behind the phenomenon of network effects is an increasing benefit or network value when the network is growing. Matutes/Regibeau (1996, 183-209) describe benefits from network effects as depicted in Figure 2 where U_i denotes the utility of agent i derived from the technology (or stand-alone) effect a_i and the network effect $b_i n$.

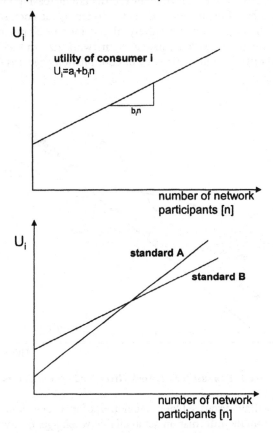

Figure 2: General network effects

Since positive feedback systems exhibit multiple equilibria, the question arises if network effect goods are efficiently allocated e.g. on a decentralized market. Here, in contrast to "traditional" externalities in the economics literature a frequently observed proposition is not an inefficient externality inducing activity level but rather an inefficient standards choice. An early prominent contribution analyzing unfavorable standards choice when network effects rise at different rates has been presented in section 2.2.2 (see also Figure 2, bottom).

But although the notion of network effects is intriguingly intuitive, there are necessary conditions for system behavior as evident in the figures above that are easily overlooked and that must be considered when interpreting and applying results. Among them are the implicit assumption of no or decreasing costs of network size and inexhaustible positive network effects. These premises certainly lead to efficient monopolies, since only networks consisting of all agents can possibly be efficient.

But if network effects were exhaustible, or if costs are increasing faster than benefits, there can also be efficient solutions characterized by the coexistence of multiple standards. Generally, there is a variety of possible developments of network costs and benefits with regard to an increasing network size and with different associated implications regarding efficiency or coordination concerns (Figure 3).

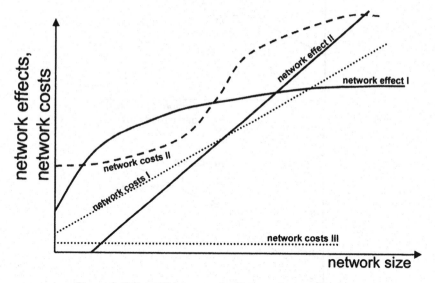

Figure 3: Exhaustible network effects and network costs

Additionally, as will be discussed later, the notion of inefficiency or market failure is not separable from the information set available when agents have to decide: is, in the example of Figure 2 (bottom), the future path of network effect development known? Is the ultimate network size known? Changing these premises certainly changes the outcome. That is why the whole of chapter 4 analyses the implications of different decision environments for agents having to decide on the use of standards. Changes in prices, decision sequence (and thereby information availability), agent size or network topology will aid in modeling realistic standardization problem scenarios with various individual influences and making network effects dependant upon the communication partners they are tied together with.

Additionally, while traditional models as described in large parts of network effect literature greatly contributed to the understanding of a wide variety of particular problems associated with the diffusion of standards, they seem not to be applicable to many real world problems. Furthermore, with regard to the discussion above, the results seem to be somewhat over-exaggerated and especially over-generalized since, although there is basically no situation without (direct and/or indirect) network effects, the laissez-faire coordination of decentralized markets has outperformed systems of centralized authority in almost every region of the world as well as in most recent management and organizational approaches. Not all markets seem to fail. The frequent notion of indefinitely persisting lock-in situations [David/Greenstein 1990, 8-9] or market failure under network effects in most of the contributions fails to explain practical issues, from the existence of cars to versioning of products, the emergence of new suppliers or more generally speaking any technological progress at all. Additionally, there are very few contributions aimed at supporting standardization decisions from a users' perspective.

The scrupulous simplifications [Wiese 1990, 101] of most proposed network effect models make them basically useless for deriving managerial implications. The simulations in section 4 will serve as a step towards incorporating a variety of network determinants and their interrelations as a response to these findings.

As has been discussed several times before, most contributions to network effect literature are concerned with the implications of the existence of network effects on market efficiency from an anti-trust point of view or the strategic situation of technology vendors. As a result, their focus is on vendor side standardization phenomena like pricing and monopolization strategies and the decision if products ought to be designed in order to be compatible with others or not. Thus, large parts of the literature cover standardization problems of technology providers in sponsored networks while in this work user problems in unsponsored networks are analyzed. Since the basic laws of network behavior are analogous, of course, an important first step of our analysis is a critique of the findings of network effect literature. The integration of the diffusion model in section 4.5 is a foundation for combining both views.

Much of the theoretical critique in this section is based on the writings of professors Liebowitz and Margolis who take a view diametrically opposed to much of traditional network effect literature, in that they have started a discussion of whether network effects are really that particular and especially different from other economic problems that are easily solved by markets. Their work again is criticized for example by Regibeau (1995) and Gandal (1995). But first some drawbacks of traditional approaches towards modeling standardization problems need to be studied more precisely to identify the determinants of the (proposed) results in terms of network behavior. The findings will be used as a set of requirements for the development of the model in sections 3 and 4 and for deriving methodological proposal for a possible future theory of network effects in section 6.2.

2.3.1 Network effects versus network externalities

Liebowitz/Margolis (1994, 1995a) argue that not all network effects are in fact externalities. Generally speaking, in accordance with traditional literature on economics or externalities in particular, a network externality exists if market participants fail to somehow internalize the impact of a new network actor on others (see section 6.1.1); with positive network externalities the private value derived from another actor is smaller than the social value, leading to networks being smaller than is efficient. Although an individual standards adopting actor is not likely to internalize his effect (from joining the network) on others, in owned ("sponsored") networks there is no essential obstacle to a network owner internalizing these effects. Thus, the existence of network effects does not necessarily imply market failure, especially in the case of competing sponsored technologies. Liebowitz/Margolis (1995a) show under what conditions the profit maximizing network size is also socially optimal. One finding in this contribution is that market failure due to network effects is possible in unsponsored networks. But failure is manifested in sub optimal size of network, not network choice itself: in contrast to the problem of internalizing network externalities (focusing on a reduction of the generating activity), the discrete problem of choosing the right network has been the focus of most literature on network externality. Under positive effects, only a monopoly network consisting of the whole population is efficient. Thus, corresponding to the literature on conventional externalities, it is not the relative but the total level of network activity that is affected by the difference between private and social values.

Katz/Shapiro (1986, 825) show problems of sponsored technologies when competing with unsponsored technologies and second-mover advantages, i.e. the advantage of one sponsored technology that will be superior over another in the future. Still, the proposed ubiquity of failing markets remains doubtful. Generally speaking, it appears to be difficult to find examples of inferior standards having prevailed over superior ones, partly because of the uncertainty of paths not pursued and their results inherent in a non-deterministic world and the imperfect foresight of individuals (ex ante vs. ex post efficiency, see the concept of second-degree path dependence in section 2.3.3), and possibly because – in a world with potential Schumpeterean entrepreneurs - there is no such situation. The reason could be perhaps exhaustible networks effects and heterogeneous preferences and therefore parallel or equally desirable networks or the fact that most standards are somehow supported by actors with patents, copyrights or other forms of property rights. A similar argument can be made focusing on satisfying instead of maximizing actors (e.g. Simon 1981, 122-126; see also section 5.3.1.3.3 for an empirical case). If we suppose that the QWERTY keyboard really is superior (see Liebowitz/Margolis 1990 for a critical discussion) the question remains: who benefits from being able to type 300 words a minute when typing skills restrict one to a fraction of this:

"...the QWERTY keyboard appears to be fast enough for almost all uses of it. If you are just driving around town you do not need a 500 horsepower V8" [Poole 1997]. This argument somewhat resembles what Liebowitz/Margolis call first-degree path dependence (section 2.3.3): There is a sensitivity to early historic events but no implied inefficiency. And if, therefore, different standards are equally beneficial after all, "efficiency models cannot be expected to predict which of several equally efficient possibilities will be chosen" (Liebowitz/Margolis 1995b).

Furthermore, the century-old discussion about pecuniary externalities is brought forward by Liebowitz/Margolis. They argue that many network 'externalities' are not externalities in the modern sense of the word that implies market failure but rather pecuniary externalities (which do not constitute market failure since they only transfer rents from one market side to the other): "Indeed, if we are consistent in our treatment of network externalities, and treat increasing costs industries as networks, we ought to conclude that most forms of consumption and production involve 'negative indirect network externalities'. Pecuniary external diseconomies, however, involve no inefficiency. Internalizing these externalities is harmful: such internalization merely mimics monopsony power" [Liebowitz/Margolis 1995a].

The point made here is not to indicate the irrelevance of externalities but rather to identify areas of improvement on modeling diffusion processes of standards and to raise the question if standards really are that different in terms of economic implications from 'traditional' goods in that mechanisms of ownership and contract can internalize the effects.

2.3.2 Direct vs. indirect network effects

Although the distinction between direct and indirect network effects (as introduced by Katz/Shapiro 1985) is almost commonplace in the introductions of articles about standards, there is very little consideration of these differences in the models. But indirect network externalities may have different economic implications [Katz/Shapiro 1994]. One possible reason is that indirect network effects are often pecuniary externalities (see section 2.3.1) and therefore should not be internalized [Young 1913, Knight 1924, Ellis/Fellner 1943]: "Indirect network externalities thus appear to be either pecuniary externalities, which require no remediation, or the reflection of conventional market failures in upstream markets" [Liebowitz/Margolis 1995a].

Empirical research shows that direct and indirect network effects are evaluated differently by potential buyers and also depend on the category of the network effect product. Still, the distinction is not carried out in the models, adding to the vagueness of their results.

The results from our Fortune 1,000 study support these findings. To find empirical substantiation for the relation between direct and indirect network effects and stand alone properties such as functionality and also price we asked the MIS managers for the categories business software (SAP etc.), EDI solutions, and office communication software (Microsoft Office etc.) about the importance of those categories using the indicators shown in Table 4. The respondents were asked to evaluate the importance of various decision criteria in the context of buying and implementing software from these categories. The criteria were evaluated by choosing from a five category scale with the extremes "very important" and "unimportant".

Table 4: Indicators for network effects as used within the Fortune 1,000 study

for software categories ▲ business software (e.g. SAP) ▲ EDI solutions ▲ office communication software (e.g. MS Office)	direct network effects	indirect network effects	stand-alone properties
	"Our business partners predominantly use the same solution"	"There are consulting services and complementary goods for this solution available on the open market"	"The functionality of the solution exactly fits our needs"
	"The solution is currently in widespread use"	"Employees know how to use the solution"	"The solution is cheap"
	"The solution is expected to be widespread in the future"		

For a particular comparison between results from the German and the US sample in the different software categories see Westarp/Buxmann/Weitzel/König (1999). Overall, the results are very similar. In the context of direct versus indirect network effects an interesting finding is that in fact the evaluation of direct and indirect effects differs. Also, substantial differences in the assessment of the importance of a solution being widespread and being used by business partners - both intended to capture direct network effects as defined in the literature - show the importance of an agent's individual environment. Although the finding that neighborhood is less important than the entire network in two of the three categories at first sight contradicts the conclusions of Westarp [2003], the respondents might have had the indirect benefits in mind. The findings are summarized in Figure 4.

It also appears that for different software categories the various network and stand-alone effects are significantly differently evaluated. While in the case of business software it does not really matter to the decision makers if the business partners use the same solution, for EDI direct effects are more important (because EDI solutions are generally operated centrally by a few employees, we skipped the criterion "knowledge of employees" in this category since it would have had different implications than in the other categories). Or for office software current and future market penetration are the most important decision criteria while at the same time the use of the same solution among business partners is not on the same high level of importance (all of these three criteria are indicators for (the widespread general notion of) direct network effects).

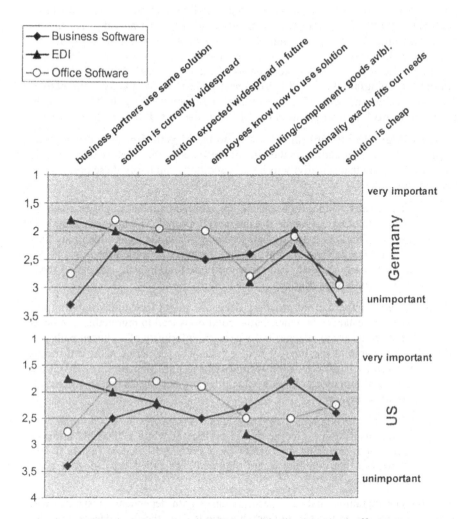

Figure 4: Importance of direct and indirect network effects

2.3.3 Inefficiency and market failure

A very emotionally discussed question is the alleged market failure property of network effects. If network effects are externalities there is a possibility of allocative inefficiency (see sections 2.2.7 and 6). But this, of course, is true for all externalities including those without networks. Thus, are there allocative inefficiencies associated with network effects that are not solvable by internalization mechanisms that seem to work well for other goods? For example, in sponsored networks the network owner can implement strategic prices to allow favorable diffusion. Analogous examples found in the literature include urban sprawl scenarios (buying huge amounts of inexpensive land and selling the first parcels below price to attract a threshold number of early investors), or bars that provide a social network and charge Whisky prices higher than a consumer would have to pay for his own bottle. In other words: are there inefficiencies that are remediable or that could have been prevented? According to Williamson (1993, 140) an allocation can only meaningfully be called inefficient if there have been known alternatives that are feasible and preferable. According to Liebowitz/Margolis (1998), other authors have made similar points [Coase 1964; Calaebresi 1968; Dahlmann 1979].

Liebowitz/Margolis (1995b) identify three forms of path dependence that make progressively stronger claims on the kind of inefficiency they impose on economic systems. They say that sensitivity to initial conditions can imply these possible efficiency outcomes:

> ▸ The sensitivity does no harm: we are set on a path that might be costly to change but that is (maybe not uniquely) optimal. The famous example is the decision to comb one's hair to the left or to the right which may lead to a lifetime of left (or right) parting. Instances in which there is a sensitivity to early incidents but with no implied inefficiency are called **first-degree path dependence**.

> ▸ There is imperfect information: decisions might look unfavorable in retrospect. Instances in which initial conditions lead to regrettable outcomes (that are costly to change) but where the inferiority of a chosen path was unknowable at the time of choice (and when superior paths are recognized only later) are called **second-degree path dependence**. Given the assumed limitations on knowledge, they are not "inefficient in any meaningful sense".

> ▸ The outcome is a remediable inefficiency: instances in which initial conditions lead to an outcome that is inefficient while a "feasible arrangement for recognizing and achieving a preferred outcome [exists or existed], but that outcome is not obtained" are called **third-degree path dependence**.

In economics literature, first- and second-degree path dependence instances will often be found, e.g. in the form of durable goods. It is the third-degree path dependence that conflicts with the neo-classical model of rational behavior implying efficient outcome (see section 6.1) [Liebowitz/Margolis 1995b]. While many authors quote the case of the QWERTY keyboard, among others, as a perfect case of market failure, Liebowitz/Margolis have a different view and have still been unable to find any empirical example of third-degree path dependence in the literature: "Our reading of the evidence is that there are as yet no proven examples of third-degree path dependence in markets. In non-market arenas, where there may be less opportunity for entrepreneurs to profit from removing inefficiencies, third degree path dependence is more likely to occur" [Liebowitz/Margolis 1998]. Poole (1997) identifies another common misconception when trying to identify winning inferior standards. He argues that the often-cited DOS vs. Macintosh example is different from e.g. U.S. 110 volt 60 cycle AC vs. European 220 volt 50 cycle AC since the U.S. AC standard is stable and DOS/WINTEL is still evolving.

Especially the notion of "lock-in" (or: persistent monopoly) is not unproblematic. Liebowitz/Margolis (1999, 227) find "large and rapid" swings in market-share. Hence there are short lock-in periods, i.e. periods of high market concentration in favor of a certain product, the markets tend to tip frequently. This has been called "serial monopoly".

Liebowitz/Margolis (1999) empirically show that instances of a third-degree path dependence are rarely to be found in markets for computer software. Based on quality evaluations from computer magazines, they find that monopoly products frequently fade away and are replaced by a product that is "of far higher quality, or is cheaper, or is more advanced in some other way" [Liebowitz/Margolis 1999, 227].

2.3.4   Costs of network size

It is commonly stated that the baseline case of information goods is that they have large fixed costs of production (or first-copy costs), but small variable costs of re-production [Varian 1997, 1999]. Therefore, networks based on information assets tend to have high up-front and low variable costs [Mauboussin/Schay/Kawaja 2000]. Additionally, the proposition of indefinitely increasing positive network effects as described in the literature [e.g. Chou/Shy 1990, 260; Katz/Shapiro 1986, 829; Farrell/Saloner 1992; 16] implies natural monopolies: the bigger the better. "...fixed costs, together with constant marginal costs, installs an inexhaustible economy of large scale operations. This, in turn, installs an externality if goods are priced at average costs" [Liebowitz/Margolis 1995a].

If optimal networks under network externalities are the size of the whole population (monopolies), all networks are too small. If network effects were exhaustible multiple networks could coexist. Even though IT might be less subject to physical limitations going together with the law of diminishing returns, there might be organizational or managerial problems restraining optimal network size [Radner 1992]. Thus the question raised by the existence of traditionally described network effects is not optimal network size but optimal network. While Arthur (1989) proposes an example consisting of one technology that has greater value in earlier but smaller in later diffusion stages leading - under increasing returns - to (ex post) regrettable market outcomes Liebowitz/Margolis (1995a) argue that "synchronization effects" are more likely to be uniform as there is no difference in the value of one more user of video recorder technology to others in either a VHS or Beta network.

The existence of network effects is not sufficient for natural-monopoly-type results. A sufficient condition for this could be average production costs that are zero, falling or constant (i.e. constant or falling (average) costs of adding new members to a network). But these costs are largely ignored in the literature on network effects, and most models assume (sometimes implicitly) constant marginal costs of network size and network effects increasing without limit. Thus network effects are not sufficient for natural monopoly and one single standard is not a compulsory social optimum. Instead, there can be optimal network sizes below the entire population and different standards can coexist.

Using the historical debate on externalities, Liebowitz/Margolis (1995a) argue that the importance of increasing returns is largely based on anecdotes and suffers from confusing movements along cost curves with movements of cost curves [see also Ellis/Fellner 1943, 243; Stigler 1941, 68-76]. An example is the interpretation of the coincidence of (first) enormous price declines and (second) tremendous growths in sales as in the VCR, computer or cellular phone markets or, in their earlier stages, refrigerators or automobiles. One reason could be increasing returns: bigger is cheaper. Another reason could be technological advances over time shifting the average cost curve downwards. They extend their argument to modern software and find that although it is said to be knowledge based with high upfront fixed costs and very small and constant costs per unit sold (even zero) (and thereby indefinitely falling average costs while output increases) a major part of the real costs is not fixed but variable, i.e. all service and sales costs. That is why they expect even software markets to exhibit U-shaped cost curves: with increasing output, the decrease in average fixed costs decreases itself and is more than set off by increases in (average) variable costs due to management, service and individualization complexity, among others. Hayashi (1992, 206) introduces the concept of a "second critical mass" that causes network effects to become negative when a certain amount of network participants is reached because of complexity costs and increased power of the network owner.

2.3.5 Homogeneous network effects

Another limiting assumption is that of similar and actor-independent valuation of networks and growth of network effects. Heterogeneity of preferences can have substantial impact on the evaluation of different competing networks as well as on the value assigned to new actors. For example, a close colleague of an engineer will add more value to the engineer's network than a sociologist from China. Another example is VHS with, compared to Beta, possibly inferior picture quality but longer recording times [Poole 1997; Liebowitz/Margolis 1990] (see section 2.3.7.2 for details on the case). Heterogeneous preferences increase the chance of efficient coexistence of networks and overcome natural monopoly tendencies. Good examples of asymmetric partner contingent valuations of network effects can be found between intra-group communications standards such as those used in corporate intranets between specialized professionals and the inter-group communication standards within and outside that same company. Thus, installed base effects cannot be generalized without regard to who is part of the personal network and who else uses compatible technologies outside the usual interaction scope of the relevant individual. See sections 4.3.6 and 4.3.7 for the influence of network topology and installed bases.

A similar argument can be used to distinguish between direct and indirect network effects. Indirect effects are - if desired - very hard to internalize in terms of the many transactions required between all network participants. Direct effects, in contrast, often involve only dedicated groups as can be seen with the famous telephone example: although one could reach so many others, there is a high probability that the Smith family can engage in family member coordination in order to select a commonly advantageous phone provider. The choice of many German students in the second half of the 1990s between various mobile service providers consisted of finding the particular group of a few friends with frequent intragroup communication to choose the same network (because internal calls are cheaper).

2.3.6 Confusion of centralized and decentralized decision making

Different instances of standardization problems are subject to different institutional backgrounds. For example, in corporate intranets, there are - at least in principle - different possibilities of approaching strategic situations in the case of interdependent actors. Thus, we propose a distinction between centrally and decentrally coordinated networks (section 3.1). In contrast to the distinction between sponsored and unsponsored technologies, the institution of centralized control within a hierarchy could coordinate dependencies due to network effects even of non-proprietary standards. Additionally, autonomous actors could change their institutional background by founding and submitting to a central authority and therefore transform the problem of market failure to a traditional agency problem, for example (sections 5.2 to 5.5); this is basically how the emergence of enterprises is explained in organization theory.

Additionally, Poole (1997) describes the institutional impact of corporate cultures and the associated path dependent properties on innovation diffusion using the failure of the steam locomotive industry in the first half of the 20th century as an example.

2.3.7 Ambiguous empirical evidence

> "The great tragedy of science --
> the slaying of a beautiful hypothesis by an ugly fact."
> *Thomas Huxley*

There are some empirical cases frequently cited to demonstrate typical system behavior when there are network effects, the QWERTY keyboard design, the VHS video system and light water reactors being the most renowned [David/Greenstein 1990, 7-9].

2.3.7.1 Keyboards: QWERTY vs. Dvorak's DSK

One of the most frequently quoted examples of standardization and inferior products winning against better ones is the case of QWERTY, followed by VHS vs. Beta VCR systems. In the following, these historic cases are analyzed, trying to avoid the bias frequently found in such studies. As so often in life, there are more sides to these stories than is intuitively and emotionally self-evident at first sight. Or at least there could be more. This story is also the basis of a somewhat heated scholarly dispute between Paul David and Liebowitz/Margolis [David 1985; Liebowitz/Margolis 1990].

In the late 1860s, Christopher Latham Sholes was awarded copyrights for a simple typewriter. In fact, Sholes was not the first but the 52nd inventor of a typewriter. Back in those days, typewriters faced a major problem: the jamming of type bars when certain keys were struck in close succession. To address this problem, in a trial and error approach, Sholes looked for a keyboard arrangement where letters that were often typed one after the other were physically remote, i.e. such that the keys which were most likely to be struck in succession approached the type point from opposite sides of the machine. In 1873 he sold his design, a keyboard with the letters QWERTY at the upper left, to E. Remington & Sons who after adding some mechanical improvements, started producing typewriters mostly based upon Sholes' design.

The general problem of jamming type bars was not solved until 1879, when Lucien Stephan Crandall invented the ball head typewriter [David 1985, 334].

In the years that followed, Remington established its typewriters and the QWERTY keyboard as the de-facto standard. One driving force often described in the literature as the moment of QWERTY's decisive triumph was victories in speed typing contests, especially by Frank McGurrin, who is known to have been the world's first touch-typist, who not only used all his fingers for typing but had also memorized the whole keyboard [Liebowitz/Margolis 1990, 6]. On July 25, 1888 he beat Louis Taub (who was using a 72-letter keyboard providing all upper and lower keys).

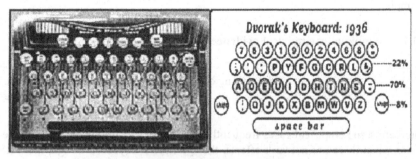

Figure 5: QWERTY (left) and DSK (right) keyboard
(Source: Beacon 2000a)

Some decades later, in 1936, August Dvorak patented his Dvorak Simplified Keyboard (DSK). His keyboard arrangement was based upon the idea of ergonomic efficiency. Frequently used letter sequences ought to be close to one another, thus reducing finger movement, the change of hands should be most frequent and balanced, and frequently used letters should be typed with stronger fingers. Dvorak claimed that his keyboard was easier to learn and faster to type with than QWERTY, while not being as fatiguing. However, we all use QWERTY, and in spite of its claims of superiority DSK remained unsuccessful. What went wrong?

The QWERTY case has been used for decades to prove market failure under network effects. It is said that the installed base of QWERTY users suffers from lock-in and does not want to change because changing the keyboard used for typing is associated with the switching costs of retraining. Enterprises buy QWERTY keyboards because typists are available, and typists learn the keyboard design they expect to be successful with in their job search, i.e. a positive feedback-loop. The superiority of DSK was mainly proved by a U.S. Navy research report of 1944, saying that efficiency increases when using DSK would compensate for the costs of retraining professional typists within ten days [Liebowitz/Margolis 1990, 7]. First, if DSK is known to be that superior, why would a rational actor not use it? This question leads to the core of debating the efficiency implications of network effects and the relation between network effects, path dependencies and market efficiency; see Arthur (1989; 1996), David (1985), Katz/Shapiro (1985; 1994) and Liebowitz/Margolis (1990; 1994; 1995a; 1995b). And second, there is more to the story.

One interesting fact that is often overlooked, is that there is no official Navy Study on that topic. The paper that has for decades served as proof of market failure – and one which is never correctly referenced – is a personal report by an individual naval officer: and that officer was Lieutenant Commander August Dvorak (sic!). That doesn't, of course, make it a bad study per se, but it made Professors Liebowitz and Margolis look deeper into the story. For one thing, the study's methodology is not sound. For example, the test typists for the two systems were of completely different ages and abilities. Then there may be a confusion of 180 and 108 words per minute. And so on. Furthermore, various other studies and simulations conducted by other people (e.g. Earle Strong in 1956 [Liebowitz/Margolis 1998]) came up with quite different results showing no or no significant superiority of DSK compared to QWERTY. The whole story is presented by Liebowitz/Margolis in their instructive paper *The Fable of the Keys* [Liebowitz/Margolis 1990].

One hypothesis is that DSK is theoretically superior - it is an ergonomic approach, after all. But what if that is way beyond the speed humans are physically capable of typing? In other words: who benefits from being able to type 200 words a minute instead of 180 when typing skills restrict one to a fraction of this? This argument somewhat resembles what Liebowitz/Margolis call first-degree path dependence [Liebowitz/Margolis 1995b; see section 2.3.3].

2.3.7.2   The battle for VCR standards: beta isn't always better

"You can't research a market for a product that doesn't exist"
Masaru Ibuka, co-founder of Sony, about the VCR market
[Rosenbloom/Cusumano 1987, 56]

Another famous example of a conflict used to show that markets fail by some standards and not by others is the history of video cassette recording. Most of the literature focuses on VHS and Beta, but the internationally less renowned Video 2000 is especially interesting, as will be shown.

In 1956, Ampex Corporation introduced the first device for audiovisual playback and recording [Liebowitz/Margolis 1995]. The advent of transistors allowed the devices to become sufficiently small for the first plans for private use to evolve in the early 60s [Gerwin/Höcherl 1995, 18]. In 1969 Philips announced the first VCR, with an eventual product release in 1972 that had poor picture quality, 30 minute capacity and cost DEM 2,800. It was as unsuccessful as the U-matic, produced by Sony, Matsushita and JVC a few months earlier and offering 63 minutes recording time. Due to the breakup of the Japanese alliance, Sony and JVC/Matsushita decided to develop their own cassette-based video system. In 1974, Sony tried to sell licenses for its Betamax system to JVC/Matsushita who refused, since they considered their VHS system superior. Betamax was released in April 1975, VHS one and a half years later at the end of 1976 [Gerwin/Höcherl 1995, 21]. From a technological perspective, both systems were basically identical; an explicit insight into physical tests and the like is presented in Liebowitz/Margolis (1995b). But they used different tapes. While Sony considered small cassettes more useful, JVC optimized playing time rather than cassette size. Thus, JVC's first product generation had a playing time of two hours, almost twice the Sony time. Each tried to sell licenses to the other; Sony turned down requests by Hitachi and did not license Betamax to Toshiba, Sanyo and Zenith until February 1977. In contrast, JVC was giving away VHS licenses to Hitachi, Sharp, and Mitsubishi for nothing even before its official market introduction. In addition, JVC offered to sell their partners complex system parts already assembled at JVC [Gerwin/Höcherl 1995, 21]. Maybe more importantly, JVC managed to win RCA, the only American television provider bigger than Zenith, as a license partner. Interestingly, RCA had already turned down an offer by Sony; they considered recording times of two hours - a whole movie – to be the key to the American market [Liebowitz/Margolis 1995].

When RCA entered the market with VHS in 1977, it soon became obvious what consumers demanded. In the following years, the battle for video cassette standards was a battle for recording time. When Betamax offered two hours, VHS already had four, when Beta had five, VHS had eight - though always at the cost of decreased picture quality (of long play modes).

Then, in 1979, Philips and Grundig announced their Video 2000, a system with impressive advantages: The cassettes were double-sided, thus offering recording times of 2x4 hours, later with longplay 2x8 hours, Video 2000 had a real time counter, stereo sound and superior picture quality, at least with the introduction of chromium-dioxide tapes. Production prices for Video 2000 tapes were about 20-30 % above the competition; but due to longer recording times the price per minute was significantly lower. The main reason for not setting the eventual standard was Grundig's license policy, involving only European partners and completely neglecting the important U.S. and Japanese markets. When Video 2000 finally hit the market in 1980, it faced an already established Japanese competition which was in the midst of hefty price wars [Gerwin/Höcherl 1995, 22-24]. And a deal in 1983 restricting the import of Japanese VCRs to Europe remained ineffective.

Maybe the real problem of Video 2000 was the establishing of a video rental market in the late 70s. At that time, VHS, though younger than Beta dominated the market due to their licensing strategy which was more focused on establishing an installed base. The new rental tapes were all VHS, triggering VHS recorder sales and vice versa. This is basically the same mechanism Microsoft was accused of using when their dominance in a market (operating systems) gives them advantages in complementary markets (web browsers). Grundig understood these principles and tried to establish their own video rental system, but the European market was too small and Grundig was too late [Gerwin/Höcherl 1995, 24-29]. Thus, possibly not the worse system won but the superior network effect internalization strategy.

Interestingly, a decade later Sony and Philips jointly agreed on a standard for Compact Discs and licensed it to competitors to avoid reiterating their VHS/Beta disaster.

2.3.7.3 Nuclear power reactors

To produce nuclear energy, most reactors use thermal fission. In the reactor core uranium isotope U-235 is shot with neutrons leading to its fission (or splitting, breakdown) into two unequally sized nuclei that are the major contributors of heat and two or three neutrons are produced which bounce around inducing a chain reaction. The thermal heat produced heats water and the steam drives a turbine that powers a generator that produces electricity [Gonyeau 2000].

Two things are crucial, the moderator and the coolant. Since pure U-235 is rare there is most likely to be some U-238 in the reactor core as well, attracting fast neutrons but not being split by them. In order for the neutrons to split the U-235, they have to be slowed down. For this purpose, a moderator is used. Usually, a coolant is used to transport the heat produced, sometimes cooling the moderator, too. The reactor types discussed below use different types of coolants and moderators: Light Water Reactors (LWR) use light water (H_2O) as coolant and moderator, Heavy Water Reactors (HWR) use water isotope D_2O and Gas Graphite Reactors (GGR) use gas (mostly helium or carbon dioxide) as coolant and graphite as moderator. There are other types as well (see for example http://www.cannon.net/~gonyeau/nuclear/rx-types.htm) but these are sufficient for an intuitive discussion of technological diffusion processes.

44

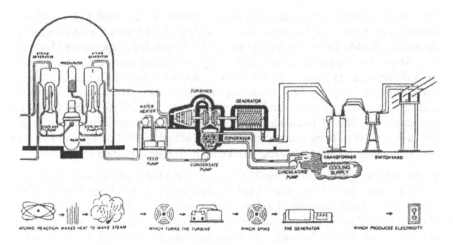

Figure 6: Thermal reactor [Gonyeau 2000]

Nuclear history basically starts in the 1940s with the development of nuclear weapons. But the military soon saw a wider range of applications for nuclear energy. The U.S. Navy was seeking for ways of equipping their submarines with a longer lasting energy supply system. After World War 2 Captain Hyman Rickover had the duty of evaluating atomic energy for that purpose. Although there have been no elaborate studies of the advantages and disadvantages of the different methods of producing nuclear energy, Rickover decided in favor of light water technology since it had caused the least trouble so far and met the Navy's demands. He asked Westinghouse to develop a prototype. It was called Mark I and its successor Mark II passed all tests on board the Nautilus in 1954. Another system was used two years later on board the Seawolf but this reactor, constructed by General Electric and using liquid metal as coolant and beryllium as moderator, caused various substantial problems [Cowan 1990, 559-560]. Thus, the Navy decided to use LWR technology.

After the first Russian nuclear explosions in 1949, the U.S. changed their restrictive information policy towards their former allies concerning nuclear energy, since they feared that Russia could become too attractive a future partner for European countries as a technology provider. Civil use of nuclear power became a top priority, and Rickover was again asked to lead the project of developing the world's first stationary reactor. In the meantime, other countries started to become interested in nuclear power and began their own research. The U.K. (first bomb in 1953) and France became Europe's nuclear leaders. Interestingly, the prevalent technology in Europe was gas graphite reactors, and the first European nuclear reactor was in fact a gas graphite reactor in the U.K. in 1956. The first American reactor became fully operational one year later and was an LWR [Cowan 1990, 545-548].

In 1954, the U.S. founded the Atoms-for-peace project to collaborate closely with Europe's Euratom from 1958 on. Of course, American (financial and technological) funding was available for LWR technology research. As a consequence, an LWR was built in Garigliano, Italy, and the development in the U.S. caused Europe to reconsider. In 1969, France decided to switch to LWR technology due to fear of technological isolation, followed by Great Britain in 1977. When Canada had their first HWR in 1967 there were already 10 LWR; five years later with Canada's second HWR there were 27 active LWR [Cowan 1990, 549-556].

Why did the world decide in favor of LWR? Reactor technology is a complex topic. The informational lead of the U.S. Navy in the LWR area also meant substantial informational gaps for civil uses. It was especially smaller countries that did not want to spend money on their own nuclear research who decided in favor of the best-researched and soon - due to the learning curve - less expensive technology. In view of subsequent developments, however, LWR's superiority is not undisputed. Few studies show LWR to be a superior technology, it is more the opposite. HWR and GGR are possibly safer because due to their construction they offer longer reaction times in case of accidents; they are more efficient because on average they are more time per period fully operational and have a longer life cycle which results in electricity costs from LWR that are about 20-25 % higher. GGR in particular have a higher thermal efficiency and are less subject to the safety risks associated with LWR. These examples certainly provide a good possible example of learning effects as in the models of Arthur (section 2.2.2). But they are problematic as evidence for government regulation to overcome market failures due to the existence of network effects especially when considering the available information at early stages. Rather, since this seems to be an instance of what Liebowitz/Margolis call a second-degree path-dependence one could ask what would have turned out for instance had Captain Rickover carried out extensive technological research prior to his decisions. This, of course, will ultimately have to remain unanswered.

2.3.7.4 Automobiles: Gas vs. Gasoline

Discussing alternative methods of individual transportation is not a new phenomenon. Especially during the years after World War II, much effort and hope was put into gas turbine engines. In 1945 Chrysler was appointed by the U.S. Navy to develop a regenerative airplane engine. A prototype presented in 1948 generated positive results, however the project was stopped due to budget cuts. But Chrysler continued its research into a gas turbine for automobiles. One problem was the high fuel turnover due to the fact that the turbine wasn't constantly running at high velocity as in an airplane. Having solved this with the help of a temperature exchange mechanism Chrysler produced a Plymouth Sedan with a gas turbine engine in 1953, resulting in a mini-series of 50 cars in 1963. Gas turbine development was quite slow over the following years, but was triggered by two events: First, strict governmental exhaust regulations (1966-1970) and second, the energy crisis of 1973. Cars should now be able to run on different types of fuel, a genuine property of the gas turbine. But reducing NO_x emissions demanded new materials for high temperature areas within the turbine, which was an expensive research task. What are the reasons why in this situation the development of gas turbine engines wasn't promoted in such a way as to take over the whole market? First, the money needed for further research had to be earned by selling traditional combustion engine cars which in turn were improved in the process. Thus fuel efficiency soon increased and technologies were developed to reduce emissions, which met the U.S. requirements.

The additional costs of equipping a car with a gas turbine are estimated at DEM 3,000-7,000 for a car and DEM 8,000-10,000 for trucks. Due to lower fuel costs, cars reach a breakeven after 22,000 kilometers, trucks after 45,000. A problem, of course, is the very rudimentary network of filling stations. In 1998, there were eighty in Germany, but the annual expected growth rate is 30% [Bundesumwelt-ministerium 1998]. What is the lesson to be learnt? Again, uncertainties about the future path of technological improvement made early decisions difficult to compare to later findings. In addition, development goals might change during the course, e.g. from high mileage to low emission. Again the question of what measures should have been taken in the 1940s in order to meet recent goals must remain at least partially open.

2.3.8 Normative Implications

Closely related to the problem of designing advantageous coordination designs is the need for normative results. Whether or not public intervention is necessary in network effect markets is a common controversy in the literature. Recommendations vary from centralized standard setting or restriction of market power by the government on the one hand to total laissez-faire without intervention on the other. Since network effects don't stop at national borders, the question arises whether public intervention might be outdated. Newly emerging phenomena like the Internet show the power of decentralized coordination, while the basic implications of network effects remain the same. Despite this, approaches to improving decentralized coordination of standardization - especially in the context of particular groups of individuals, e.g. within enterprises - cannot be found in the traditional models. Finding advantageous coordination designs, efficient intermediaries and network specific cost and incentive structures may lead the way to answering questions like that of the optimal network size or the trade-off between architectural (open) standards as XML and - based upon these - (proprietary) complementary technologies.

Thus, most traditional approaches towards diffusion processes of standards fail to properly consider costs and character of network effects and lack consideration of actor contingent knowledge and of institutional personal neighborhood structures. Moreover, the overall aim is an analysis of software vendor strategies and antitrust implications, leaving individual users and user groups with no theoretical or practical support concerning their standardization decisions.

2.3.9   Summary

The commonality property inherent in standards implies an externality problem. The commonality is that all networked activities are based upon compatibility between network agents. Thus standards are a necessary prerequisite for reaping network benefits, i.e. internalizing network effects. Network effects thus imply coordination problems that might on an individual level result in unfavorable decisions and from an aggregate perspective in market failure.

Common results found in the literature on network effects are the following:

▸ Demand-sided positive network effects exhibit multiple equilibria and the market will finally lock-in to a monopoly with one standard gaining total market share. In many cases, market solutions are Pareto-inferior.

▸ Instability is a typical property describing the fact that multiple, incompatible technologies are rarely able to coexist and that the switch to a single, leading standard can occur suddenly ("tippy networks").

▸ The start-up problem prevents the adoption even of superior products; excess inertia can occur as no actor is willing to bear the disproportionate risk of being the first adopter of a standard.

▸ On the other hand, excess momentum can occur, e.g. if a sponsoring firm uses low prices in early periods of diffusion to attract a critical mass of adopters.

In a systematic critique theoretical, empirical, and practical deficiencies in network effect literature have been identified as a foundation for developing the standardization model in sections 3 and 4. The main drawbacks are:

▸ No sufficient distinction between direct and indirect network effects is made in the models although it can be shown empirically and analytically [Katz/Shapiro 1994] that they have different economic implications. Additionally, not all network effects need to be externalities. One possible reason is that indirect network effects are often pecuniary externalities and therefore should not be internalized [Young 1913, Knight 1924, Ellis/Fellner 1943].

▸ Generally, in a world with incomplete information and rational agents (which is a common assumption in traditional models) the notion of redeemable market failure seems problematic. Problems of finding unambiguous empirical evidence for market failure due to the existence of network effects make this fundamental discussion especially interesting.

▸ If optimum networks under network externalities are monopolies, "all networks are too small". This hypothesis only holds where there are constant or falling costs when adding new members to a network. The costs of network size are ignored in almost all models. Thus, even with traditional definitions of network effects, a natural monopoly is not a compulsory social optimum. Instead, there can be optimum network sizes smaller than the entire population and different standards could coexist.

▶ The frequent proposition of indefinitely increasing positive network effects is problematic. If network effects were exhaustible, multiple networks could co-exist.

▶ Another limiting assumption is that of similar and agent independent valuations of networks and the growth of network effects. Heterogeneity can have substantial impact on the evaluation of different networks as well as on the value assigned to new actors. Heterogeneous preferences increase the chance of the efficient coexistence of networks.

▶ Traditional literature offers few decentralized solution proposals, making inefficiencies appear more dramatic, for no cure seems available. At the same time, no decision support for corporate standardization problem can be derived.

The standardization model described in sections 3 and 4 serves as a first step towards addressing some of the problems mentioned above by considering micro-economic decision-making by actors embedded in individual informational and communicational environments, the structural determinants of diffusion in networks, and by providing the basis for agent-based simulation models representing real-life actors. In the simulations based on the model, in section 4 many of the phenomena identified in the literature on network effects as described above will be supported. At the same time, though, it will be shown that these phenomena are often dependent on particular parameter constellations.

3 A standardization framework

> "If the dominant symbol of the industrial economy is a factory,
> then the emblem of the modern economy is a network"
> *[Mauboussin/Schay/Kawaja 2000]*

The standardization model developed in this section is a first step towards addressing some of the drawbacks discussed in the previous section. While modeling basically the same phenomenon, i.e. technology choice under increasing returns, the standardization model was developed to consider:

▶ individual decision-making, i.e. the particular informational and economical environment of all network actors, especially their heterogeneous costs and benefits and the information sets available

▶ clear direct network effects, i.e. explicit and separate indirect dependencies will be added in future versions to explicitly analyze their implications

▶ the influence and interplay of determinants such as network topology and density, agent size and choice sequence, or installed base on network behavior

▶ applicability to real-world problems, i.e. the model as well as its software implementation should be adjustable to both particular problem instances incorporating empirical data as well as generalized networks

Thus, in order to incorporate the individuality of incentives and disincentives in terms of standards adoption (i.e. network participation), an individual valuation of network effects and network costs in the respective context of other relevant determinants is crucial. The basic concept of the standardization models is described below.

3.1 Modeling the standardization problem: A basic model

There are various benefits and costs to implementing standards. The common use of IT standards generally simplifies transactions carried out between actors or eases the exchange of information between them. While the use of standards can lead to direct savings resulting from decreased information costs due to cheaper and faster communication [Kleinemeyer 1998, 63], standards often induce more strategic benefits and allow the realization of further savings potential. In short, avoiding media discontinuities eliminates errors and costs. The immediate availability of data allows an automation and coordination of different business processes, e. g. enabling just in time production [Picot/Neuburger/Niggl 1993]. As a result, an enterprise can reduce its stock drastically, capital investment in stock decreases, it can react faster to changes in its competitive environment. In addition, standardization can enhance the exchange of information so that more and better information can be exchanged between communications partners. Because information provides the foundation for any decision, better information implies better decisions. Economically, this is represented as an increase in the information value. Often, long-term strategic benefits are modeled like this, see Buxmann (1996) for a first operationalization for standardization problems and section 5.3.1 for an empirical case.

Potential benefits of using standards besides being able to reach more communication partners include less converting and friction costs [Braunstein/White 1985; Thum 1995, 14-15]. See section 5.1 for empirical data and sources of costs and benefits associated with EDI standards.

As we will later empirically substantiate, the implementation of an IT standard, on the other hand, is accompanied by the costs of hardware, software, switching, and introduction or training – in short, standardization costs. Furthermore, the interdependence between individual decisions to standardize occasioned by network externalities can yield coordination costs of agreeing with market partners on a single standard [Kleinemeyer 1998, 130]. More generally, coordination costs embody the costs of developing and implementing a network-wide communications base comprised of a specific constellation of standards which considers the individual, heterogeneous interests of all actors. Concretely, these include costs for time, personnel, data gathering and processing, and control and incentive systems. Depending upon the context, these standardization costs can vary widely [Buxmann 1996; Westarp/Buxmann/Weitzel/König 1999].

The abstract system of communication between actors can be described as a network [for networks in graph theory see e.g. Müller-Merbach 1973, 238-241; Neumann 1991, 11]. A communications network then is a directed graph. Let the nodes represent the communications partners ($i \in \{1,...,n\}$) (e.g. human, machine, firm) that are characterized by their ability to process, save and transfer information[1] and the network edges represent the communications relationships. In the standardization models, as introduced by Buxmann (1996) for centralized networks, the nodes of a network embody the costs of standardization (K_i) for the particular network agent i while the edges show the cost of their communications relations (c_{ij}) with their respective partners that could be saved in case of standardization. These costs include the above-mentioned cost of information exchange, as well as opportunity cost of sub-optimal decisions. Because information provides the foundation for decisions in all areas of the firm, better information implies better decisions [Buxmann 1996]. From an economic perspective, this can

---

[1] Note that in previous publications about the network diffusion model which will be integrated in section 4.5 "i" denotes not network agents but is the index used for products: $i \in \{1, ... , v\}$.

be seen as an increase in the value of information. Cost reductions can be realized only when both communicating nodes i and j have introduced the same (or a compatible [Wey 1999, 34]) standard. This does not mean that no costs whatsoever occur for the transfer of information when both nodes are standardized. Rather, the c_{ij} can be interpreted as the difference between the information costs before (c_{ij}^b) and after (c_{ij}^a) standardization along the respective edge, so that $c_{ij}^b - c_{ij}^a = c_{ij}$. With explicit regard to changes in the information value before (w_{ij}^b) and after (w_{ij}^a) standardization, the information costs savings potential resulting from standardization is: $c_{ij} = c_{ij}^b - c_{ij}^a + w_{ij}^a - w_{ij}^b$. This concept was first introduced by Buxmann (1996). Thus, the decision problem arises which nodes should be equipped with which standard. In our model, there is a tradeoff between the node-related costs of implementing a standard and the edge-related savings of information costs. Analogously, a possible stand-alone utility of any standard which is often important in the models described in section 2.2 may directly be deducted from the price which then corresponds to the individual standardization cost.

The benefits of implementing a communications standard must be determined for each node i. In order to do so, the costs of standardization (i.e. node costs K_i) must be compared to the savings c_{ij}. If the savings are greater than the costs, then the standard will be implemented. The savings of the edge cost c_{ij} can only be realized, however, if the partner node j also implements this same standard, while the node costs K_i occur independently of the decision of the partner node.

In the case described in figure 1, nodes 1 and 2 have information costs c_{12} and c_{21}, respectively. If node 1 or 2 standardizes, it pays the relevant standardization costs K_1 or K_2.

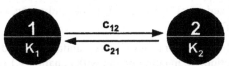

Figure 7: Standardization and information costs

If both nodes implement the same standard, they save c_{12} and c_{21}, respectively. If these standards are not compatible however, nodes 1 and 2 pay the costs K_1+c_{12} and K_2+c_{21}, respectively. In this simplified situation with two actors, coordination of the decision leads to a total benefit of $(c_{12}+c_{21}) - (K_1+K_2)$ and prevents the firms from paying standardization costs without realizing cost savings. The more actors involved and the more different standards available, the more difficult this agreement becomes and the less likely the coincidental, completely uncoordinated implementation of a favorable constellation of standards becomes.

From the perspective of the entire network, standardization is advantageous when total savings on information costs exceed aggregate standardization costs. While in the 2 player network above this implies complete or no standardization, in networks with n>2 determining the optimum solution requires identifying the optimal set of agents participating in standardization that yields a maximum excess of information cost savings over standardization costs. This approach implicitly applies a collective or centralized utility function as a measure of the quality of decisions. We refer to the standardization problem from the perspective of a central decision-making unit (e.g. the state or a parent firm, credited with the aggregate results) as the *centralized standardization problem*.

In those cases in which autonomous actors make standardization decisions and are credited individually with the results and responsibility for the effects of these decisions however, this collective measure at the aggregate level of the entire network is unsuitable. The optimization of the individual objectives of each actor with respect to the implementation of communication standards in the absence of a central, controlling unit is described by the *decentralized standardization problem*.

Both approaches describe extreme perspectives in the consideration of coordination mechanisms, providing the basis for examination and evaluation of various hybrid forms of coordination.

3.1.1   A standardization model for centrally coordinated networks

In centrally coordinated networks, an optimal (first-best) solution for any given network can be determined using the mixed integer problem formulation in Equation 1 [Buxmann 1996]. The binary indicative variable x_i takes on a value of 1 if node i is standardized and 0 if not (no investment). If i is standardized (i.e. $x_i=1$), then standardization costs K_i occur. The standardization costs for the entire network are described by $\sum_{i=1}^{n} K_i x_i$. The binary variable y_{ij} equals 0 if both nodes i and j are standardized ($x_i=1 \wedge x_j=1$). Then, and only then, can the information costs on the edge <ij> be saved.

Equation 1.1 describes the overall costs of a standardization decision. For $x_i = 1$ and $x_j = 1$, the restriction 1.2 in combination with equation 1.1 requires that $y_{ij} = 0$. More precisely, equation 1.2 requires the indicative variable y_{ij} to take on a value of 1 for $x_i+x_j < 2$. If $x_i+x_j = 2$, meaning bilateral standardization, $y_{ij} = 0$ because of the objective function 1.1. For a multi-period multi-standard extension of the centralized standardization model see Buxmann (1996).

The centralized model is based on the assumption that all agency or coordination costs (data, complexity, and implementation problems, see section 5.2.2) are resolved (at zero cost) and that there is a central manager who can determine and implement the optimum result network-wide. Its purpose is to serve as the first-best benchmark solution for the evaluation of standardization strategies under realistic information assumptions.

$$OF = \sum_{i=1}^{n} K_i \, x_i + \sum_{i=1}^{n} \sum_{\substack{j=1 \\ j \neq i}}^{n} c_{ij} \, y_{ij} \quad \rightarrow \quad Min!$$

s.t.:

$$x_i + x_j \geq 2 - M \, y_{ij} \qquad\qquad \forall \, i, j; \; i \neq j$$

$$x_i, x_j, y_{ij} \in \{0,1\} \qquad\qquad \forall \, i, j; \; i \neq j$$

**Equation 1.1-3: The basic standardization model
in centralized networks [Buxmann 1996]**

The example in Figure 8 clarifies the tradeoff between standardization and information costs [Buxmann/Weitzel/König 1999]. Shown as the total network-wide costs, the advantage of each standardization constellation is given under each figure.

No nodes are standardized in the upper left-hand constellation, represented by light gray nodes. There are no standardization costs for this constellation, but all edge costs must be considered. This yields a total cost of 217 monetary units (MU). In the upper right-hand constellation, only node 3 is standardized. That leads to 36 MU in standardization costs. As the implementation of standards in a single node does not improve the exchange of information, the edge costs remain 217 MU, yielding total costs of 253 MU. If node 5 is also standardized, then the costs of standardization reach 61 MU (lower left-hand constellation). In exchange however, the edge costs of 45 MU (20+25) between these two nodes can be saved, yielding total costs of 233 MU. Should node 1 be standardized as well (lower right-hand constellation), the costs of standardization increase by 30 MU. As compensation however, edge costs of 100 MU ((15+20)+(20+25)+(10+10)) between the three standardized nodes can be saved. This constellation leads to standardization costs of 91 MU and edge costs of 117 MU, or total costs of 208 MU. This is at the same time the optimal centralized solution.

54

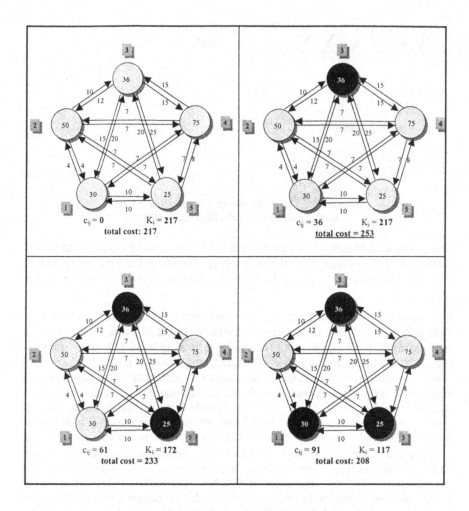

Figure 8: Example of a centralized standardization problem
[Buxmann/Weitzel/König 1999, 142]

3.1.2 A standardization model for decentrally coordinated networks

If individual agents are in focus, the situation changes. Figure 9 exemplifies the difference for the particular situation of $c_{12}<K_1$ and $c_{21}>K_2$ while $K_1+K_2<c_{12}+c_{21}$: With centralized coordination, both nodes will be standardized resulting in overall benefits of MU $((30+9)-(10+20))=9$. If agents decide individually, they will probably not standardize at all since standardizations means net losses of MU 1 for agent 1.

Generally, given autonomous agents and the availability of a realistic information set, the *decentralized standardization problem* is mainly a problem of anticipating

55

the standardization decisions of others. Each node i needs to anticipate the behavior of the other nodes j ($j \in \{1,...,n\}$; $i \neq j$).

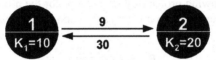

Figure 9: Centralized vs. decentralized standardization problems [Buxmann/Weitzel/König 1999, 139]

It is assumed that all nodes i know the various standardization costs occurring in every other node j and the costs along the edges which directly affect them, i.e. the information costs c_{ij} which they themselves pay and the costs c_{ji} assumed by their direct communications partners. Further data, like the information costs between other nodes, are unknown, as estimation is either too inaccurate or too expensive. Assuming that all other nodes standardize, so that savings of c_{ij} are certain, actor i will also standardize when Equation 2 is true:

$$\sum_{\substack{j=1 \\ j \neq i}}^{n} c_{ij} - K_i > 0$$

Equation 2: Standardization condition

However, actor i does not know the strategies pursued by nodes j beforehand, and vice versa. We assume that the actors are risk-neutral decision-makers.

$$E[U(i)] = \sum_{\substack{j=1 \\ j \neq i}}^{n} p_{ij}\, c_{ij} - K_i$$

Equation 3: The expected utility[2] of standardization in decentralized networks

p_{ij} describes the probability with which actor i believes that node j will standardize.[3] If $E[U(i)] > 0$ then actor i will standardize. If actor i were certain of the behavior of his communications partners, p_{ij} would take on a value of 0 or 1. The decentralized model, however, implies uncertainty. Given our assumptions about the availability of data, p_{ij} can be heuristically computed as follows. Every edge <ij> with costs c_{ij} contributes to the amortization of the standardization costs of the incidental node i. Because the standardization costs K_j and the information costs c_{ji}

---

[2] The problematic concept of utility is not explicitly discussed in this work. For associated problems see sections 3.2.4 and 6.

[3] "Probability", of course, does not imply that $\sum p_{ij}=1$. Note that **prob**$_{ij}$ is used in section 4.5 since p denotes price in the diffusion model.

are the only costs regarding j known to node i, actor i can assume that the edge <ji> is representative of all of j's edges. Combining all assumed data, node i can then develop the following probability estimate p_{ij} for the probability of standardization in node j by attempting to imitate j's decision making behavior:

$$p_{ij} = \frac{c_{ji}(n-1) - K_j}{c_{ji}(n-1)}$$

Equation 4: Anticipation of partners' standardization behavior

The numerator describes the net savings possible through the standardization for node j, assuming that all nodes standardize and that the edge <ji> is representative of all of node j's communications relationships (best case). The denominator normalizes the fraction for non-negative K_j as a value from 0 to 1. Should the fraction have a value less than 0, that is $c_{ji}(n-1) < K_j$, then $p_{ij} = 0$ holds. This suggests Equation 5:

$$E[U(i)] = \sum_{\substack{j=1 \\ j \neq i}}^{n} \frac{c_{ji}(n-1) - K_j}{c_{ji}(n-1)} c_{ij} - K_i = \sum_{\substack{j=1 \\ j \neq i}}^{n} p_{ij} \, c_{ij} - K_i$$

Equation 5: Expected utility using the anticipatory decision heuristic

Whenever more precise information is available, it can be used, of course (see sections 3.3 and 4). See section 4.1 for a decision function in incomplete networks (no full density, i.e. V<1) to incorporate individual neighborhood relations, i.e. to model the network effects in the utility function in order to capture *relevant* network effects as being dependent only on the decisions of the decider's direct neighborhood (the individual communication partners) and not on an abstract overall network or installed base. See section 4.4 for a different anticipatory decision function (different derivation of p_{ij} that is based on the concept of second degree neighborhood) and its implications on the results of the model.

As long as the individual actors are unable to influence the standardization decisions of their communications partners, they can do no more ex ante than estimate the probability that their partners will standardize. *Ex post* of course, the communications costs either remain or are no longer applicable, but the situation of uncertainty described here results from the assumption of limited knowledge of available data. The decentralized model allows the prediction of standardization behavior in a network, thereby creating a basis for predicting the effects of various concepts of coordination. Such measures for influencing the decision to introduce standards also generally apply to influencing the development of expectations regarding the future spread of standards (installed base) or to forms of cooperation which would allow partners to jointly reap the profits of standardization through the partial internalization of network effects.

In the example of Figure 8, decentralized coordination would have no agent standardize. Results are summarized in Table 5:

Table 5: Results from decentralized coordination of the network in Figure 8

E[U(1)]=	E[U(2)]=	E[U(3)]=	E[U(4)]=	E[U(5)]=
-18,25	-46,75	-9,43	-67,47	-9,7

3.2 Equilibria in standardization problems

The standardization models developed in the last section allow us to look deeper into standardization decisions. In this context, decisions about communication standards have been found to be subject to network effects, the evaluation of one agent's decision being highly dependant upon other agents' decisions. What happens if agents have to decide about using standards, i.e. what information infrastructures can we expect to see emerge under the coordination regimes described above? And how can we influence the standardization process to produce favorable outcomes? And when - if possible at all - is influencing the standardization process necessary? To learn about the possible results of standardization processes, it is useful to apply basic game theory to systematically identify and evaluate potential equilibria. This fits in with the view of Alstyne (1997) describing - among others - game theory and utility theory as "tools used to probe network organizations" from an economic perspective. While traditional decision theory is focused on decision patterns when there is no influence of the deciding agent's action on his environment, game theory provides an extension to that view by incorporating the interactivity of agents' behavior.

When deciding about standards (or in this context more generally IT infrastructures), individual as well as aggregate results are determined by many individual agents' decisions that can be quite loosely correlated, and all agents are aware of these interdependencies [Holler/Illing 2000, 1] although they might be incapable of perfectly considering them due to institutional, rational and informational bounds (see section 6). The resulting conflicts of interest are typical of strategic decision problems. Game theory provides an abstract formal way of describing these conflicts and interdependencies and evaluating possible solutions [Feess 2000, 42-43].

In this section, applying basic game theory to the standardization problem will disclose some general properties of the problem that are useful for further developing a framework for standardization. In particular the extent to which deciding agents have access to information about their own and their partners' costs and benefits determines the structure of the resulting network. These findings are elaborately explored in the course of the numerical simulations in section 4.

58

3.2.1 Information

Complete information describes the case in which all agents have all relevant information about their own and their partners' payoffs, i.e. complete multilateral knowledge of all payoff matrices [Harsanyi 1967-68, 163; Güth 1999, 1-4]. This very restrictive assumption, of course, is rarely to be found in practice but instructive for identifying basic properties of network interaction, e.g. in the form of benchmark equilibria. The centralized standardization problem rests upon the assumption of a central decider with complete information (section 3.1.1). *Incomplete information* describes a situation when players do not have access to all relevant facts in advance (ex ante) and thus have to use probabilistic decision approaches [Harsanyi 1967-68, 163; Feess 2000, 625]. This is the situation modeled within the decentralized standardization problem (section 3.1.2). If players know all the former decisions of all other players then they have *perfect information* [Mycielsky 1992, 41-43]. If they do not "forget" they also have *perfect recall* [Holler/Illing 2000, 42-45]. In this work, agents are always assumed to have perfect recall. These differentiations become important in the dynamic decision scenarios of section 4.2.2 and 4.3. When imperfect information exists players cannot know what decisions were made by other players, they are not observable. In economics, this phenomenon is often referred to as hidden action [Feess 2000, 579-582] resulting in sub optimal outcomes compared to a situation with perfect information (moral hazard) [Varian 1991, 570-573].

3.2.2 Basic games

If there are only two players, their complete set of strategies can be described by a bi-matrix (strategic form) [Neumann/Morgenstern 1967, 46-48; Güth 1999, 152-160]. This is applicable for static as well as dynamic games [Holler/Illing 2000,14]. Dynamic or sequential games (players decide about their strategies in different periods simultaneously or one after the other; see section 4) with more than two players can be described using a tree notation (extensive form) where all boughs represent different decisions [Luce/Raiffa 1957, 39-44]. Under perfect information, a player always knows where he is within that tree while under imperfect information he might not.

A very important distinction has to be made concerning the degree to which players can communicate before their decisions and make joint binding agreements, i.e. the extent to which cooperation designs are exogenously enforceable [Güth 1999, 215; Luce/Raiffa 1957, 89]. In a cooperative game, contracts are enforceable by third parties [Holler/Illing 2000, 23; Luce/Raiffa 1957, 114-154]. A legal system and its enforcement means, for example, guarantee to a certain extent that rules are obeyed. In non-cooperative games contracts cannot be relied upon; thus, desired equilibria have to be self-enforcing for no player can be prevented from changing his strategy in cases where he is better off doing so.

The famous prisoners' dilemma [e.g. Fudenberg/Tirole 1995, 6-7, 9-10] is a dilemma due to its uncooperative structure: although both prisoners could possibly bargain not to confess, either (single) party would win by reneging, in other words cheating pays. Regularly, non-cooperative games imply Pareto-inefficient equilibria [Luce/Raiffa 1957, 110-114]. Contracts are possible but ineffective [Dixit/Nalebuff 1995, 217-219]. Contract law as well as, in some sense, the Mafia provide ways of controlling the prisoner's dilemma.

It is important to note that the (decentralized) standardization problem as formulated in this work is not a strictly competitive game, thus mutual coordination gains are possible [Luce/Raiffa 1957, 89].

3.2.3 Equilibria

In static games under complete information, Nash equilibria [Varian 1991, 445-447; Amann 1999, 11] are plausible solutions to standardization games [McKelvey 1996, 5]. But there can be multiple equilibria [Feess 2000, 47-54]. Sub-game perfect Nash equilibria (SPNE) [Feess 2000, 390] are based upon backward induction for finite games [Holler/Illing 2000, 21-23]. A strategy is a SPNE if a player chooses the optimum strategy in every sub-game. But backward induction is applicable only under complete information and if the sequence of decisions is fixed. In cases of incomplete information Bayes equilibria can be determined. Without further information it is also possible that no Nash equilibrium is actually reached at all, e.g. in a battle of the sexes game (if the players cannot communicate or coordinate their decisions, see section 3.3) one can end up at the boxing arena while the other goes to the opera.

3.2.4 Efficiency of equilibria

As shown multiple equilibria can exist. Among the criteria discussed in the literature for distinguishing and evaluating different equilibria [Neumann/Morgenstern 1967, 49-52], Pareto efficiency and Kaldor-Hicks (or Hicks-Kaldor) efficiency [Fees 2000, 54-57] are useful for the standardization equilibrium analysis in the next section.

3.2.4.1 Pareto efficiency

A central concept in welfare economics, an equilibrium is called Pareto-efficient if no one can be made better off without at least someone being worse off. More formally, an allocation x is considered to be Pareto-optimal (or Pareto-efficient, respectively) if and only if no other allocation y exists which is weakly preferred over x by all individuals and strongly preferred by at least one individual. In neoclassic economics, markets move toward a Pareto optimum, since no individual would willingly trade goods or services in a manner that would harm his own welfare (see section 6.1).

Pareto optimality is not an undisputed concept, though. Among others, it relies on consumer sovereignty, i.e. the premise that each agent perfectly knows his real preferences. Yet, in most realistic cases those might have been quite improperly formed or the agent does not have enough information or judgment capacities.

More important, though, is the problem of how to handle situations where there is more than one possible equilibrium, i.e. of identifying the "right point" on the contract curve of an Edgeworth Box. In addition, in politics there might be few positive sum games, i.e. political reality is typically described by choices between a status quo and a policy change that will make some better off and others worse off, at least in a subjective ex ante evaluation. But even in positive sum games, there is no clear answer as to the distribution of booty, which has redistributive consequences. For a discussion about problems associated with the notion of utility and equilibrium transitions as well as the implications of the validity of certain premises of the "fundamental theorems of welfare economics" on market efficiency see section 6.1.

3.2.4.2 Kaldor-Hicks efficiency

The concept of Pareto efficiency conserves the ordinality of utility theory in avoiding interpersonal utility comparisons. Yet there can be multiple Pareto-efficient equilibria. The Kaldor-Hicks criterion describes a preference order for various Pareto-efficient equilibria [Feess 2000, 56-67; Böventer/Illing 1995, 259-260].

The basic idea is a possible compensation between players such that everyone is better off or at least not worse. A change (in policy or policy regime) from the present state should be undertaken if the gainers from the change *could* compensate the losers and still be better off. The criterion does *not* require that the compensation actually be paid, which, if it did, would make this the same as the Pareto criterion. If the payoff matrix shows monetary values the Kaldor-Hicks criterion ranges the Pareto-efficient equilibria by aggregate values. That is why problems of fairness are often discussed in the context of Kaldor-Hicks optimality (see also section 5.3.1). In comparison, Kaldor-Hicks-superiority is a more lenient test than is Pareto superiority; the Kaldor-Hicks criterion is sometimes termed the "potential" Pareto criterion. A problem of Kaldor-Hicks as a yardstick for wealth maximization or evaluating legal rules, however, is that it implies the very interpersonal comparisons of utility that the Pareto criterion set out to avoid. The reason is that adding the losses to determine the compensation implies that a transfer of wealth reflects a transfer of utility in the same proportion (for associated problems see Kelly (1978); Bossert/Stehling (1990)).

Table 6: Two Pareto-efficient Nash equilibria but only one is Kaldor-Hicks-efficient

player 1	player 2	
	s_{21}	s_{22}
s_{11}	(3,4)	(2,3)
s_{12}	(1,2)	(5,3)

The game in Table 6 has two Nash equilibria: (s_{11}, s_{21}) and (s_{12}, s_{22}). Both are Pareto-efficient but with regard to the Kaldor-Hicks criterion only (s_{12}, s_{22}) is efficient.

Table 7: Kaldor-Hicks equilibrium is not trembling hand perfect (condition: Equation 6)

	player 2	
player 1	s_{21}	s_{22}
s_{11}	(0,100)	(0,100)
s_{12}	(-10,-10)	(40,40)

Again, the game in Table 7 has two Pareto-efficient Nash equilibria in (s_{11}, s_{21}) and (s_{12}, s_{22}). (s_{11}, s_{21}) is Kaldor-Hicks-efficient, too, but not trembling hand perfect, though, for strategy s_{22} will dominate even when the probability ε of choosing a wrong strategy is very low [Aruka 2000, 8-9; Holler/Illing 2000, 102-106].

$$E(s_{21}) = (1-\varepsilon)100 - \varepsilon10 = 100 - \varepsilon110 < (1-\varepsilon)100 + \varepsilon40 = 100 - \varepsilon60 = E(s_{22})$$

Equation 6: Trembling hand perfection condition for Table 7

For all $0<\varepsilon\leq k$ player 2 will choose strategy 2 instead of one. Thus, according to the Pareto criterion, both equilibria are efficient, according to Kaldor-Hicks only (s_{11}, s_{21}) is a plausible equilibrium, and according to the trembling hand criterion it is (s_{12}, s_{22}). It is therefore important to explicitly check which concept is suitable for particular problem instances. In the next section these differentiations will prove useful for the analysis of the standardization problem.

3.3 Standardization games

3.3.1 Standard standardization games

There are some basic games used in game theory to explain general strategic situations that have been borrowed by parts of network effect literature to illustrate standardization problems. Coordination games are particularly characterized by multiple Nash equilibria (i.e. "somewhat" diverging interests as in the battle of the sexes game [Feess 1997, 49-50; Holler/Illing 2000, 11-12]) while discoordination games do not have any Nash equilibria at all (i.e. a "real" social dilemma [Rieck 1993, 53-64; Feess 1997, 50-54]). Famous examples of coordination games include television standards PAL versus SECAM in Europe.

Generally, positive network effects can be identified by the on-diagonal of the payoff matrix exceeding the off-diagonal as in the battle of the sexes coordination game of Table 8 that got its name from the strategic situation of a couple yearning for quality time together but disagreeing whether there is more quality in going to a boxing match or to the opera together.

Since almost all models in the literature only consider positive network effects most standardization problems are found to have a battle of the sexes structure [Farrell/Saloner 1988, 238], among them such famous cases as television standards (PAL, SECAM, NTSC) [Crane 1979] or AM stereo [Besen/Johnson 1986].

Another set of famous games is introduced by Besen/Farrell (1994) as part of their analysis of standard vendors' strategies towards horizontal competitors. Although vendor strategies are not analyzed in this work, the strategies might also prove useful when discussing user coalitions later. According to a firm's horizontal compatibility strategy these basic forms of competition are found:

If all firms prefer competing for the eventual industry standard the situation is called **Tweedledum and Tweedledee**. Thus, the off-diagonal exceeds the on-diagonal payoffs. In this situation (both want incompatibility, i.e. their own technology to win), tactics include building an early lead, attracting the suppliers of complements, product preannouncements, and price commitments.

If all firms want compatibility but only disagree on the particular choice of a universal standard the situation is called **Battle of the Sexes**. As explained above, compatibility is the overwhelming goal. Tactics focus on bargaining and include commitments and concessions. One interpretation of the victory of VHS vs. Beta was that there were concessions by JVC to their license partners to jointly carry out future product development while Sony sought to monopolize further development [Besen/Farrell 1994, 126]. Similarly, shifting product development to Open Source Communities is another means a technology owner can use to attract rivals to the own network.

If one firm prefers to see its technology as a proprietary standard and the other favors compatibility this asymmetric situation is called Pesky Little Brother (like a big brother who wants to be left alone and the pesky little brother who wants to be with his bigger brother). It is often found if one technology is exceptionally good or has a huge installed base and the other does not. The payoff matrix resembles Table 10. Tactics that seem more available to firms than to older brothers are asserting property rights and frequent technology changes.

If players chose simultaneously, it is also possible that ultimately (*ex post*) no equilibrium is reached at all, of course. This happened, for instance, when Germany and France had to decide on a television standard (PAL vs. SECAM). In that battle of the sexes game (as in Table 8 with $(s_{12}, s_{22})=(1, 2)$) both preferred their own system but mostly they wanted to use a common system. Since making the first move could tip the strategic situation, both made a "first" move simultaneously resulting in two different TV systems (s_{11}, s_{21}). For strategy randomization (or mixed strategies) in cases where there are no or multiple Nash equilibria in pure strategies see Holler/Illing (2000, 86-94; Rieck 1993, 54-57, 150-152) and Farrell/Saloner (1988).

Table 8: A coordination game: The battle of the sexes

player 1	player 2	
	s_{21}	s_{22}
s_{11}	(3, 2)	(0, 0)
s_{12}	(0, 0)	(2, 3)

Table 9: A pure coordination game

player 1	player 2	
	s_{21}	s_{22}
s_{11}	(1,1)	(0, 0)
s_{12}	(0, 0)	(1,1)

Table 10: A discoordination game

player 1	player 2	
	s_{21}	s_{22}
s_{11}	(1, -1)	(0, 0)
s_{12}	(0, 0)	(2, -2)

The standardization problems in this work – as will become clear in the course of the analysis - are mostly instances of coordination games, for we have so far only modeled the positive effects of standardization. Extending the standardization model by incorporating negative competitive effects from standardization as e.g. less differentiation from competitors would imply considering more properties of discoordination games.

A pure coordination game can be solved by "cheap talk" [Farrell 1987; Wärneryd 1990; Cooper/DeJong/Forsythe/Ross 1992], i.e. just by simple communication as prominently executed in so-called breakfast cartels. Cooper/DeJong/Forsythe/Ross (1989) show that even in battle of the sexes situations, cheap talk can be advantageous. Evaluating the possibility of communication designs for overcoming standardization problems will be an important part of the analysis of erroneous standardization decisions in decentrally coordinated networks in sections 4.2.4, 4.3.4, and 5.

3.3.2   Static non-cooperative 2-player standardization games

This simple two-player game provides an easy foundation for the later discussion about the implications of available information sets and dynamic properties of standardization processes. Using the notation of the standardization model, with two players standardization is – from an aggregate perspective – in principle advantageous if $(c_{12}+c_{21}) > (K_1+K_2)$, i.e. if cumulative savings are greater than cumulative standardization costs (which is the Kaldor-Hicks solution). The problem becomes more complex if one considers the individual incentives to standardize. To better understand the decentralized case compared to centralized coordination, the different equilibria resulting from these institutional environments need to be systematically compared.

Table 11: The basic two-player standardization game

	player 2	
player 1	s_{21} (no standardization)	s_{22} (standardization)
s_{11} (no standardization)	(c_{12},c_{21})	$(c_{12},c_{21}+K_2)$
s_{12} (standardization)	$(c_{12}+K_1,c_{21})$	(K_1,K_2)

It is important not to prematurely generalize findings of the simple two-player standardization game with simultaneous single choice (as in Table 12 and Table 13) that does not allow for modeling the fundamental uncertainty about the other players' cost and benefit data to a general n-player standardization game. To understand the importance of available information sets, choice sequence etc. in the following, some rules are subsequently changed to prepare the ground for the simulations in section 4.

As will be shown later, a sequential instead of simultaneous choice order certainly alters the outcome. At first, we assume that agents decide simultaneously and are tied to their decision afterwards. In addition, information is assumed to be complete (we will relax this assumption later). This is a most common set-up (e.g. in the prisoners' dilemma) and will be called scenario I (simultaneous single choice scenario) in the course of section 4.

To identify Nash equilibria, assumptions about parameter constellations are necessary. Let s_{i1} describe the strategy of "no standardization" and s_{i2} "implementing the standard". If for each player costs are smaller than benefits ($c_{12}>K_1$ and $c_{21}>K_2$)

there are two Nash equilibria ((s_{11},s_{21}) and (s_{12},s_{22})): bilateral non standardization and bilateral standardization. Thus, in contrast to a centrally coordinated network, the sub optimal case of both players not standardizing is also an equilibrium. If one player benefits from standardization, but not the other ($c_{12}<K_1$), a unique equilibrium of non-standardization results for standardizing is dominated for player 1 ($c_{12}<c_{12}+K_1$ and $c_{12}<K_1$). Table 12 summarizes the equilibria resulting from the different parameter constellations.

Table 12: Existence of equilibria (static 2-player standardization problem)

parameters	results centralized coordination	results decentralized coordination
$c_{12}>K_1$ and $c_{21}>K_2$	bilateral standardization	? (2 Nash equilibria)
$c_{12}<K_1$ and $c_{21}<K_2$	no standardization	no standardization (unique Nash equilibrium)
$c_{12}<K_1$ and $c_{21}>K_2$ while $K_1+K_2<c_{12}+c_{21}$	bilateral standardization	no standardization (unique Nash equilibrium)
$c_{12}<K_1$ and $c_{21}>K_2$ while $K_1+K_2>c_{12}+c_{21}$	no standardization	no standardization (unique Nash equilibrium)
$c_{12}<K_1$ und $c_{21}>K_2$ while $K_1+K_2=c_{12}+c_{21}$	indifferent	no standardization (unique Nash equilibrium)
$c_{12}=K_1$ und $c_{21}=K_2$	indifferent	? (2 Nash equilibria)

One can see that within the settings of Table 12 there is no (pure strategy) unique standardization equilibrium under decentralized coordination: either no standardization is the only equilibrium or there are two equilibria. Hence, a key finding is that an important property of decentralized networks is a smaller propensity to standardize (see e.g. Figure 17 on page 86). We call this phenomenon the standardization gap, see section 4.2.1.1 for elaborate simulation results showing the gap. Additionally, if $c_{12}>K_1$ and $c_{21}>K_2$ not only are there 2 possible equilibria but under simultaneous choice *ex post* there is also the possibility of one agent having standardized and the other not, as in the PAL vs. SECAM case. The dynamic fundamentals behind this discrepancy in a multi-period and multi-standard context are the main research subject of the analysis in section 4. Especially in sections 4.2.4 and 4.3.4 the essentials behind those "decision errors" in decentralized networks are disclosed.

When comparing the different equilibria with regard to the coordination form, it becomes obvious that whenever there are multiple equilibria, Kaldor-Hicks efficiency equals the centralized solution.

Table 13: Efficiency of equilibria (static 2-player standardization problem)

parameters	decentralized coordination (static)	solution optimal from centralized perspective	Pareto-efficient	Kaldor-Hicks-efficient
$c_{12}>K_1$ and $c_{21}>K_2$	no standardization	no	no	no
	standardization	yes	yes	yes
$c_{12}<K_1$ and $c_{21}<K_2$	no standardization	yes	yes	-
$c_{12}<K_1$ and $c_{21}>K_2$ while $K_1+K_2<c_{12}+c_{21}$	no standardization	no	yes	-
$c_{12}<K_1$ and $c_{21}>K_2$ while $K_1+K_2>c_{12}+c_{21}$	no standardization	yes	yes	-
$c_{12}<K_1$ and $c_{21}>K_2$ while $K_1+K_2=c_{12}+c_{21}$	no standardization	yes	yes	-
$c_{12}=K_1$ and $c_{21}=K_2$	no standardization	yes	yes	yes
	standardization	yes	yes	yes

In most cases, decentralized coordination can achieve Pareto-efficient results. But the optimum solution of centralized coordination is not reached in all cases. Especially if one player's benefits are below his costs but total benefits exceed total costs collectively unfortunate decisions result from decentralized coordination. This is, for example, typical of small and large enterprises within a single value chain and their frequent failure to exploit possible network gains (see section 5.1.6 for empirical data).

Thus, the discrepancy between centralized and decentralized standardization decisions (the standardization gap) consists of a twofold standardization predicament: First, in cases where overall standardization is individually advantageous but there is no unique equilibrium ($c_{12}>K_1$ and $c_{21}>K_2$) players need more information (communication or some other form of information intermediation) to overcome the standardization gap that results purely from uncertainty about the other player's actions. Furthermore, there are situations like for example $c_{12}<K_1$ and $c_{21}>K_2$ at the same time as $K_1+K_2<c_{12}+c_{21}$ that are characterized by the need to somehow arrange for a redistribution of benefits or costs for agents in a decentralized network. In other words, unexploited network gains can, according to the strategic situation of the deciding agents, be internalized either by improving the information available to the agents to find advantageous equilibria or by mechanisms like side-payments to jointly reap network gains. Solution proposals are developed in sections 5.3 - 5.6.

3.3.3 Sequential non-cooperative 2-player standardization games

If agents decide sequentially, the game, and thereby network behavior, changes compared to the static games described in the previous section in that explicit assumptions about information concerning observability of past moves have to be made.

3.3.3.1 Complete, perfect information

With complete and perfect information, both agents 1 and 2 have equal information before the game starts. Let agent 1 first, and then agent 2 decide who can base his decision on his observations of the other agent's action. The tree of Figure 10 depicts the situation.

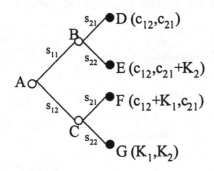

Figure 10: Sequential standardization decision with two agents under perfect information (extensive form)

As in the static game, strategy s_{i1} describes „no standardization" for i while s_{i2} is the implementation of a standard. The game can also be described using a normal (reduced) form.

Table 14: Sequential standardization game

agent 1	agent 2			
	s_{21}/s_{11} s_{21}/s_{12}	s_{21}/s_{11} s_{22}/s_{12}	s_{22}/s_{11} s_{21}/s_{12}	s_{22}/s_{11} s_{22}/s_{12}
s_{11}	(c_{12},c_{21})	(c_{12},c_{21})	$(c_{12},c_{21}+K_2)$	$(c_{12},c_{21}+K_2)$
s_{12}	$(c_{12}+K_1,c_{21})$	(K_1,K_2)	$(c_{12}+K_1,c_{21})$	(K_1,K_2)

To check the plausibility of existing Nash equilibria, backward induction is used. Before determining possible Nash equilibria, assumptions about the parameters need to be made. If for both agents information cost savings exceed standardization costs ($(c_{12}>K_1)$ and $(c_{21}>K_2)$) there is a SPNE in (s_{12},s_{22}). Agent 2 has a dominant strategy in s_2 the best answer to which is - from the perspective of agent 2 - to standardize as well. This result can be confirmed using backwards induction: Starting at the end of the tree and looking for the relevant best strategies for agent 2 reveals s_2 as the optimum strategy given that agent 1 starts playing strategy 2. If agent 1 plays s_1 then agent 2 should also not standardize. Since agent 1 can anticipate his influence on agent 2, he chooses to standardize, resulting in the centrally optimal solution (s_{12},s_{22}).

Table 15: Existence of equilibria (2 sequential players)

parameter constellation	result centralized coordination	result decentralized coordination (sequential choice)
$c_{12}>K_1$ und $c_{21}>K_2$	standardization	standardization (SPNE)
$c_{12}<K_1$ und $c_{21}<K_2$	no standardization	no standardization (SPNE)
$c_{12}<K_1$ und $c_{21}>K_2$ while $K_1+K_2<c_{12}+c_{21}$	standardization	no standardization (SPNE)
$c_{12}<K_1$ und $c_{21}>K_2$ while $K_1+K_2>c_{12}+c_{21}$	no standardization	no standardization (SPNE)
$c_{12}<K_1$ und $c_{21}>K_2$ while $K_1+K_2=c_{12}+c_{21}$	indifference	no standardization (SPNE)
$c_{12}>K_1$ und $c_{21}<K_2$ while $K_1+K_2<c_{12}+c_{21}$	standardization	no standardization (SPNE)
$c_{12}>K_1$ und $c_{21}<K_2$ while $K_1+K_2>c_{12}+c_{21}$	no standardization	no standardization (SPNE)
$c_{12}>K_1$ und $c_{21}<K_2$ while $K_1+K_2=c_{12}+c_{21}$	indifference	no standardization (SPNE)
$c_{12}=K_1$ und $c_{21}=K_2$	indifference	no standardization (SPNE)

If $c_{12}<K_1$ and $c_{21}<K_2$ then the only Nash equilibrium is the bilaterally dominant strategy not to standardize, resulting in the centrally optimal SPNE (s_{11},s_{21}). In the

case of $(c_{21}>K_2)$ and $(c_{12}<K_1)$ there is a unique SPNE in (s_{11},s_{21}). To determine aggregate (Kaldor-Hicks) efficiency additional information about parameter values is required. If aggregate savings exceed (are less than) costs, (no) standardization is the optimal solution that will only be reached in centrally coordinated networks.

Since this decision process is sequential, the case of reversed parameter value constellations needs to be considered, too. Reversing parameters in this case is equivalent to reversing the decision order, however the results remain the same. Thus with complete and perfect information, in this context the sequence of decisions is irrelevant.

As before, in the sequential game there are sub optimal decisions from an aggregate perspective. Compared to the static analysis, if $(c_{12}>K_1)$ and $(c_{21}>K_2)$ then bilateral standardization is achieved (unique Nash equilibrium); in the static game, that equilibrium could not be reached with certainty.

Equilibria in this sequential 2-player game are different from the simultaneous game in that they are unique, i.e. there is one particular equilibrium for every parameter constellation (SPNE only allow for solutions deductible qua backwards induction). The reason is a reduced uncertainty for the 2nd player concerning the strategy choice of player 1. This phenomenon will be analyzed explicitly in sections 4.2.3 and 4.3 as part of a comparison between different simulation designs.

Table 16: Efficiency of equilibria (2 players, sequential decision)

parameter constellation	decentralized coordination	optimal (centralized network)	Pareto-efficient
$c_{12}>K_1$ and $c_{21}>K_2$	standardization	yes	yes
$c_{12}<K_1$ and $c_{21}<K_2$	no standardization	yes	yes
$c_{12}<K_1$ and $c_{21}>K_2$ while $K_1+K_2<c_{12}+c_{21}$	no standardization	no	yes
$c_{12}<K_1$ and $c_{21}>K_2$ while $K_1+K_2>c_{12}+c_{21}$	no standardization	yes	yes
$c_{12}<K_1$ and $c_{21}>K_2$ while $K_1+K_2=c_{12}+c_{21}$	no standardization	yes	yes
$c_{12}=K_1$ and $c_{21}=K_2$	no standardization	yes	yes

The Kaldor-Hicks criterion compares different equilibria and is therefore not applicable. For $(c_{12}>K_1)$ and $(c_{21}>K_2)$ standardization is optimal from a central and a

70

decentral perspective and Pareto-efficient as well. In the opposite case, too, decentralized coordination implies efficient equilibria.

Inefficiencies can still occur, though, in the dilemma situation $(c_{12}>K_1)$ and $(c_{21}<K_2)$ or $(c_{12}<K_1)$ and $(c_{21}>K_2)$ respectively. Here, equilibria are always Pareto-efficient but not centrally optimal (Kaldor-Hicks sub optimal). If standardization costs equal potential savings $((c_{12}=K_1)$ and $(c_{21}=K_2))$ no player standardizes for s_1 is a weakly dominating strategy for both players. This result is efficient from an aggregate view. All equilibria for different parameter constellations are summarized in Table 16.

Compared to static standardization games, there are fewer centrally inefficient equilibria resulting from decentralized coordination.

3.3.3.2 Complete, imperfect information

Sequential choice under imperfect information is depicted in Figure 11.

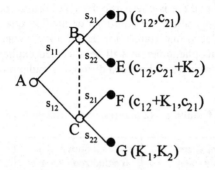

Figure 11: Standardization decision with 2 players and imperfect information

The dotted line between nodes B and C symbolizes that agent 2 cannot know in which node he is for he cannot observe 1's behavior. In contrast to the situation with perfect information no differentiation between all possible cases is required. The reduced form of this game equals that of the static analysis because one player's action does not influence the other's. Equilibria and efficiency properties are equivalent, respectively.

3.3.3.3 Incomplete information

So far, the players have had full and true information available. In realistic decision situations this is rarely to be found (see section 6.1 for a discussion about properties and problems of the homo oeconomicus). Information asymmetries due to incomplete information can originate from different information about strategies or the evaluation of their results. In other words, there is private information available to some players but not to others ("hidden information").

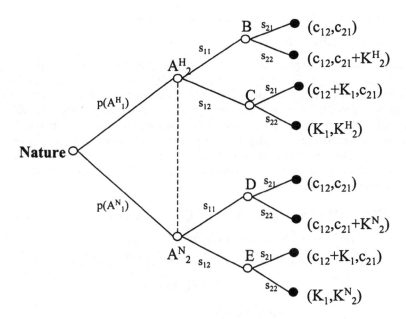

Figure 12: Standardization decision with 2 players and incomplete information

To demonstrate the strategic implications let K^H_i be a player with standardization costs higher than savings potentials and K^N_i another player with cost savings exceeding standardization costs. Only player i knows i's standardization costs. Other information asymmetries can be analyzed analogously. To start, let player 1 – not knowing the standardization costs of 2 – estimate a probability of $p(A^H_1)$ for player 2 being of type H, i.e. high standardization costs (K^H_2) so that standardization will not pay off $(K^H_2 > c_{21}$ and $K^N_2 < c_{21})$. It is common in game theoretical analysis to model this by adding a third player "nature" to provide the first step in choosing the player type (thereby transforming games with incomplete information to games with complete but imperfect information [Harsanyi 1967/68]).

Again, the dotted line in Figure 12 shows the first player's incapability of knowing whether he is in A^H_2 or A^N_2. The solution to the game can be found by backwards induction. In the last stage (in B, C, D, or E) player 2 chooses his strategy. In B and C he would choose s_{21} because of $c_{21} < K^H_2$ and $c_{21} < K^H_2$, it is the same for D; starting in E he would play s_{22}. Player 1 now has to choose a strategy based upon his anticipation of the other player's behavior. If we suppose that the players are risk neutral they maximize the expected value of their respective strategies:

$$E(s_{11}) = p(A^H_2)c_{12} + p(A^N_2)c_{12}$$
$$E(s_{12}) = p(A^H_2)(c_{12} + K_1) + p(A^N_2)K_1$$

**Equation 7: Determination of expected value of standardization
(asymmetric information distribution, 2 players)**

Thus, probability estimation of agent 1 determines eventual equilibria.

3.3.3.4 *Bayes-Nash-Equilibria*

The equilibria under incomplete information are called perfect Bayesian equilibria or Bayes-Nash-Equilibria [Feess 2000, 381]. Generally, a strategy combination is a Bayes-Nash equilibrium if all players choose their optimal strategy taking as given that all others play their optimal strategy as well while also considering all players' probability estimates. In this case, the probability distribution of player 1 over the standardization costs of player 2 is important. Thus, in the example above the game has a solution if the character of player 2 as well as assumptions about player 1's probability estimates are considered. Generally speaking, player 1 chooses strategy s_1 if $E(s_{11}) < E(s_{12})$:

(1) $\quad E(s_{11}) = p(A_2^H)c_{12} + p(A_2^N)c_{12} < p(A_2^H)(c_{12} + K_1) + p(A_2^N)K_1 = E(s_{12})$

(2) $\quad p(A_2^N) = 1 - p(A_2^H) \quad \perp \quad 0 \le p(A_2^N) \le 1$

(3) $\quad p(A_2^H)c_{12} + (1 - p(A_2^H))c_{12} < p(A_2^H)(c_{12} + K_1) + (1 - p(A_2^H))K_1$

$$c_{12} < p(A_2^H)c_{12} + K_1$$

$$p(A_2^N) < \frac{K_1}{c_{12}}$$

Equation 8: General condition for the probability estimation of the first agent

Player 1 chooses strategy s_1 if he estimates probability $p(A_2^N)$ to be smaller than K_1/c_{12}. If $K_1 > c_{12}$ player 1 chooses strategy s_1 since standardization cannot be advantageous for him.

Table 17 shows that assumptions about player 1's probability estimation about the type of player 2 are as important as standardization costs. In contrast to the game under complete information, the decision sequence is important.

The analysis of the dynamic 2-player game under incomplete information also shows situations with unilateral standardization (i.e. only one agent standardizes). This can result from the first player's standardizing due to his estimation of the other's cost situation being that player 2 will with high probability profit from standardization, too. A wrong decision results from a wrong probability estimation (see sections 4.2.4.2 and 4.3.4 for simulation results concerning this phenomenon). The first mover can anticipate this risk and apply somewhat more moderate estimations. An extreme case is player 1 never standardizing. This situation could be interpreted as what is called the start-up problem in network effect theory and is discussed in sections 4.2.1.1 and 4.2.7. Table 18 summarizes possible equilibria and their efficiency.

Table 17: Existence of equilibria (2 players, incomplete information)

parameter constellation		result decentralized coordination	result centralized coordination
K_1,K_2,c_{12},c_{21}	$p(A^N_2)$		
$c_{12}>K_1$ and $c_{21}>K_2$	$p(A^N_2)<K_1/c_{12}$	no standardization (s_{11},s_{21})	standardization (s_{12},s_{21})
	$p(A^N_2)>K_1/c_{12}$	standardization (s_{12},s_{21})	
	$p(A^N_2)= K_1/c_{12}$	indifference	
$c_{12}<K_1$ and $c_{21}<K_2$	-	no standardization (s_{11},s_{21})	no standardization (s_{11},s_{21})
$c_{12}<K_1$ and $c_{21}>K_2$ while $K_1+K_2<c_{12}+c_{21}$	-	no standardization (s_{11},s_{21})	standardization (s_{12},s_{21})
$c_{12}<K_1$ and $c_{21}>K_2$ while $K_1+K_2>c_{12}+c_{21}$	-	no standardization (s_{11},s_{21})	no standardization (s_{11},s_{21})
$c_{12}<K_1$ and $c_{21}>K_2$ while $K_1+K_2=c_{12}+c_{21}$	-	no standardization (s_{11},s_{21})	indifference
$c_{12}>K_1$ and $c_{21}<K_2$ while $K_1+K_2<c_{12}+c_{21}$	$p(A^N_2)<K_1/c_{12}$	no standardization (s_{11},s_{21})	standardization (s_{12},s_{21})
	$p(A^N_2)>K_1/c_{12}$	uni-lateral standardization (s_{12},s_{21})	
	$p(A^N_2)= K_1/c_{12}$	indifference	
$c_{12}>K_1$ and $c_{21}<K_2$ while $K_1+K_2>c_{12}+c_{21}$	$p(A^N_2)<K_1/c_{12}$	no standardization (s_{11},s_{21})	no standardization (s_{11},s_{21})
	$p(A^N_2)>K_1/c_{12}$	uni-lateral standardization (s_{12},s_{21})	
	$p(A^N_2)= K_1/c_{12}$	indifference	
$c_{12}>K_1$ and $c_{21}<K_2$ while $K_1+K_2=c_{12}+c_{21}$	$p(A^N_2)<K_1/c_{12}$	no standardization (s_{11},s_{21})	indifference
	$p(A^N_2)>K_1/c_{12}$	uni-lateral standardization (s_{12},s_{21})	
	$p(A^N_2)= K_1/c_{12}$	indifference	
$c_{12}=K_1$ and $c_{21}=K_2$	$p(A^N_2)<K_1/c_{12}$	no standardization (s_{11},s_{21})	indifference
	$p(A^N_2)>K_1/c_{12}$	indifference	
	$p(A^N_2)= K_1/c_{12}$	indifference	

Table 18: Efficiency of equilibria (2 players, incomplete information)

parameter constellation		decentralized coordination	optimal from centralized perspective	Pareto-efficient
K_1,K_2,c_{12},c_{21}	$p(A^N_2)$			
$c_{12}>K_1$ and $c_{21}>K_2$	$p(A^N_2)<K_1/c_{12}$	no standardization (s_{11},s_{21})	no	yes
	$p(A^N_2)>K_1/c_{12}$	standardization (s_{12},s_{21})	yes	yes
	$p(A^N_2)=K_1/c_{12}$	indifference	no	yes
$c_{12}<K_1$ and $c_{21}<K_2$	-	no standardization (s_{11},s_{21})	yes	yes
$c_{12}<K_1$ and $c_{21}>K_2$ while $K_1+K_2<c_{12}+c_{21}$	-	no standardization (s_{11},s_{21})	no	yes
$c_{12}<K_1$ and $c_{21}>K_2$ while $K_1+K_2>c_{12}+c_{21}$	-	no standardization (s_{11},s_{21})	yes	yes
$c_{12}<K_1$ and $c_{21}>K_2$ while $K_1+K_2=c_{12}+c_{21}$	-	no standardization (s_{11},s_{21})	yes	yes
$c_{12}>K_1$ and $c_{21}<K_2$ while $K_1+K_2<c_{12}+c_{21}$	$p(A^N_2)<K_1/c_{12}$	no standardization (s_{11},s_{21})	no	yes
	$p(A^N_2)>K_1/c_{12}$	unilateral standardization (s_{12},s_{21})	no	no
	$p(A^N_2)=K_1/c_{12}$	indifference	yes	yes
$c_{12}>K_1$ and $c_{21}<K_2$ while $K_1+K_2>c_{12}+c_{21}$	$p(A^N_2)<K_1/c_{12}$	no standardization (s_{11},s_{21})	yes	yes
	$p(A^N_2)>K_1/c_{12}$	unilateral standardization (s_{12},s_{21})	no	no
	$p(A^N_2)=K_1/c_{12}$	indifference	no	no

Table 18: Continuation

parameter constellation		decentralized coordination	optimal from centralized perspective	Pareto-efficient
K_1, K_2, c_{12}, c_{21}	$p(A^N_2)$			
$c_{12} > K_1$ and $c_{21} < K_2$ while $K_1 + K_2 = c_{12} + c_{21}$	$p(A^N_2) < K_1/c_{12}$	no standardization (s_{11}, s_{21})	yes	yes
	$p(A^N_2) > K_1/c_{12}$	unilateral standardization (s_{12}, s_{21})	no	no
	$p(A^N_2) = K_1/c_{12}$	indifference	yes	yes
$c_{12} = K_1$ and $c_{21} = K_2$	$p(A^N_2) < K_1/c_{12}$	no standardization (s_{11}, s_{21})	yes	yes
	$p(A^N_2) > K_1/c_{12}$	indifference	yes	(yes)
	$p(A^N_2) = K_1/c_{12}$	indifference	yes	(yes)

Asymmetric information implies possible efficiency losses compared to complete information. Some Pareto-efficient equilibria are sub optimal from a centralized perspective.

3.3.4 Dynamic n-player standardization games

> "However, it has long been recognized in sociology, and in practical affairs, that between two-person situations and those involving three or more persons there is a qualitative difference which is not as simple as the difference between 2 and 3"
>
> *[Luce/Raiffa 1975, 155]*

While the analysis of the strategic standardization situations above was restricted to 2 players to identify fundamental properties of system behavior in terms of the existence and efficiency of equilibria, it is now focused on n-player standardization games. Again there is a problem of graphically displaying the strategic situations especially if n is not known. Therefore, it is instructive to analyze particular decision situations under incomplete information, first with imperfect and later perfect information. Since the number of network actors may not be determined, the assumption of incomplete information ensures that the results are applicable in networks of any size n. An abstract comparison of equilibria as in the last section

76

is not possible since parameter constellations cannot be seen independently of network size.

If n is not known ex ante, a problem results from the impossibility of easily visualizing the strategic dependencies. In a network with bilateral communication relations between n agents there can be as many as $2\binom{n}{2} = n(n-1)$ individual communication relations. This is also referred to as "Metcalfe's Law" [Shapiro/Varian 1998, 184]. Every agent has up to (n-1) communication relations with different communication costs. Under the information assumptions described above there is uncertainty about the other agents' actions. Given autonomous agents as in the decentralized standardization model and a realistic knowledge of the data, the standardization problem is first and foremost a problem of anticipating the standardization decisions of others as modeled in section 3.1.

3.3.4.1 Incomplete, imperfect information

With incomplete and imperfect information, players know very little about the entire system. Neither do they have ex ante knowledge of all other players' potential payoffs or actions nor can they observe their partners' decisions. Regardless of the sequence of decisions, the individual decision situation is equivalent, as shown in Figure 13.

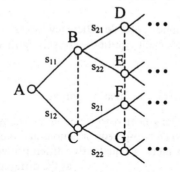

Figure 13: n-player standardization decisions (incomplete, imperfect information)

Since the players cannot differentiate between the different initial situations and the game has no definite end, backwards induction is not applicable. A forward deduction is not sensible, either, for no additional information will be available during iteration through the tree. In this situation, the dynamic property of sequential choice does not alter the strategic situation compared to the static game.

3.3.4.2 Incomplete, perfect information

A particular property of the n-player standardization game with incomplete but perfect information is different information sets among the players. While the first mover does not have any information about other players' moves and has to make his decision under maximum uncertainty, the second mover has some additional information in that he can observe the actions of player 1 and incorporate this information into his own decision and so forth (see previous section). The n-th player decides without any uncertainty. Again, assumptions about the particularities of the incompleteness of information can vary. As before, in this work it is assumed that all agents know their own standardization costs and potential benefits as well as those of their direct partners.

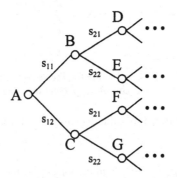

Figure 14: n-player standardization decisions (incomplete, perfect information)

The decision situation (in terms of information structure) of different players is different. Therefore, the particular case of each of the first three players is analyzed and then generalized for the i-th player.

The first mover in this dynamic process does not have more information than in a static game. Using the anticipatory decision function introduced in section 3.1.2 he cannot do more than weigh all information costs c_{1j} with the probability p_{1j}. If the expected value is positive, he implements the standard.

$$E(s_{12}) = \sum_{j=2}^{n} p_{1j}c_{1j} - K_1 = \sum_{j=2}^{n} \frac{c_{j1}(n-1) - K_j}{c_{j1}(n-1)}c_{1j} - K_1$$

Equation 9: Expected value for the first agent
(n-player network, incomplete, perfect information)

The second mover is faced with the same situation but an improved information set, i.e. the fact that he can incorporate the first mover's decision with certainty into his decision.

The difference now is that the information cost savings potential with the first mover is certain, thus player 1 can use a binary coefficient p^*_{21} taking a value of 1 if player 1 decided in favor of the standard and 0 otherwise.

$$E(s_{22}) = p_{21}^* c_{21} + \sum_{j=3}^{n} p_{2j} c_{2j} - K_2 = p_{21}^* c_{21} + \sum_{j=3}^{n} \frac{c_{j2}(n-1) - K_j}{c_{j2}(n-1)} c_{2j} - K_2$$

$$p_{21}^* = \begin{cases} 1 & \text{for } E(s_{12}) = \sum_{j=2}^{n} p_{1j} c_{1j} - K_1 = \sum_{j=2}^{n} \frac{c_{j1}(n-1) - K_j}{c_{j1}(n-1)} c_{1j} - K_1 > 0 \\[4mm] 0 & \text{for } E(s_{12}) = \sum_{j=2}^{n} p_{1j} c_{1j} - K_1 = \sum_{j=2}^{n} \frac{c_{j1}(n-1) - K_j}{c_{j1}(n-1)} c_{1j} - K_1 < 0 \end{cases}$$

**Equation 10: Expected value for the second agent
(n-player network, incomplete, perfect information)**

The third mover has information about the decisions of players 1 and 2 but not the rest of his partners.

$$E(s_{32}) = p_{31}^* c_{31} + p_{32}^* c_{32} + \sum_{j=4}^{n} p_{3j} c_{3j} - K_3 = p_{31}^* c_{31} + p_{32}^* c_{32} + \sum_{j=4}^{n} \frac{c_{j3}(n-1) - K_j}{c_{j3}(n-1)} c_{3j} - K_3$$

$$p_{31}^* = \begin{cases} 1 & \text{for } E(s_{12}) = \sum_{j=2}^{n} p_{1j} c_{1j} - K_1 = \sum_{j=2}^{n} \frac{c_{j1}(n-1) - K_j}{c_{j1}(n-1)} c_{1j} - K_1 > 0 \\[4mm] 0 & \text{for } E(s_{12}) = \sum_{j=2}^{n} p_{1j} c_{1j} - K_1 = \sum_{j=2}^{n} \frac{c_{j1}(n-1) - K_j}{c_{j1}(n-1)} c_{1j} - K_1 < 0 \end{cases}$$

$$p_{32}^* = \begin{cases} 1 & \text{for } E(s_{22}) = p_{21}^* c_{21} + \sum_{j=3}^{n} p_{2j} c_{2j} - K_2 = p_{21}^* c_{21} + \sum_{j=3}^{n} \frac{c_{j2}(n-1) - K_j}{c_{j2}(n-1)} c_{2j} - K_2 > 0 \\[4mm] 0 & \text{for } E(s_{22}) = p_{21}^* c_{21} + \sum_{j=3}^{n} p_{2j} c_{2j} - K_2 = p_{21}^* c_{21} + \sum_{j=3}^{n} \frac{c_{j2}(n-1) - K_j}{c_{j2}(n-1)} c_{2j} - K_2 < 0 \end{cases}$$

**Equation 11: Expected value for the third agent
(n-player network, incomplete, perfect information)**

$$E(s_{i2}) = \sum_{j=1}^{i-1} p_{ij}^* c_{ij} + \sum_{j=i+1}^{n} p_{ij} c_{ij} - K_i = \sum_{j=1}^{i-1} p_{ij}^* c_{ij} + \sum_{j=i+1}^{n} \frac{c_{ji}(n-1) - K_j}{c_{ji}(n-1)} c_{ij} - K_i$$

$$p_{ij}^* = \begin{cases} 1 & \text{for } E(s_{j2}) = \sum_{i=1}^{j-1} p_{ji}^* c_{ji} + \sum_{i=j+1}^{n} p_{ji} c_{ji} - K_j = \sum_{i=1}^{j-1} p_{ji}^* c_{ji} + \sum_{i=j+1}^{n} \frac{c_{ij}(n-1) - K_i}{c_{ij}(n-1)} c_{ij} - K_j > 0 \\[4mm] 0 & \text{for } E(s_{j2}) = \sum_{i=1}^{j-1} p_{ji}^* c_{ji} + \sum_{i=j+1}^{n} p_{ji} c_{ji} - K_j = \sum_{i=1}^{j-1} p_{ji}^* c_{ji} + \sum_{i=j+1}^{n} \frac{c_{ij}(n-1) - K_i}{c_{ij}(n-1)} c_{ij} - K_j < 0 \end{cases}$$

**Equation 12: Expected value for the i-th agent
(n-player network, incomplete, perfect information)**

Equation 12 describes the decision for an i-th mover. The first sum determines the certain savings potential based upon observed decisions of earlier movers. The second sum determines the uncertain savings potentials.

$$E(s_{i2}) = \underbrace{\sum_{j=1}^{i-1} p_{ij}^{*} c_{ij}}_{\substack{\text{certain savings potential;} \\ \text{based on decisions up to the (i-1)th mover}}} + \underbrace{\sum_{j=i+1}^{n} p_{ij} c_{ij}}_{\text{uncertain savings potential}} - \underbrace{K_i}_{\text{standardization costs}}$$

Equation 13: General decision function of agent i
(n-player network, sequential choice)

The distinctions made will prove to be useful when analyzing different choice scenarios as part of the computer-based simulations in the next section that will help disclose some properties of systems subject to network effects (i.e. Q-standards choice in n-player networks). The differentiation between simultaneous choice (as in the static games in section 3.3.2) and sequential choice (as in the sequential games in section 3.3.3) will be used to analyze the influence of determinants like agent size, network topology and density, number of available standards and standardization costs and benefits on size and location of the standardization gap.

4   A simulation model for the standardization problem

"The future is already here,
it's just not evenly distributed"
William Gibson

In this section, computer-based simulations based upon the standardization model developed in section 3 are used to analyze the different coordination designs under different assumptions about network structure, decision determinants such as choice sequence, agent size or network density, and their implications for local and aggregate network efficiency.

This work thus uses a numerical rather than an analytical approach. Associated disadvantages like smaller analytical transparency or results that cannot be presented in the form of an equation are compensated for by the ability to analyze more complex and dynamic structures and discrete choice scenarios. Since an incumbent property of network effect markets is the absence of a stopping rule such as *marginal costs equal marginal revenues* in the neo-classical analysis (see sections 2 and 6) relevant results cannot possibly be marginal conditions [Arthur 1996]. See section 6.2 for the paradigm of computational economics.

Firstly, a simulation based upon standardization processes within the basic standardization model (one standard, one period) discloses fundamental diffusion phenomena. Later, in an analogous structure extensions towards multi-period, multi-player decisions between different standards within different decision contexts and using different information sets are examined.

4.1   Simulation design

"Computers are incredibly fast, accurate, and stupid:
humans are incredibly slow, inaccurate and brilliant;
together they are powerful beyond imagination."
Albert Einstein

All simulation results were generated using JAVA 1.2 applications. For data analysis SPSS 9.0 was used.

4.1.1   Decision functions

Individual benefits E_i to agent i (i $\in$ {1,...,n}) from implementing a standard (see section 3.1) are:

$$E_i = \sum_{\substack{j=1 \\ j \neq i}}^{n} c_{ij} \cdot x_j - K_i$$

Equation 14: Individual benefits E$_i$

The binary variable x_i is one if i standardizes. GE denotes aggregate network-wide savings resulting from standardization, i.e. the horizontal aggregation of all individuals' benefits.

$$GE = \sum_{i=1}^{n} E_i = \sum_{i=1}^{n} \sum_{\substack{j=1 \\ j \neq i}}^{n} c_{ij} \cdot (1 - y_{ij}) - \sum_{i=1}^{n} K_i \cdot x_i = \underbrace{\sum_{i=1}^{n} \sum_{\substack{j=1 \\ j \neq i}}^{n} c_{ij}}_{\text{ex ante costs}} - \underbrace{\left(\sum_{i=1}^{n} K_i \cdot x_i + \sum_{i=1}^{n} \sum_{\substack{j=1 \\ j \neq i}}^{n} c_{ij} \cdot y_{ij} \right)}_{\text{ex post costs}}$$

Equation 15: Network-wide savings as the sum of all individual net savings

The transformation in Equation 15 enables deduction of GE from *ex ante* costs (before standardization) and *ex post* costs. As before, y_{ij} takes a value of zero if both agents, i and j, have standardized.

The interpretation of aggregate savings, GE, is not unproblematic in a decentralized network, as will be elaborated in this section. But it measures overall decision quality in decentrally coordinated networks, especially in contrast to the potential coordination efficiency that is achievable in centrally coordinated networks in the ideal situation of complete absence of coordination costs (see section 3.1). The individual implications are explicitly discussed in sections 4.2.4 and 4.3.4.

The strategic uncertainty about other agents' standardization behaviors is modeled as in section 3.1. n_j denotes the number of direct neighbors of j where $c_{ji}>0$. Where there are complete networks (see 4.2.5) all agents communicate with one another so that $n_j = n-1$. Although formally networks are always complete in the simulations, information costs of zero describe situations with no relevant relations between agents.

An agent only implements the standard if expected net savings are greater than zero. Expected savings for each agent are determined as described in section 3.1.2.

$$E[U(i)] = \sum_{\substack{j=1 \\ j \neq i}}^{n} p_{ij} \cdot c_{ij} - K_i = \sum_{\substack{j=1 \\ j \neq i}}^{n} \left(\frac{c_{ji} \cdot n_j - K_j}{c_{ji} \cdot n_j} \right) \cdot c_{ij} - K_i$$

Equation 16: Decentralized anticipatory decision function

The decision structure extending the simulation to Q standards ($q \in \{1,...,Q\}$) remains basically the same and is introduced in section 4.3. The standardization decision is then no longer compatibility yes/no but rather a selection between various standards. Information cost savings can only be achieved between partners using the same standard. Partial compatibility could easily be incorporated into the simulation model. This additional parameterization would not substantially contribute to more sophisticated results without losing sharpness at the same time. Thus, in this work, partial compatibility is not considered. See section 7.2 for possible extensions to the framework incorporating hierarchical dependencies between standards.

4.1.2 Simulation parameters and pattern

> "Sampling is one of the easiest, yet most complex, problems in mining"
> *Gold Prospectors Handbook*

First, a network is initialized assigning approximately[4] normally distributed random values for K_{iq} to all agents (network vertices) i and c_{ij} to all communications relations (network edges) <ij> based upon network density V ($0 < V \leq 1$). V denotes the relative amount of "existing" edges (with probability (1-V) an edge's value is zero instead of (ND~($c_{ij}| \mu, \sigma^2$)), see sections 4.2.5 and 4.3.6 for the relation between density and network topology). In case of $c_{ij}=0$ it is irrelevant whether agent i does not have any relation to agent j or if there are just no savings potentials (see section 7.2 for extensions to that view).

Table 19: Simulation parameters

n	network size (number of agents)
$\mu(K)$, $\sigma(K)$	parameters of the normal distribution (standardization costs)
$\mu(C)$, $\sigma(C)$	parameters of the normal distribution (information costs)
V	relative network density
Q	number of available standards
T	total periods
B, B(q)	relative size of installed base of standard q

---

[4] No negative cost values are used.

In later simulations, installed base effects are also considered. B (0≤B≤1) or, in the Q standards case, B(q) (0≤B(q)≤1) denotes the fraction of the network that already uses standard q. Besides learning about the implications of the existence of a number of users of a legacy technology and discrepancies to diffusion processes with completely new technologies that have not been adopted at all this is essential for identifying what prospective network participants a principal (such as a software vendor, a "network owner" in enterprises or a government) could "pre-standardize" in order to start a bandwagon or domino effect e.g. by subsidizing early adopters or giving away software for free. Table 19 summarizes the simulation parameters.

Having generated a network, the centralized solution is determined according to the centralized model described in section 3.1 providing the best possible value for the objective function. For this purpose, a linear program with all network data is formulated and solved using JAVA-packages drasys.or by DRA Systems (http://www.opsresearch.com) and lp.solve 2.0 by M. Berkelaar (http://siesta.cs.wustl.edu/~javagrp/help/LinearProgramming.html).

Min

$$\text{total costs} = \sum_{i=1}^{n} K_i \cdot x_i + \sum_{i=1}^{n} \sum_{j=i+1}^{n} (c_{ij} + c_{ji}) \cdot y_{ij}$$

$s.t.$

$$x_i + x_j + y_{ij} \leq 2 \qquad\qquad\qquad \forall i, j \in n; \ i < j$$

$$x_i + y_{ij} \geq 1 \qquad x_j + y_{ij} \geq 1 \qquad \forall i, j \in n; \ i < j$$

$$y_{ij} \geq 0 \qquad\quad y_{ij} \leq 1 \qquad\qquad \forall i, j \in n; \ i < j$$

$$x_i \geq 0 \qquad\quad x_i \leq 1 \qquad\qquad \forall i \in n$$

Equation 17.1-5: Linear program for determining the centralized solution (adapted from Buxmann (1996))

Note that the formulation as a linear program is a relaxation of the original integer program: x_i and y_{ij} have not been defined as binary variables. Since the simplex algorithm is not suitable for solving integer problems, integer requirements are replaced by Equation 17.4/5. This, of course, is not a sufficient substitution, but the reason for the deviation from the simpler problem formulation in equation 1 (see also Domschke/Mayer/Wagner 2002). The additional restriction of Equation 17.3 and the altered restriction 17.4 create a coefficients matrix assuring an integer solution since all corners of the solution space are integers; the unimodularity of the basic (one standard) centralized standardization problem guaranteeing that the solution to the relaxation is also the solution to the integer program has recently been proven in Konstroffer (2001, 35-39), see section 5.2.2.2. Still, the computational complexity of the centralized model becomes clear when we see that the number of variables (x_i for all agents and y_{ij} for all communication relations) and restrictions is polynomialy dependent upon the problem size n as described by Equation 18.

$$\text{number of variables} = \underbrace{n}_{(agents)} + \underbrace{\sum_{1}^{n-1} i}_{(edges)} = \sum_{1}^{n} i = \frac{n \cdot (n+1)}{2} = \frac{n^2 + n}{2}$$

$$\text{number of restrictions} = n + 4 \cdot \sum_{i=1}^{n-1} i = \frac{(n-1) \cdot n}{2} \cdot 4 + n = 2n^2 - n$$

Equation 18: Complexity of the standardization problem
(apart from non-negativity conditions)

That is why most simulations use a network consisting of 35 agents corresponding to 630 variables and 2,415 restrictions. Where appropriate, network size has been altered (as e.g. in section 4.2.5 to n=250).

Although $c_{ij} = c_{ji}$ is not required in the course of the simulations, both directed edges can be considered for the linear program using one variable y_{ij} by connecting the sum of both costs in the objective function of Equation 15.1. That does not make any difference because individual savings are irrelevant to the centralized solution.

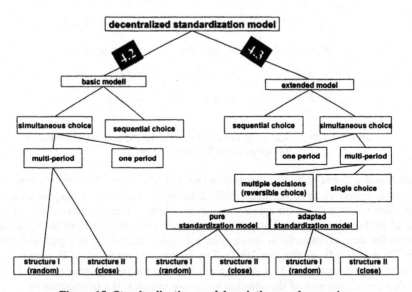

Figure 15: Standardization model variations and scenarios

After determining the centralized solution, the decentralized decisions are computed. Either the process stops after one period, or the agents can reconsider their decisions using additionally available information about their partners' decisions according to the relevant decision scenarios. The whole simulation process is repeated 50 times in most cases before altering particular parameters such as mostly reducing $\mu(K)$ and then starting anew. In case of obvious solutions, the number of repetitions was sometimes reduced or a heuristic solution for the centrally coordinated network was used as is always noted in the relevant scenarios. Unless otherwise noted, the default simulation configuration consists of changing $\mu(K)$ in steps of 125 or 250, V in steps of 0.03. On average the figures in this section consist of about 4,500 simulation runs each. Figure 15 summarizes all the scenarios used.

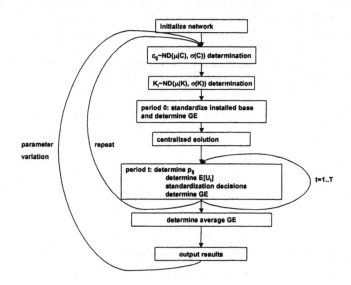

Figure 16: Simulation pattern

4.2 The basic standardization problem

4.2.1 The single-period basic standardization problem

4.2.1.1 The standardization gap

Centralized and decentralized standardization decisions are compared using mean standardization costs that vary between 45,000 and 0. The number of agents standardizing is denoted with *no_stan*(z) (centralized) and *no_stan*(dz) (decentralized). GE describes total savings. Standardization costs are varied and assumed to be normally distributed with a standard deviation of $\sigma(K)=1,000$; information costs are also normally distributed with $\mu=1,000$ and $\sigma=200$.

Table 20: Simulation parameters (basic standardization problem)

μ(C) = 1,000	σ(C) = 200	μ(K) = *var.*	σ(K) = 1,000	
n = 35	T = 1	V = 1.0	B = 0.0	Q = 1

As the results from both forms of coordination are identical when standardization costs are either very high or very low relative to information costs, leading either to absolutely no or complete standardization respectively, this analysis focuses on more interesting 'moderate' values. To compare the quality of decision-making in both extreme forms of coordination, Figure 17 shows the results from randomly generated networks according to the parameter values as described in Table 20. Cost savings for the entire network are graphed against decreasing expected values μ(K) on the abscissa. Structurally equivalent phenomena result from varying information costs instead [Buxmann/Weitzel/König 1999].

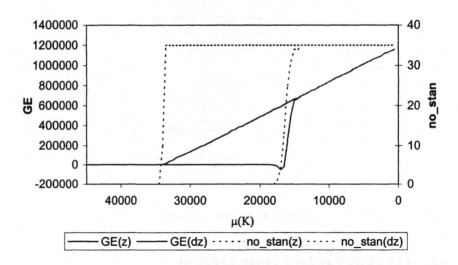

Figure 17: The standardization gap

In a centrally coordinated network, all agents standardize if μ(K) ≤ 34,000. Here, the mean sum of standardization costs is smaller than information costs. For the parameters used, there was no mixed standardization solution, i.e. central coordination always resulted in either network-wide or no standardization at all. Strongly increasing standard deviation evidently increases the probability for mixed solutions (see also section 4.2.6.2 and 4.3.2).

In a decentrally coordinated network, agents standardize much later[5], i.e. only at significantly lower standardization costs do they consider standardizing to be an advantageous strategy. Uncertainty about their partners' standardization behavior and thereby their ability to reap network effects implies a start-up problem or excess inertia (section 2.2) since no agent is willing to bear the disproportionate risk of being the first adopter of a standard: all actors perceive an incentive to wait and see which standard prevails in order to avoid the risk of a premature and possibly unfavorable decision. At lower K ($\mu(K)$=[19,000; 16,700]) some agents decide in favor of standardizing but not all their expected partners which results in negative savings subsequently. From the perspective of the entire network this means that the wrong decision was made because the deteriorations in the individual positions of each node outweigh the improvements. In contrast, wrong decisions are impossible under centralized coordination, as the ex post results cannot deviate from the ex ante planned results. Measured against centralized coordination, too few actors standardize (similar to the unilateral standardizations in section 3.3.3.4).

For $\mu(K)$<14,000 decentralized decisions equal those in centrally coordinated networks. Thus there is an intuitive discrepancy between centralized and decentralized networks that takes on the form depicted in Figure 17 for the basic standardization problem. In the course of this chapter, this discrepancy will be looked at in much more detail when extending the decision scenario step by step. We call this perpendicular distance between GE(z) and GE(dz) the *standardization gap* quantifying the magnitude of the standardization problem. Examples of standardization gaps are manifold and include e.g. EDI networks.

Narrowly interpreted, these correlations are only valid for the constellations of parameters upon which they are based. Structurally however, other values and distribution assumptions yield analogous results. Generally, it can be said that given decentralized coordination, the frequency of standardization ceteris paribus increases with c_{ij} or a growing installed base and decreases with K_j. The risk of incorrect decisions under decentralized coordination leads to less willingness to standardize within the moderate range of values. Measured in cumulative, network-wide costs, the accuracy of the solution achieved in the centralized model cannot be attained by the decentralized network. On the other hand, there are no coordination costs in the decentralized model. Network-wide savings attainable through centralized coordination determine the critical value for the costs of coordination above which a centralized solution is no longer advantageous. This value corresponds to the (vertical) size of the standardization gap.

---

[5] "Later" in this context does not describe a later period in time regarding one particular diffusion process, of course, but rather "at parameter constellations farther to the right of the abscissa" (as mostly lower K). Since the relevant scenario is always clear, this use of language makes a discussion of the results easier.

4.2.1.2   Stability of the standardization gap

The standardization gap is determined by the parameters $\mu(C)$, $\sigma(C)$, and $\sigma(K)$. For further analysis, it is described using three $\mu(K)$ coordinates:

> **A**: Left border of the standardization gap (i.e. the maximal $\mu(K)$ with centralized standardization)

> **B**: Maximal $\mu(K)$ at which at least one agent standardizes in a decentralized network (i.e. when decentralized standardization begins)

> **C**: Right border of the standardization gap (i.e. the maximal $\mu(K)$ of all agents standardizing in both coordination forms)

For analyzing the position of these points and their stability, six different network sizes (n={5; 15; 25; 35; 45; 55}) and different cost parameters ($\mu(C)$={1000; 2000; 3000), $\sigma(C)$={200; 400; 600}, $\sigma(K)$= {500; 1000; 2000}) were used. Since in all simulations described above centralized coordination showed no mixed solutions, exchanging accuracy for simulation runs the centralized results were determined using the heuristic that all agents standardize if $\Sigma c_{ij} \leq \Sigma K_i$ or no agents, otherwise. Possible deviations from the real optimum at very high $\sigma(K)$ and $\sigma(C)$ are possible but would only slightly change the position of A.

As one could expect, the position of points A, B, and C is mostly determined by n und $\mu(C)$.

4.2.1.2.1   A: First centralized activities

A could always be explained by $(n-1)*\mu(C)$. At small $\mu(C)$, increases of $\sigma(K)$ raised A slightly by up to 2,000 towards higher $\mu(K)$ values, mostly independent of n. Due to the obvious multiplicative properties, regression analysis is not appropriate here. The correlation between $\mu(K_A)$ and the mean deviations was close to 0 and not significant (to 0.05) while there was a significant correlation (0.01 level) between $\mu(K)$, $\mu(C)$, and n with $r(\mu(K), \mu(C))=0.54$ and $r(\mu(K), n)=0.78$.

4.2.1.2.2   B: First decentralized activities

B showed similar correlations but also a systematic influence of both deviation parameters. As shown in Table 21 an increase of both deviations implied moving the abscissa values of B towards higher $\mu(K)$ values. A formalization of these dependencies is not easy due to the non additive relationships. For large networks (n $\geq$ 35) in which the influence of deviation values decrease, the relation can be approximated by

$$\mu(K) = \frac{n \cdot \mu(C)}{2}$$

with deviations of less than 10% in 94% of all cases.

Table 21: μ(K)-coordinates of B depending on n and other parameters

μ(C)	σ(C)	σ(K)	n=5	n=15	n=25	n=35	n=45	n=55
1000	200	500	2750	8000	13000	18000	23000	28000
1000	200	1000	3750	8500	13500	18500	24000	29500
1000	200	2000	5750	10500	15000	20000	25000	30000
1000	400	500	3000	8500	14000	18500	24000	29000
1000	400	1000	4000	8750	14000	19500	24000	29000
1000	400	2000	6000	10750	15500	21000	25500	31000
1000	600	500	3250	9000	14500	20500	25000	31000
1000	600	1000	4000	9250	15500	20000	25500	30000
1000	600	2000	6750	11250	16500	21000	25500	32000
2000	200	500	5000	15250	25000	35000	45000	55000
2000	200	1000	5750	15500	25500	35500	45500	55500
2000	200	2000	7750	17000	27000	38000	47500	57000
2000	400	500	5000	15250	26000	36500	46500	56000
2000	400	1000	5750	16000	26000	36500	46500	56500
2000	400	2000	7250	18000	27000	37500	47000	57500
2000	600	500	5250	16000	26500	36000	46500	57000
2000	600	1000	6000	16250	26500	38000	47000	57500
2000	600	2000	7500	17500	28000	38000	47500	58500
3000	200	500	7000	22000	37500	52000	67500	82500
3000	200	1000	7500	22500	37500	52500	68000	83000
3000	200	2000	9500	24250	39000	54500	70000	84000
3000	400	500	7250	22250	37500	53000	68000	83500
3000	400	1000	8000	22750	38000	53500	68500	84000
3000	400	2000	9750	24250	39000	55000	70500	84500
3000	600	500	7250	23250	39000	53500	69500	86000
3000	600	1000	8000	23500	38500	54000	70000	84500
3000	600	2000	10250	24750	39000	55000	71000	85500

4.2.1.2.3   C: Right border of the standardization gap

The position of **C** is dissected not in its absolute position but relative to B. Table 22 shows the difference between B and C, i.e. those constellations where there are standardization activities in a decentralized network but no centralized solution quality is attained, however.

Table 22: Difference of μ(K)-coordinates of B and C
depending on n and other parameters

μ(C)	σ(C)	σ(K)	n=5	n=15	n=25	n=35	n=45	n=55
1000	200	500	2000	2500	3000	3500	4000	4000
1000	200	1000	3450	3500	4500	4500	5000	6500
1000	200	2000	5750	6750	7000	7500	7000	7500
1000	400	500	2500	4250	6000	5500	7000	8500
1000	400	1000	3600	4500	6500	7500	8000	8500
1000	400	2000	6000	8000	9000	10500	10000	11500
1000	600	500	3150	5500	8000	9500	10000	12500
1000	600	1000	4000	6000	8500	9500	11000	11500
1000	600	2000	6750	9250	11000	11000	11000	15000
2000	200	500	2000	2500	3000	3000	4000	3500
2000	200	1000	3750	3500	4000	4000	4500	4500
2000	200	2000	7050	6250	7000	8000	8000	7000
2000	400	500	2500	3750	6000	6500	7500	7500
2000	400	1000	4000	4750	5500	6500	7500	8500
2000	400	2000	6450	7750	7500	9000	9500	10500
2000	600	500	3250	5000	7500	8500	11000	12000
2000	600	1000	4500	6250	8500	10500	11000	12500
2000	600	2000	7500	8750	10500	12000	11500	14000
3000	200	500	2000	2250	3000	3000	4000	4000
3000	200	1000	3500	3250	4000	4000	5500	5000
3000	200	2000	6750	6750	7000	8000	8500	7000
3000	400	500	2500	3250	4500	5500	6000	7500
3000	400	1000	4000	4500	5500	6500	7000	8000
3000	400	2000	6500	7250	7500	9000	10500	10000
3000	600	500	3250	5750	7500	8000	10000	12500
3000	600	1000	4500	6000	8000	9000	10500	12000
3000	600	2000	8000	8250	8500	11000	12500	14000

Again, as well as the movement of B towards higher $\mu(K)$ values, a systematic dependency on $\sigma(K)$ and $\sigma(C)$ can be seen expanding the gap with increased deviation. This can be explained as follows: since every agent has to anticipate his partners' decisions and since this anticipation implies estimating the partners' information costs to the partners' partners, a decrease in $\sigma(C)$ also lowers uncertainty for known c_{ji} become more similar and thus the estimations improve closing the gap between B and C.

The effect of different $\sigma(K)$ affects the aggregate network: the smaller the differences in standardization costs, the more similar the agents' decisions. With huge deviations of standardization costs, some agents standardize even "earlier", others always "later". The aggregate effect is an extension and flattening of both, the GE and the *no_stan* graph.

Figure 18 summarizes the findings concerning the fundamental coordinates determining the standardization gap. In the next section, a multi-period analysis of the standardization gap shows the dynamic aspects of standardization processes.

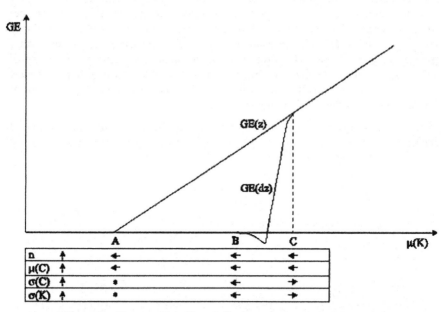

Figure 18: Changes of A, B, and C when varying cost parameters
(* = no significant correlation)

4.2.2 The multi-period basic standardization problem

4.2.2.1 The standardization gap

In this section, a dynamic extension of the basic standardization model shows the influence of broadening the decision horizon to T periods and especially allows us

92

to identify the number of periods before stable equilibria can be reached, i.e. no additional agent standardizes. The simulation parameters used in this section are summarized in Table 23.

Table 23: Simulation parameters (multi-period basic standardization problem)

$\mu(C) = 1,000$	$\sigma(C) = 200$	$\mu(K) = $ var.	$\sigma(K) = 1,000$	
$n = 35$	$T = 35$	$V = 1.0$	$B = 0.0$	$Q = 1$

Firstly, it is assumed that an agent can only decide to implement a standard once and that after this decision he is tied to it. In other words, he can choose not to standardize until - if at all - he finds it advantageous at any one time. Therefore, in this constellation, an agent cannot de-install or change a standard ($Q=1$). Incomplete but perfect information is assumed. If an agent can see that a partner has standardized, the uncertainty about this partner's action vanishes ($p_{ij}=1$). This common setting will be called the (multi-period) simultaneous single choice scenario (as opposed to simultaneous reversible and sequential choice introduced later) (see section 4.2.3 for an exact analogy to the scenario presented by Arthur (section 2.2)). Thus, the state of the network (as binary $1*n$-vector consisting of all agents' x_i) and therefore the available information' set can change up to $(n-1)$ times; no later than in period n all agents will eventually have made a decision in favor of standardization or they will no longer do so.

Figure 19 and Figure 20 show the development of GE in the first and last period and over time.

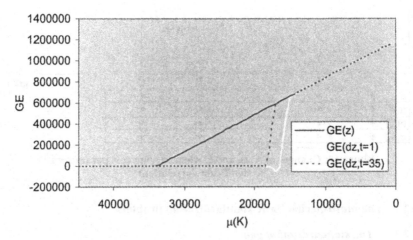

Figure 19: GE (centralized and decentralized) in t=1 and t=35

The centralized solution is obviously the same for each period and thus only depicted once. One can see that the negative values of GE(dz,t=1) are neutralized over time. Uncertainty for later adopters is reduced by the costly standardizations of a few early adopters in period 1. Then, they also standardize. The first movers' additional costs are neutralized and later yield benefits. This phenomenon is often called the penguin effect in network effect literature (section 2.2).

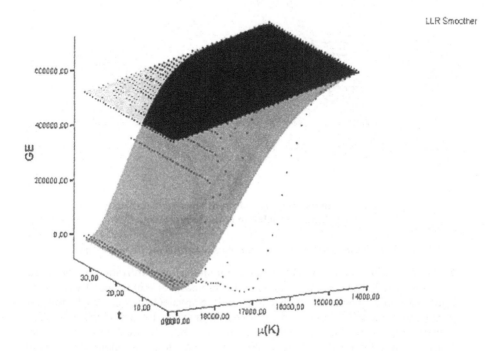

Figure 20: GE(z) and GE(dz) depending on μ(K) and t

Figure 21 gives a detailed impression of the dynamics behind the penguin effect: the area between points B and C of the standardization gap shows the "speed" of the standardization process towards the centralized equilibrium. The figure shows only seven periods because afterwards there was no longer any network activity. The linear graph in the background is the centralized solution.

The penguin effect is very apparent, since the network reacts quite quickly to the actions of the first movers. As early as period 3, there only are marginal discrepancies with the stationary graph. The question as to the period in which a stationary equilibrium can be expected is dealt with in section 4.2.5.

94

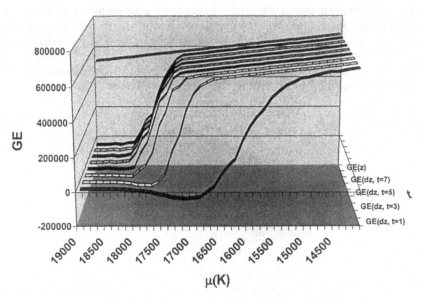

**Figure 21: GE in different periods until reaching a stationary state
(centralized solution in the background)**

4.2.2.2 Single standard implementation vs. continuous license costs

So far simulations were based on the assumption that standardization implies costs in every period. This resembles software license costs or more generally the operating costs of running a standard. Structurally equivalent findings result from assuming that standardization costs *only* occur in the very first period the standard is actually implemented (i.e. pure implementation costs). To prove this, the simulations shown in Figure 19 and Figure 20 above were altered to capture the effect of standardization costs in only one period. Results are shown in Figure 22 and Figure 23.

In periods after standardization, savings equal the sum of saved information costs and therefore are constant (on average) throughout the simulation because only $\mu(K)$ varies. But in periods t=2 to t=8 - it is here that the last agent standardized - there are hidden compensations since some agents standardize only then, reducing (summed) GE of the first movers afterwards.

The standardization model only considers the costs for one period. Thus, results are necessarily identical. Since the analyzed phenomena become much clearer using the license cost assumptions (as demonstrated in Figure 19 and Figure 20 and as will become more evident later) we will use this assumption throughout this work. This assumption becomes problematic when substantial technology price changes over time need to be considered as proposed in section 7.2 to incorporate vendor side intertemporal pricing strategies. In that case, the anticipation calculus would have to be adapted. In a slightly different context, Habermeier (1989) pro-

95

poses to model prohibitive switching cost using a single choice scenario. Our empirical data about standardization problems from EDI networks also suggest modeling the license or operations costs scenario, see section 5.1.5.

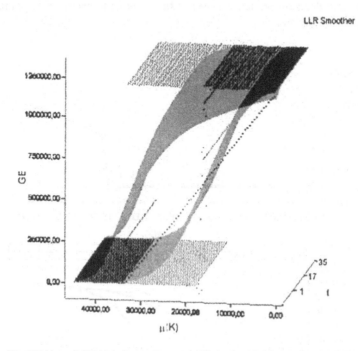

Figure 22: GE(z) and GE(dz) depending on μ(K) and t (single implementation costs)

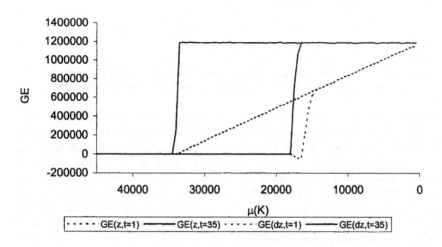

Figure 23: GE(z) and GE(dz) (single implementation costs)

4.2.3 Sequential choice

The above simulations used a simultaneous decision assumption within the relevant periods, i.e. each actor had a chance to adopt a standard in each period. We now alter the decision sequence to see if there are differences when using a sequential choice model.

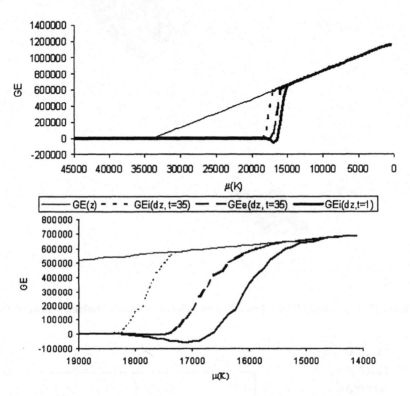

Figure 24: GEe (sequential single choice), compared to GEi (simultaneous choice)
(bottom: magnified area between points B and C of standardization gap)

To separate decision choice phenomena, we will now use a different interpretation of "period" that does not focus on finding out WHEN there is an equilibrium. In one period, one agent decides. In contrast to the situation before, each agent has one chance (one "period" or rather "sub period") when he can decide and he can take advantage of his knowledge of all his precedents' decisions (incomplete, perfect information). As modeled in 3.3 for agents deciding after him he uses the anticipatory decision function of section 3.1.2 and for those having already decided p_{ij} is either 1 or 0 (see above). Thus, the period when a stationary equilibrium is reached in the multi-period simultaneous case is comparable (if at all) only with the n-th period in the sequential model because then every agent has had a chance to standardize. While in the simultaneous model results for each period had a sensible meaning, here "period" is no more than an artificial means of altering some properties of the constellation when using the decentralized coordination design. The differentiation between simultaneous and sequential choice will be particularly needed when discussing multi-standard decisions later on. Sequential choice settings are often used throughout network effect literature without considering the influence of this special setting when generalizing results. See for example section 4.2.3 for an analogy to the sequential choice scenario presented by Arthur (but with no foresight, i.e. anticipation of others' behavior; section 2.2).

Figure 24 compares GE of the sequential (GEe) model in t=35 to the centralized and decentralized simultaneous GE (GEi) (t=1; t=35) from Figure 19. Again, the advantage of using periodic standardization costs is obvious.

As a result, the sequential model dominates the first period results of the basic model due to decreased average uncertainty but in terms of eventual efficiency remains behind the simultaneous case at stationary state because agents can only make one yes/no decision at one particular informational state. There are fewer standardization incentives because - due to higher certainty - partners' decisions not to standardize (which are revocable in the simultaneous model) are more important (reducing positive probabilities to zero). The negative part of GEe results from early deciders under high uncertainty.

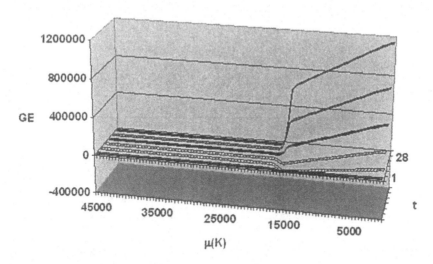

Figure 25: GEe in t={1;7;14;21;28;35}

Figure 25 shows the GEe pattern for different periods (t=1;7;14;21;28;35). Total savings reach their low in t=7 to increase later with further standardization decisions. Sequential choice will become more important when studying multi standard problems in section 4.3.3.

98

The influence of variations of fundamental parameters of the standardization model on network behavior and efficiency in centralized and decentralized networks over time was explored. Multi-period decisions were modeled using two different approaches that capture many of the scenarios found in the literature in network effects. These general results are the basis for the further analysis of the effects of various extensions to the model. They will serve as a reference and to pinpoint similarities, regularities, and deviations. Next, we focus on the consequences of standardization decisions on individual agents.

4.2.4 Individual consequences

4.2.4.1 Individual gains and losses

The importance of the different institutional backgrounds and implications associated with the notion of centrally and decentrally coordinated networks has been discussed earlier. Network wide savings are relevant, among others, in closed user networks such as intranets when there might actually be a principal trying to internalize network effects. Still, GE has primarily been used to benchmark diffusion processes in decentralized networks. In this section, a more profound analysis of individual decisions and savings in context with the simulations showing the standardization gap in the previous sections is described.

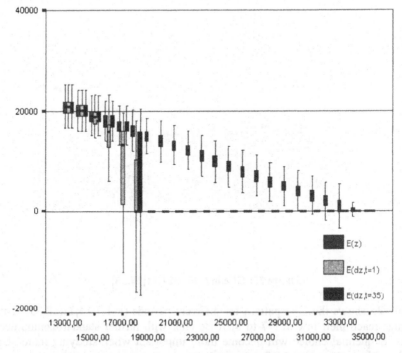

Figure 26: Individual savings E_i for different $\mu(K)$ (reverse $\mu(K)$ scale)

Figure 26 shows box plots for individual savings E_i at different values of $\mu(K)$. The box borders denote the 0.25 and 0.75 quantiles and the bar in the box shows the median. The antennas show the whole range of resulting E_i (except few extreme outcasts). To clearly show changes of E_i over time, "true" individual savings in period 1 and 35 (resulting from decentralized coordination) as well as the individual's situation when participating in a centralized solution without any redistribution of the costs or benefits are depicted in Figure 26. The data presentation required an abscissa with increasing $\mu(K)$ values. Figure 27 shows a magnification of the standardization gap between points B and C.

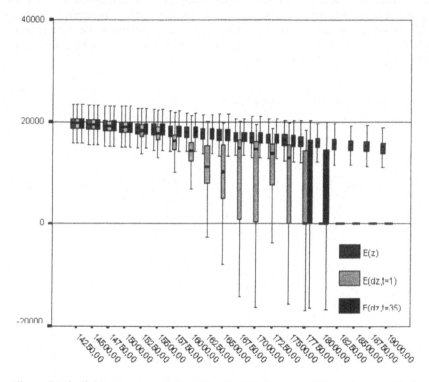

Figure 27: Individual savings E_i for different $\mu(K)$ (reverse $\mu(K)$ scale, magnified)

Interestingly, relatively few E_i are negative, especially in the case of centralized coordination. This means that cases of agents that are forced to standardize against their will (or that would require compensations ex post in a decentralized context) are scarce. In other words, predators will rarely have eaten penguins. This, too, shows the relevance of designs that try to internalize network effects. Obviously, not only the whole network but also the vast majority of individuals are better off getting the optimal solution from a central principal. The fraction of these individuals is of course highly responsive to $\sigma(C)$ and $\sigma(K)$.

In certain constellations, decentralized coordination leads to individual net losses for up to 25% of all agents. In an ordained centralized solution, at $\mu(K)$=33,000 this is also the case but losses are significantly smaller (minimal $E_i(z)$=-4,360 compared to $E_i(dz,t=1)$=-17,089 and $E_i(dz,t=35)$=-16,461).

In addition to the quartiles, Figure 28 shows for the highlighted area ($\mu(K)$ for $E_i(z)$, $E_i(dz,t=1)$ and $E_i(dz,t=35)$) a pattern for average savings and the risk corridor, i.e. the area between *average ± standard deviation*. One can clearly see how risk vanishes over time. Only for $\mu(K) = [17,500; 18,250]$ individual ex post savings remain uncertain as in period 1. That is why in this constellation there are few agents having standardized in the stationary state (on average between 10 and 15). The causality, of course, works in reverse in the simulations, i.e. uncertainty - which is only implicitly captured by the decision function - is high due to the small number of standardizing agents.

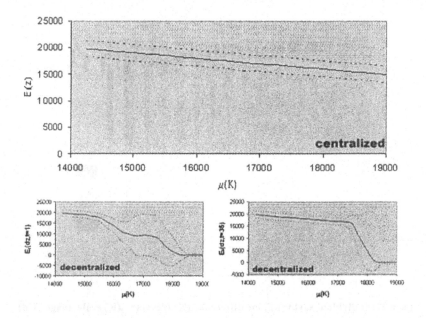

Figure 28: Risk corridor (avg. E±σ) t=1 and t_{stat} (reverse scale)

4.2.4.2   Wrong decisions

In the previous section it could be shown that only in rare cases are there agents who are part of a centralized solution and do not also profit individually from standardizing. But in the decentralized case agents are not facing the centralized solution ex post. Thus, a very interesting question is what type of wrong decisions agents make in the decentralized case if there are deviations from the centralized solution. There are two possibilities of deviations between *ex ante* and *ex post* savings in a decentralized network:

1. an agent standardizes but regrets it afterwards
2. no standardization ex ante although it would have been advantageous

In both cases, standardization decisions by the communication partners have been wrongly anticipated. The relative error occurrence f denotes the number of agents having made a wrong decision ex post relative to all agents. Let f_{pos} be the error of the first kind and f_{neg} that of the second so that $f = f_{pos} + f_{neg}$. It is important to note that "error" does not constitute deviations from the centralized solution but rather from the "real" (ex post) result of decentralized coordination in the relevant periods. For example, if both agents in a two player network do not standardize even though it would have made sense (see e.g. section 3.3.2), then this is not an error in the decentralized meaning, since individual standardization by one agent in that situation would have been unfavorable ex post (which would have resulted in an f_{pos}). Here, the individuality of the decentralized approach shows: decisions can only turn out to have been wrong if partners behave in a way different from that anticipated by the deciding agent. At the same time, the other agents incorporate *their* anticipation of the others' decisions and cost structures into their own decision and so forth. In this manner, the costs and decisions of each agent influence the subsequent state of his environment. Besides this complexity, this is the reason why any definition of error in a decentralized scenario needs to restrict itself to an ex post state *assumed* to be *given or stable respectively* in terms of the neighbors. In other words, the bilateral property of the network effect between any two agents needs to be switched off during the individual analysis and period.

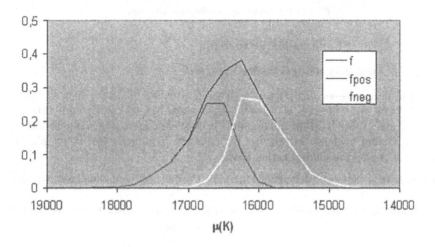

Figure 29: Errors depending on μ(K) in t=1

Errors only occur in the dynamic area between points B and C. This area is magnified in Figure 29. At $\mu(k) = 18,000$ not one agent standardizes. Because there is no network activity at all, no unfavorable decisions can be made. For $\mu(K) \leq 14,000$ all agents standardize in period 1 which is also the optimal solution. At $\mu(K) < 15,800$ so many agents adopted a standard that standardization could no longer be wrong.

During the standardization process errors became increasingly rare (Figure 30). In the first four periods, errors of the first and second kind had a similar frequency. In period 5 there were only errors of the second kind. In period six, the last standardization activities (correcting the errors of period 5) led to the stationary state.

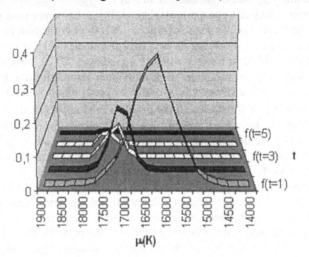

Figure 30: Errors depending on $\mu(K)$ and t

4.2.5   Agent size and standardization time

4.2.5.1   Stationary state period and agent size

In the last sections, we focused on the dynamic structure of GE dependent of $\mu(K)$ and t. Now we will look at *when* agents standardize and *when* equilibria are reached and especially if the point in time is dependent upon an agent's size. Thus, we try to find evidence of whether the common hypothesis that larger players (companies etc.) standardize earlier holds.

The size of a network participant is modeled using his "communication weight" i.e. his aggregate information costs ($\text{size}(i) = \sum_{\substack{j=1 \\ j \neq i}}^{n} c_{ij}$). Size in this context is therefore not equivalent to size in terms of number of employees etc. It is rather a

generic metric describing an agent's role in an communications network. According to the linear transformation, node size is normally distributed as well:

$$size(n) = ND \sim \left(\mu(size(n)); \sigma(size(n))^2\right) = ND \sim \left((n-1)\cdot\mu(C);(n-1)\cdot\sigma(C)^2\right)$$

Equation 19: Distribution of *size*

The longest standardization processes could be observed for $\mu(K)$ = [16500;
18000] (Figure 31). Accordingly, the four samples (quasi the cross section parallel
to the size(n)/t_{stan}-plane) were taken from $\mu(K)$ = {16500; 17000; 17500, 18000}.
$t_{stan}(i)$ denotes the period of agent i standardizing.

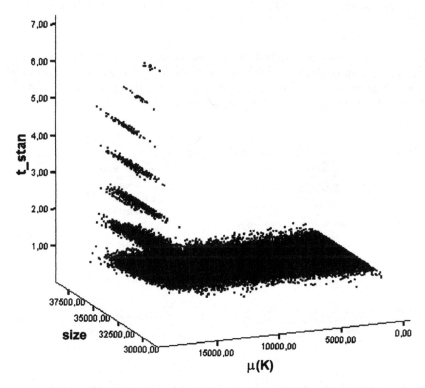

Figure 31: Standardization time depending on $\mu(K)$ and agent size

Due to the significance level, the counter hypothesis "there is no stochastic relation between agent size and standardization time" can be rejected with a probability of 99%.

Table 24: Correlation between standardization time and agent size
(**=significant to 0.01)

	correlation between $t_{stan}(i)$ and size(i)	regression
$\mu(K)$=18,000	-0.2877**	$t_{stan}(i)$ = -0.0004 size(i)+ 17.20
$\mu(K)$=17,500	-0.3568**	$t_{stan}(i)$ = -0.0003 size(i)+ 12.13
$\mu(K)$=17,000	-0.3321**	$t_{stan}(i)$ = -0.0002 size(i)+ 7.55
$\mu(K)$=16,500	-0.3242**	$t_{stan}(i)$ = -0.0001 size(i)+ 6.36

Figure 32 shows that the standardization process and thereby the time necessary for reaching a stationary state shortened with decreasing $\mu(K)$. At $\mu(K)$=16,000 almost all agents standardized in period 1 (also centralized optimum) while at $\mu(K)$=18,500 there were no standardization activities at all.

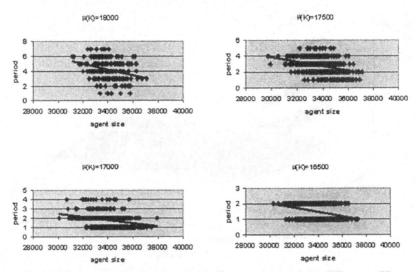

Figure 32: Standardization time depending on agent size for different $\mu(K)$

There were no stable outcomes with e.g. half of all agents standardizing. In all simulations so far one of these three processes emerged:

1) no agent standardizes

2) three or fewer agents standardize, a stationary state is reached mostly in period 1 and never later than period 3, of course, although quite rarely

3) network wide standardization. A stationary state is reached within seven periods.

This frequent network behavior pattern - no, few or all agents standardize - will be scrutinized again in more depth in the course of identifying five general diffusion patterns in the multi-standard case in section 4.3.2.

4.2.5.2 *Stationary state period and network size*

To explore whether the period taken to reach a stable state in a network depends on the network size, n was changed from n=5 to n=250. No systematic influence of overall network size could be found. The latest period of reaching stability was in period 9. Even this was a ricochet for it only occurred once (with 30 repetitions per n).

Table 25: Stationary state period depending on n

n	max. $t_{stan}(n)$	n	max. $t_{stan}(n)$	n	max. $t_{stan}(n)$
5	4	45	7	100	7
15	7	55	7	150	6
25	6	65	6	200	6
35	6	75	5	250	9

The values in Table 25 increase slightly with other parameters such as σ in particular but are independent of network size. This is not a surprise for the network structure does not change when altering n. With an increase of n, there will be more new first movers (due to their local structure), thus reducing their positive impact on the laggards. But their increase in number counterbalances this effect.

4.2.6 Variation of network structure

> "There exists the eternal fact of conflict
> And - next - a mere sense of locality."
> *Stephen Crane*

In this section, the influence of the network structure is analyzed. One of the most important insights derived from considering interdisciplinary requirements for a theory of networks was incorporating topological determinants into the models. Very instructive research in this area has recently been proposed by Westarp (2003) and Wendt/Westarp (2000). Thus, this section is also an important step towards integrating the standardization model with the diffusion model in section 4.5.

For incorporating the structural elements of networks, a new parameter V is introduced describing network density. The simulations of the basic model in section 4.2.1 are now repeated now considering different densities and therefore altering V while $\mu(K)$ is held constant.

Table 26: Simulation parameters

$\mu(C) = 1,000$	$\sigma(C) = 200$	$\mu(K) = 14,000$	$\sigma(K) = 1,000$	
n = 35	T = 1	V = var.	B = 0.0	Q = 1

The reason for $\mu(K)$=14,000 is that the right edge of the standardization gap (for $\mu(K)$<14,000 centrally as well as decentrally coordinated networks are completely standardized) is exactly here. The simulation uses two substantially different structures as introduced by Westarp/Wendt (2000) as part of their diffusion model. They have shown a significant influence of different topologies on diffusion results. We try to adapt those approaches to the standardization model as closely as possible. While Westarp/Wendt use the absolute number of direct communication links, in the standardization model the density parameter V ($0 < V \leq 1$) is used. There are two basic structures:

Structure 1:

(*random topology*)

When initializing the network, with a probability determined by V all edges are assigned positive values. This is equivalent to the "random topology" of the diffusion model.

Structure 2:

(*close topology*)

Agents are assigned to geographic coordinates (unit square) by a random generator (even distribution). This results in n*(n-1) edges. The shortest V*100% of all edges are assigned strictly positive values (as before c_{ij}~ND($\mu(C)$, $\sigma(C)$)). As a result, decreasing V leads to (increasingly) isolated clusters in the network. Also, in doing so the total number of edges decreases linearly in V, which is implicitly the case in structure 1, too. This implicitly equals the "close topology" of the diffusion model.

Both structures have the same number of edges if V is the same (for structure 1 on average). A decision to adopt a standard has a more indirect influence on other agents' decisions in structure 2 because the shortest average path between two network nodes is longer than in structure 1: more dominoes have to fall.

107

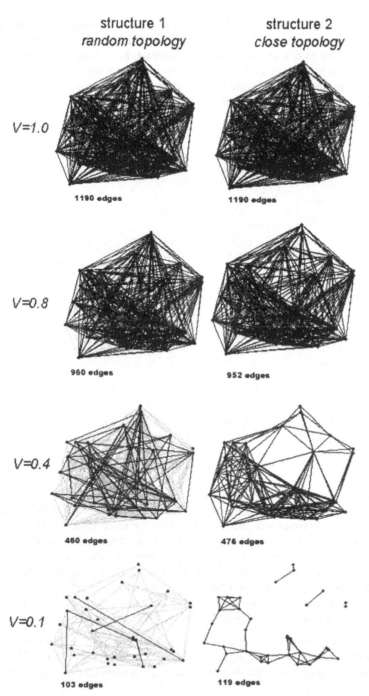

Figure 33: Network structures I (left) and II (right) for V={1,0; 0,8; 0,4; 0,1}

108

The decentralized model's individual consideration of all communication relations and their values will, especially in structure 1, lead to an increased appearance of one-sided relations as can be observed in the Internet, for instance. Formally it is important only to use those edges in the decision function where $c_{ji} > 0$, since otherwise the denominator of p_{ij} would be zero; thus if $c_{ji} = 0$ then $p_{ij} = 0$. Figure 33 shows both structures for different V to visualize the clustering. One-sided relations are of a lighter color.

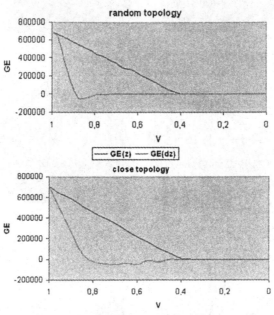

Figure 34: GE at different V

In the diffusion model, it is argued that most real-world networks represent an intermediate version of these extreme types, but since the costs of bridging geographical distance become less and less important the more information technology evolves, there is a clear tendency. Electronic markets will tend to resemble the *random* type of structure (since we select our partners by other criteria than geographical distance), while in markets for physical goods (or face to face communication) physical proximity is still a very important factor for selecting business partners and therefore, the *close* topology will be a good substitute for the real world network structure [Weitzel/Wendt/Westarp 2002, 20; Westarp 2003].

GE developed very similarly compared to the variation of $\mu(K)$ although in structure 2 there is a significantly larger area of negative total savings (Figure 34). On the other hand, in structure 2, the standardization gap is more moderate for V>0.8.

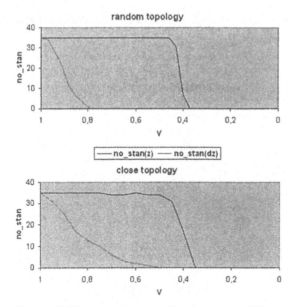

Figure 35: Number of standardizing agents at different V

In close topologies, agents start standardizing at a lower V because in random topologies the c_{ji} compulsory for determining p_{ij} are the more often zero the lower V although c_{ij} might have been positive. This could not happen in close topologies, except that an uneven number of edges has positive information costs; this phenomenon could then be seen with the geographically longest edge where $c_{ij}>0$.

4.2.6.1   Errors in different topologies

Although agents in structure 2 show a "braver" standardization behavior, they could not improve their decision quality because their network got smaller with decreasing V (clustering).

Figure 36 shows relative frequency of errors analogous to section 4.2.4. One can see that positive standardization decisions in close topologies are mostly regrettable ex post, i.e. the agents could not realize the anticipated savings. Again this is emphasized by the larger areas of negative total savings (GE) in close topologies.

Results above describe the first period. This simplification made the results easier to understand. Extending the analysis to later periods until stationary states are reached yields no additional findings; results are structurally equivalent and resemble the multi-period standardization gap of Figure 34: in later periods the decentralized total savings (GE(dz)) moved somewhat towards smaller V values due to additional standardizations' neutralizing the area of earlier (individual) errors. Relative frequency of errors continually decreased in later periods. Interestingly, from period 2 on agents made wrong decisions up to four periods longer than in random topologies: in structure 1 a stationary state could be reached no later than period 8 whereas in close topologies (structure 2) dominoes sometimes needed to fall until period 13.

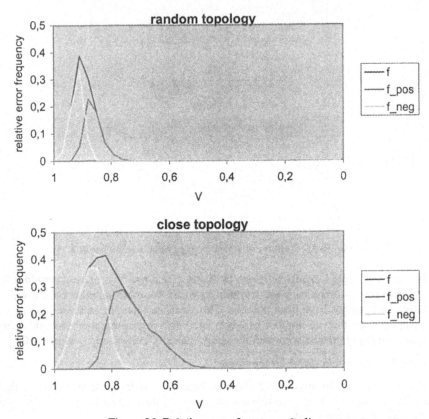

Figure 36: Relative error frequency (t=1)

4.2.6.2 Standardization costs and network density

There is a significant difference between the two network structures in centrally coordinated networks that can only faintly be seen in Figure 34 as the more thin tailed (at V=0.4) and at V>0.5 more wave like no_stan graph in close topologies. In contrast to structure 1, 9.5 % of all simulations in structure 2 showed mixed solutions while altering V. This is not representative, though, for it is not just V but the mutual influence of density and standardization costs which determines the frequency of centralized solutions with 0 < no_stan < n. To look deeper into these dependencies, in a network of size n=20 we simultaneously varied V and $\mu(K)$ to find out what proportion of the solutions consisted of partially standardized networks.

In a network with V=1 and n=20 the standardization gap is located at $\mu(K)=[7,500; 19,500]$. That means that for standardization costs below 7,500 centralized as well as decentralized coordination implies completely standardized networks. In the following simulation, the trade-off between density and standardization costs beginning at $\mu(K)=10,000$ und V=1.0 is investigated reducing both parameter values to 0. Figure 37 shows the aggregated results of a total of 2772 simulation runs.

The occurrence of partly standardized networks in structure 2 has a "corridor" pattern that runs like a ridge approximately diagonally over the plane spanned by the $\mu(K)$ and V axis. The lower (both) the parameter values the closer the fraction of mixed solutions is to 0. The ridge is approximated by Equation 20.

$$\mu(K)=12475.78*V+148.183$$

Equation 20: Approximation of ridge

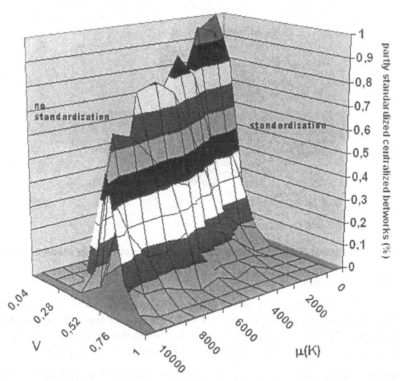

Figure 37: Fraction of partly standardized centralized networks in close topologies

This function results from a regression with $\mu(K)$ being dependent, V the independent variable, and relative occurrence as weighting factors. The resulting correlation coefficient is r=0.829.

112

Parameters to the left of the "mountain" in Figure 37 imply no (central) standardization while for high V and low K there is a propensity to standardize completely.

The equivalent simulation with structure 1 depicts a significant relative increase in
mixed solutions only for very small μ(K) and V values (Figure 38). Regression
analysis shows the following results (r=0.9088): μ(K)=25,765.80*V-613.759.

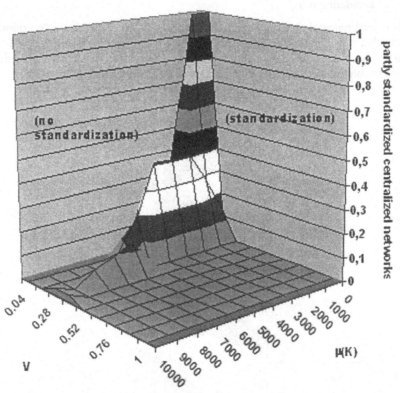

Figure 38: Fraction of partly standardized centralized networks in random topologies

4.2.6.3   Summary

Network density has an important influence on standardization processes. The
fewer communication relations in a network, the smaller the total savings potential. At low densities, there is little local incentive to standardize decentrally. This
corresponds with the findings of section 4.2.1.1 when increasing μ(K).

There is a strong influence of neighborhood structure (topology). If network structure favors clustering, individual consequences are comparatively negative. Important examples of the clustering property in networks are systems where geographical proximity is important, as in traditional corporate intranets that have significantly stronger internal than external information flows.

Finally, given that centralized coordination (solution determination and implementation) is possible, at low density and an adequate network structure the numerical complexity is especially acute because simple heuristics are quite likely to fail to deliver good solutions.

4.2.7   Installed base effects

The simulations have so far described network agents deciding about introducing new compatibility standards. Regardless of what the constituents of the actual information infrastructure are, the standard to be chosen is a new one and does not have a legacy of installations. There are two reasons for considering standard choices where the standard has already gone through some dispersion. The first reason is that many real life standardization choices are not only concerned with brand new technologies. Especially in the case of choosing between different standards as elaborated in detail in section 4.3, there are often already users of the standard to be chosen. This situation is comparable to starting a multi-period simulation at some time t>1. Thus, incorporating installed base effects broadens the applicability of the decentralized standardization model to basically all communication networks.

The other reason is trying to support centralized solutions in real life. One possible way of shrinking the standardization gap, i.e. to come closer to a centralized solution quality, is trying to identify certain parts of a network that can be used as a stepping stone to initiate further favorable diffusion processes. To put it more simply: which dominoes should be tipped to overcome the start-up problem? This is a prevalent question for software vendors trying to win a new market that is subject to network effects [Westarp 2003], for large enterprises trying to establish a communication infrastructure between autonomous business units or for governmental authorities like the EU in trying to establish electronic marketplaces or other infrastructure goals (section 5.6.5). Strategies can be selling software at low (or zero) prices in early diffusions periods or forcing particular user groups, e.g. only small or only large enterprises within the EU, to standardize.

These effects are analyzed analogously to the former simulations. To capture the installed base, the new variable B ($0 \leq B \leq 1$) is introduced with B>0 if there are already agents using a standard. In addition, to guarantee formal homogeneity with the former simulations, a new period t=0 is introduced where all pre-simulation standardization activities, e.g. by a central authority, are supposed to have happened. Consequently, there also is GE in t=0. In periods t>0 agents decide as before using the information about previous standardizations (installed base) as before when determining p_{ij} in t=2,...,T.

The simulations in this section comprise three scenarios with different values of B respectively.

I.   the largest agents (*size(i)* as defined in section 4.2.5) are pre-standardized

114

II.   random agents are pre-standardized

III.   the smallest agents (*size(i)* as defined in section 4.2.5) are pre-standardized

Table 27: Simulation parameters

$\mu(C) = 1,000$	$\sigma(C) = 200$	$\mu(K) = var.$	$\sigma(K) = 1,000$	
$n = 35$	$T = 35$	$V = 1.0$	$B = 0.1; 0.2; 0.3$	$Q = 1$

In the typically used network of n=35 the respective values of B correspond to 4, 7, and 11 network nodes. The three scenarios were simultaneously simulated to guarantee networks of identical cost structure for each run. The same data was used to determine the centralized solution. For every new value of B simulations were made using a different random seed.

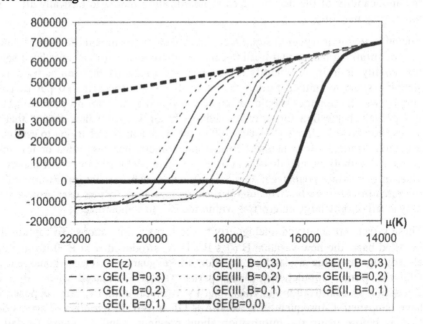

Figure 39: GE at different installed bases

Figure 39 magnifies the area between points B and C of the standardization gap. A structural deviation of the centralized solution at B=0 and B>0 is not possible except for the negative $\mu(k)$ values to the left of A (there are costs for standardizing the installed base, too; formally, the installed base is considered using an additional restriction of the type $x_i=1$. Also, there is a slight leftward move of A, because from a central perspective earlier standardization also makes sense).

The legend in Figure 39 shows the graphs from left to right in the same order as in the diagram. Additionally, there is GE(z) and GE(dz) (here as GE(B=0.0) from Figure 19) to compare the standardization process with and without installed base. The other graphs are described by the relevant scenario and the fraction of pre-standardized network nodes.

At first, increasing B by 0.1 moved the GE graph about 1,000 units to the left, shifting the start-up problem towards higher costs. But standardization is advantageous as "early" as at $\mu(K)=44,000$. In comparison, the shriveling of the standardization gap is small, especially when considering that at B=0.3 a centralized principal - trying to tip these dominoes - would have to accommodate almost one third of all standardization activities. Thus one can see that establishing an installed base in order to get some decentralized diffusion dynamics going is questionable.

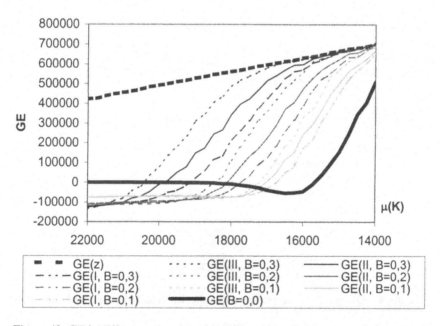

Figure 40: GE in different scenarios with different installed bases for $\sigma(C)=500$

Another finding is that structure III dominates II which dominates I. In other words, the worst idea is pre-standardizing big network participants. This is surprising at first sight. In section 4.2.5.1 it turned out that large players standardize first. Thus, one could expect that standardizing the big players causes the smaller remainder to follow immediately. But it is quite the opposite. Pre-standardizing the big players means that the remaining network is left with agents suffering from

116

a worse savings-cost ratio. They do not care about the size of installed base agents for their p_{ij} are 1 and they have to bear their standardization costs themselves anyway. But if small nodes are pre-standardized as an installed base, those left to decide are those with a higher propensity to standardize. As a result, big players will standardize at even higher $\mu(K)$. Therefore, the described phenomenon does not result from the structure of the installed base but rather the structure of the rest of the network.

A structurally equivalent simulation with the standard deviation increased by 2.5 ($\sigma(C)$=500) showed an increase in the graphs' distances by about the same proportion (Figure 40). A more precise determination of that relationship is difficult due to the simultaneous shift and flattening of the graphs.

Finally, Figure 41 shows the total effect of the existence of an installed base at stationary state. There are no new insights compared to section 4.2.2. The GE graphs with B>0 show only slightly stronger shifts over time than the original GE(dz) graphs.

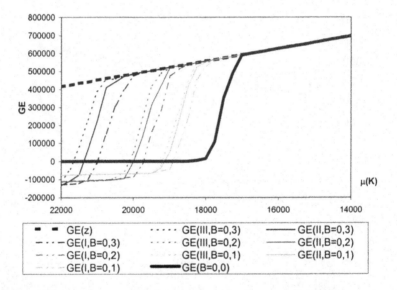

Figure 41: GE in different scenarios with different installed bases (stationary state)

Table 28 emphasizes the findings. The last standardization activities show that in scenario III (smallest agents) the stationary state can be arrived at the most quickly.

In conclusion it was possible to show that a pre-standardization (which way achieved anyway) of parts of a network can lower the start-up problem somewhat. For installed bases with B<1 it is highly improbable that in doing so a central principal could close the standardization gap at reasonable costs. This result is valid for different parameter values, too. If considering installing a standard user base, it is definitely preferable to start with those network players that show the smallest c_{ij}.

Table 28: Stationary state period in different scenarios

scenario	σ(C)=200			σ(C)=500		
	I	II	III	I	II	III
B=0.0		7			8	
B=0.1	7	7	6	8	8	7
B=0.2	7	6	6	7	8	7
B=0.3	6	6	6	7	8	7

4.2.8 Summary of multi-period one standard problems

Various aspects of the basic standardization model have been analyzed and the implications evaluated. The effects of variations of parameters like standardization costs, network structure, agent size or information sets on efficiency (total vs. local savings), position of the standardization gap, number of standardizing agents, period of reaching stable equilibria etc. have been explored considering different scenarios like neighborhood structure or installed bases. Instead of obviously possible extensions of these investigations concerning system behavior when altering parameters while also varying some parameters as in other sections, in the next chapter an extended standardization model is developed. The analyzed scenario is extended from 1 to Q standards so that in the following the selection between different standards is modeled.

Many real life standardization decisions are not primarily compatibility yes/no decisions but consist of selecting from a range of alternative standards, e.g. between different EDI standards. Many findings from this section can be sustained. But there are also very interesting new facets such as in particular the diffusion paths of different standards.

4.3 The extended standardization model

In the extended standardization model, agents can choose between Q different standards to save on information costs. Savings require two communication partners to use matching standards. Modeling multi-standard decisions requires some additional assumptions and proceedings. Standardization costs are generated for every agent and technology using the same parameters as before

$(K_{iq} \sim N(\mu(K); \sigma(K)) \quad \forall i, q)$. The decision function is the same apart from considering the availability of different technologies to choose from. Since K_{iq} are not identical the individually expected values differ with regard to the respective technology. Real life analogies include different legacy applications and data, switching costs etc. At first, it is assumed that agents decide using the technology that yields the highest expected value to the respective agent given that at least one technology's expected value is positive.

$$E[U(i,q)] = \sum_{\substack{j=1 \\ j \neq i}}^{n} p_{ijq} \cdot c_{ij} - K_{iq} = \sum_{\substack{j=1 \\ j \neq i}}^{n} \left(\frac{c_{ji} \cdot n_j - K_{jq}}{c_{ji} \cdot n_j} \right) \cdot c_{ij} - K_{iq}$$

Equation 21: Expected utility of standardization (extended model; ex ante utility)

As can be seen, potential information cost savings are independent of the technology. Thus there is no difference regarding the benefits of alternative standards, e.g. cost savings if two partners use EDIFACT or ANSI ASC X12 to exchange data electronically or different XML dialects such as xCBL or cXML [Weitzel/Harder/Buxmann 2001]. Other assumptions are possible, of course, see Weber (2000) for a critique of neglecting hierarchical dependencies between standards. This can be a valuable extension to the proposed standardization model but would not contribute additional findings in the context of the general simulative exploration brought forward in this research work.

Individual ex post savings resulting from Equation 21 are:

$$E_i = \sum_{\substack{j=1 \\ j \neq i}}^{n} y_{ij} \cdot c_{ij} - \sum_{q=1}^{Q} x_{iq} \cdot K_{iq} \qquad s.t.: \sum_{q=1}^{Q} x_{iq} \leq 1$$

Equation 22: Standardization benefits (extended model; ex post utility)

The binary variable x_{iq} has the same properties as x_i; $x_{iq}=1$ describes agent i implementing standard q. The meaning of y_{ij} remains unchanged, too. The proposition that users buy one or no unit of a standard restricting an agent to using no more than one standard at the same time is common in modeling standardization problems [e.g. Katz/Shapiro 1985; Arthur 1989; Wiese 1990].

When analyzing the standardization gap in a multi-standard scenario, the centralized solution is again used to evaluate the efficiency of the different outcomes. Due to its complexity, the centralized solution for the extended standardization model is heuristically determined. As an example of the complexity, Buxmann (1996, 49) reports a solution time, without heuristics, of 350 hours for a supposedly simple centralized standardization problem with 10 agents and seven standards (n=10; Q=7; V=1.0; B=0.0).

As described in section 4.2, the heuristic used implements the standard with the lowest aggregate standardization costs if superior to no standardization. Accordingly, if there are deviations from the actual optimum solution, the "real" GE(z) graph would always be above the one heuristically determined. According to Buxmann (1996, 87) this heuristic finds the real optimum in 96% of the cases (for the special case of V=1.0, B=0.0, and exemplary cost values but with evenly distributed costs). Since in case of V<1 and B>0 this heuristic will probably frequently miss the analytical optimum, in section 4.3.6 (variations of network structure) the GE(z) graph is omitted.

In view of the fact that multiple standards are available, it is now possible for each agent to revise a standardizing decision in favor of another standard in cases where the neighbors have decided to implement other technologies. In analogy to section 4.2.3, different choice sequence scenarios are compared:

1) simultaneous decisions (single choice)

2) simultaneous decisions (reversible choice)

3) sequential decisions

The main focus will again be the most realistic case of (multiple) simultaneous decisions.

When analyzing the one standard scenario, the outcome (in terms of monetary results) was analyzed separately from the equilibrium process towards a stationary state (sections 4.2.2 and 4.2.5). This separation is not adequate anymore since monetary results (i.e. the standardization gap) have to be explained using the diffusion pattern in order to be easily understandable. That is why - although trying to follow the structure of the last section - 4.3.1 comprises the scenarios described earlier in sections 4.2.2 and 4.2.5.

4.3.1 The standardization gap and the equilibrium process

4.3.1.1 Simultaneous decisions, single choice

As much as possible the parameters of the previous simulations are used in the multi standards case, too, to make the results comparable.

Table 29: Simulation parameters (extended model)

$\mu(C) = 1{,}000$	$\sigma(C) = 200$	$\mu(K) = var.$	$\sigma(K) = 1{,}000$	
$n = 35$	$T = 35$	$V = 1.0$	$B = 0.0$	$Q = 1, 2, 3, 4$

First, the sum of all agents' savings from t=1 are compared to GE of the single standard scenario. As expected, the standardization gap in the extended model has

120

dramatically increased in the one period scenario (Figure 42). As soon as there is a choice, there will be agents preferring standard 1 to standard 2 etc. and vice versa (for identical μ(K) for all q). Regularly, agents will choose different standards regardless of how low average costs are (that are identical across the technologies). That is why GE(dz) stay notably below the optimal solution. The standardization gap cannot be closed anymore with decreasing μ(K). Since all standards on average cost the same, GE(z) is structurally independent of Q.

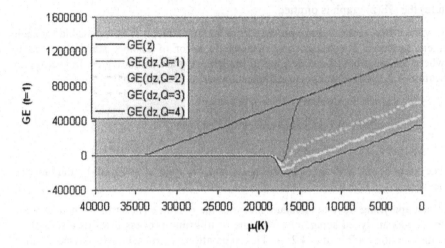

Figure 42: GE in t=1 (simultaneous, single choice)

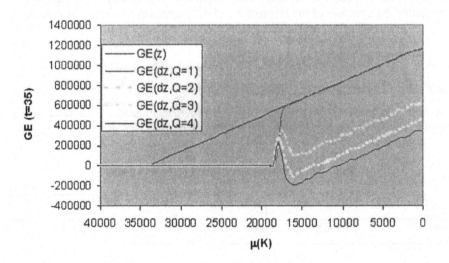

Figure 43: GE in t=35 (simultaneous, single choice)

If agents cannot revise their decisions, the errors of the first period force total savings to stay significantly below the GE(dz,Q=1) graph in Figure 43.

First decentralized activities ($\mu(K)$=[16,500;19,000]) bring first changes over time. Here, in later periods, savings can be realized that are otherwise attainable only at significantly lower $\mu(K)$. This phenomenon is an advanced penguin effect again: this time, there are Q different ponds for the penguins. At first, due to high costs, only a few agents (one, two, or three) standardize. Recurrently, they choose different standards and cannot save information costs even between one another, GE(dz) values at Q>1 are more negative in the first period than in the basic model. But later adopters can imitate the first movers' behavior. As a result, it is much more probable that a standard will spread throughout large parts of the network. Since distribution parameters are identical for all standards, the state of the network in early diffusion periods is highly unstable and first movers' decisions have a huge impact on later network participants.

These findings describe the path dependent property associated with network effects in large parts of the literature as well as the frequent notion of networks being tippy. But as will be shown later, these findings are only valid for rather high standardization costs.

4.3.1.2 An adapted Herfindahl index

To validate these findings, the diffusion over time is dissected using a Herfindahl index (aggregated squared market shares). The Herfindahl coefficient measures market concentration. It is often used in oligopoly models to show market concentration between monopoly (HK=1) and polypoly (HK=0) [Martin 1994, 114]. The Herfindahl index is therefore very appropriate for diffusion processes in the standardization model; it is also used for the analysis within the relational diffusion model of Westarp (2003). During the simulation, a Herfindahl coefficient is determined according to Equation 23.

$$HK = \sum_{q=1}^{Q} \left(\frac{no\_stan\ (q)}{n} \right)^2$$

Equation 23: Herfindahl coefficient (HK)

One problem, though, results from the fact that in contrast to the diffusion model the standardization model also allows for agents with no standard (the diffusion model requires the special case of B=1). The Herfindahl index is based upon the premise that the sum of all elements of the nominator equals the denominator. This is not problematic for market share because market size results from sales or revenue numbers. "Market size" of the standardization model is exogenous, though. Considering all agents without standards as separate "quasi market share" would lead to misleading interpretations. Both, a complete standardization and no standardization at all would yield HK=1. Instead, to separate the effect of overall network standardization from the diffusion of particular standards, an adapted

122

Herfindahl index HKa is introduced. It is based on the number of standardized nodes of a network.

$$HK_a = \sum_{q=1}^{Q} \left(\frac{\text{no\_stan}\ (q)}{\sum_{q=1}^{Q} \text{no\_stan}\ (q)} \right)^2$$

Equation 24: An adapted Herfindahl index (HKa)

In the following simulation, the default number of standards will be Q=4. Thus the Herfindahl index HK will take values between 0 (no standardization) and 1. In contrast, the minimal HKa is 0.25 with an equal number of agents having adopted all standards. For *no_stan*=0, HKa cannot be determined and will be set to zero. Smaller values in the following figures result from averaging. Figure 44 and Figure 45 show HK and HKa dependent on μ(K) and period t. μ(K) was varied between 10,000 and 24,000. Graphs on the left show simulations with the single choice scenario while on the right agents could revise their decisions in all periods. This is discussed in more detail in the next section. Figure 46 shows for the same sample the total number of agents who decided in favor of a standard (*no_stan*).

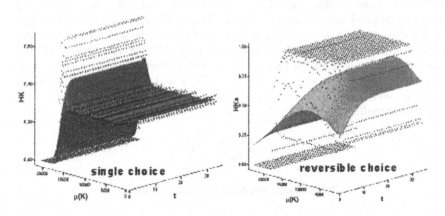

Figure 44: HK depending on μ(K) and t

For intermediate costs values (μ(K)=[16,000;19,000]), the figures on the left (single choice) support the findings concerning the equilibrium process towards a stationary state. Here, concentration is at its maximum. The maximum value of 0.8 results from the fact that one point represents 50 simulation runs. In many cases, HK and HKa reached 1.0.

HK values below HKa values are only found in a small area of standardization costs ($\mu(K)$=[15,750; 18,875] in t=1 and $\mu(K)$=[17,625; 18,875] when a stationary state was reached). Here, not all agents standardized instantly, or not at all.

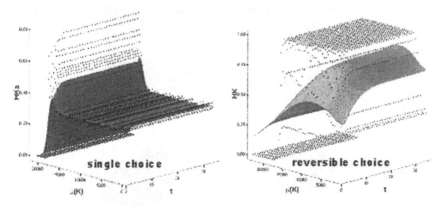

Figure 45: HKa depending on $\mu(K)$ and t

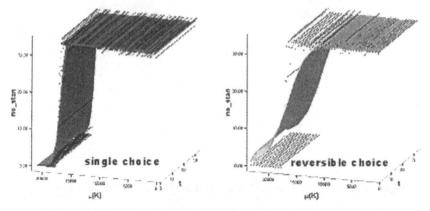

Figure 46: Number of standardizing agents depending on $\mu(K)$ and t

All these findings are based upon *average* results. To get an impression of the raw data and to see how many agents factually standardized, the histogram of Figure 47 shows results from individual simulation runs for t=1 and t=35. Data results from a simulation where $\mu(K)$ was varied from 21,000 to 1,000 in steps of 20 with each constellation simulated once.

Similar to the findings in section 4.2, in a multi period setting networks either have up to six (basic model: three) or all 35 agents standardizing. Other solutions in early periods eventually end in fully standardized networks.

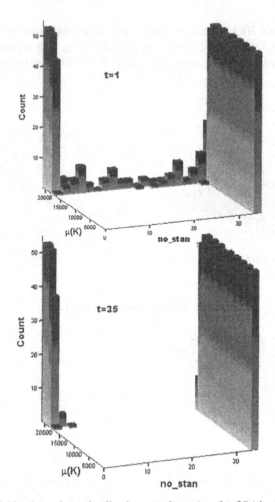

Figure 47: Number of standardized agents for t=1 and t=35 (single choice)

Below μ(K)=17,000 there is a very high probability that all agents have standard-ized when reaching the stationary state (which never happened later than in t=9). This is quite identical to the basic model. But after all a decision constellation in which agents have to bear costs for running a standard technology in each period but can only decide on the standards once is somewhat artificial. Therefore, in the next section the model is extended as before to a multiple choice scenario with re-visable decisions which exhibits some quite surprising properties.

4.3.1.3 Simultaneous choice with reversible decisions

In this section, the model is extended to the second choice sequence scenario: every agent can decide in every period about what standard to use. Thus, even though an agent might have implemented a standard, he has the opportunity to re-

consider his choice with regard to his environment which can change in any period. In this way, errors can be corrected and adaptations to the evolving eventual
network structure guarantee that after all the results are similar to those of the basic model. The relevant GE graphs are depicted in Figure 48 using the parameters
from Table 29. Only results for t=35 are shown, since first period savings equal
those from Figure 42 (see Figure 57 for t=1).

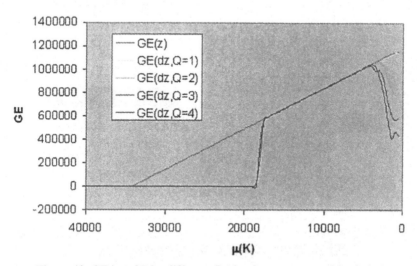

Figure 48: GE in t=35 for different Q (simultaneous reversible choice)

The graphs only partly support the findings described above. In a cost range of
$\mu(K)=[5,000; 17,000]$ centralized solution quality can almost be attained. In addition, the advanced penguin effect of Figure 43 seems almost vanished. The reason
is clear: Now, due the possibility to reverse their choice, the penguins have a lad-
der for climbing out of a pond and go fishing in another pond. But with smaller
standardization costs there is a surprising sudden decline of GE. This is the more
dramatic the more different technologies are available. To explain this phenomenon, the adaptation process towards the equilibrium is investigated in more detail.
There are more complex diffusion patterns in the multi standard case with simultaneous decisions than in the basic model.

Table 30: simulation parameters

$\mu(C) = 1,000$	$\sigma(C) = 200$	$\mu(K) = var.$	$\sigma(K) = 1,000$	
n = 35	T = 400	V = 1.0	B = 0.0	Q = 4

First, some exemplary simulation runs (without any averaging) will show typical
diffusion paths.

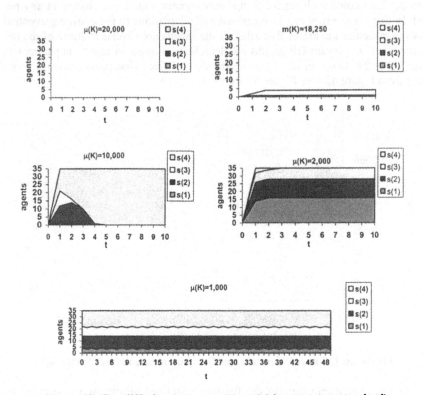

Figure 49: Five diffusion process patterns (s(q): agents per standard)

Figure 49 shows five different diffusion processes leading to equilibria. They are based on simulations using different μ(K) as can be seen above the respective paths. s(q) denotes the number of agents having implemented standard q.

The processes can be described from the top left to the bottom right as follows:

1) no standardization at all (no agent standardizes)

2) mixed solution (some agents standardize, some not)

3) complete standardization with the same technology ("monopoly")

4) complete standardization with different technologies ("oligopoly")

5) no stationary state ("dynamic equilibrium", (some) agents change technologies in a stable and repeated rhythm)

These are all possible adoption processes in the extended model. Buxmann (1996, 87) offers a similar classification for centrally coordinated networks with the exception that obviously there is no equilibrium path as number 5. Figure 50 gives an overview of the relative frequency of the different processes depending on different $\mu(K)$ (based on 4,800 simulation runs). In Figure 51 and Figure 52 the influence of variations of other parameters like $\sigma(c)$ and $\sigma(K)$ in particular is shown.

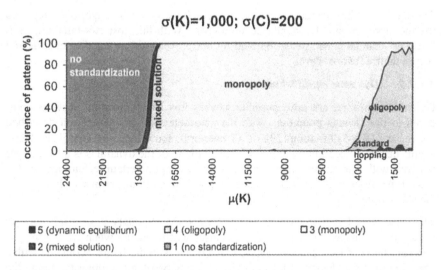

Figure 50: Relative occurrence of the different process patterns at different $\mu(K)$

4.3.2 Five diffusion patterns

Below, the five possible diffusion patterns and their implications are described in more detail.

4.3.2.1 No standardization

This case is identical to the start-up problem of the basic model.

4.3.2.2 Mixed solution

Networks that are partly standardized are not too frequent even for Q>1. If there are mixed solutions, the existence of incompatible technologies can lead to slightly more agents having standardized anyway (in this case up to 6).

4.3.2.3 Monopoly

The monopoly solution dominates large areas of the $\mu(K)$ scale. This diffusion path can often be seen in real world standardization processes although there it is difficult to speak of stationary states, since the standardization model does not allow for endogenous consideration of fundamental technology changes. To put it vice versa: When are "real" diffusion processes stable, i.e. over?

For higher values of $\mu(K)$, the marginal increase in the total number of standardizing agents is not as strong as in Figure 49 (middle left). Sometimes, only in t=6 are all agents standardized. On the other hand the battling out process is weaker, since most agents follow the first movers.

4.3.2.4   Oligopoly

The stable multiple standard equilibrium (which we will call "oligopoly") replaces the monopoly at smaller standardization costs. With this cost constellation, even "weaker" standards can resist the battling out process of "stronger" standards and secure their network share.

4.3.2.5   Dynamic equilibrium

Dynamic equilibria are only possible at very low standardization costs as compared to the savings potential. With the parameters of this simulation described above, at $\mu(K)=1,000$ about 5% of all networks show dynamic equilibria. Here, agents become "technology hoppers". An example of the dynamics is a two player network with one player expecting the other to adopt a certain technology. At the same time, the partner changes his technology choice to the former technology of his partner and so on.

This case would at first sight appear to be a static oligopoly if - as in Figure 49 (bottom) - identified by s(q). It only discloses its true nature when we see the cyclic variations of total savings. Those cases that - as in the figure - coincide with a variation of the diffusion of technologies in the network are a minority among the few dynamic equilibria.

Sometimes, stronger instances of these kinds of equilibria are called "chattering disequilibria" (no one joins a network, then everyone etc.), the phenomenon itself is also sometimes referred to as the fisheries problem: if too many fisherman show up at the top secret fishing hole, they all go home, and if no one shows up, they all want to fish [e.g. Liebowitz/Margolis 1995a].

4.3.2.6   Comparing the diffusion paths

With increasing deviation of the standardization costs ($\sigma(K)$) oligopoly can surpass monopoly (Figure 51). Because differences in standardization costs become more important the probability of technology changes declines. An increase in the deviation of the information costs leads to an opposite effect that is much weaker, though (Figure 52).

In analogy with the findings in section 4.2.2, an increased deviation implies starting standardization activities at higher $\mu(K)$.

Going back to the figures showing Herfindahl indices that were used in Figure 44 and Figure 45 (right) to compare the results to the single choice model, the diagrams of Figure 51 and Figure 52 show a distribution of the diffusion processes. This enables a more detailed analysis than the aggregated view of HK and HKa. Still, each diffusion pattern is represented by a particular development of these measures. In a monopoly case, from the second period on both coefficients, HK and HKa, deploy a strictly monotonous increase until they reach a value of 1. In the last two diffusion scenarios, they end up at significantly lower values but in most cases they are the same since all agents will eventually have standardized.

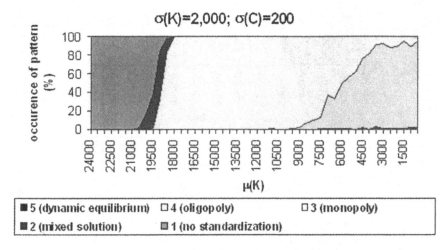

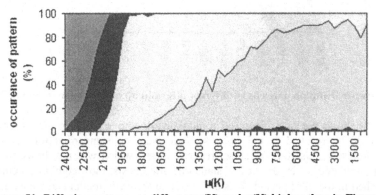

Figure 51: Diffusion patterns at different μ(K) and σ(K) higher than in Figure 50

Finally, the question of when the equilibrium is reached needs consideration. Therefore, for the above simulation we also determined the first periods showing equivalent total savings for each simulation run. In addition, the number of agents standardizing (*no_stan*) was retrieved. Results are summarized in Figure 53. Data represented by the lighter colored circles on the t_{stat}=30 plane correspond to networks without stable equilibria (diffusion pattern 5).

130

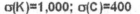

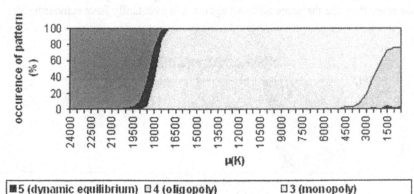

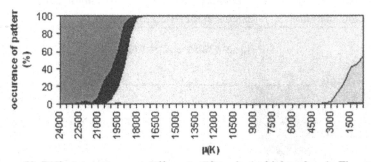

Figure 52: Diffusion patterns at different μ(K) and σ(c) higher than in Figure 50

Figure 54 shows the area of $t_{stat} < 21$ in more detail. Above μ(K)=18,000 stationary state could be reached in t=1 because there were no standardization activities (more precisely, this state is in fact reached in t=0 which was not, however, explicitly simulated for B=0). At low standardization costs, most equilibria could be established in the third period. This difference to the basic model and the extended model with single choice can be explained by the agents' being able to reconsider their technology choice and to correct errors (mostly of period 2). With this cost constellation, in the single choice model, equilibrium was mostly reached in the second period at lower GE. In the reversible decision model these decisions were often corrected in period three.

t_{stat} appears to be surprisingly negatively correlated with μ(K) which would be the opposite of the findings of the basic model (when not considering the μ(K) areas without standardization activities). Actually, for high values of μ(K) (which caused the latest standardizations in the basic model) the values are quite similar.

Due to their small frequency (in both models) they are covered behind the histogram for many parts.

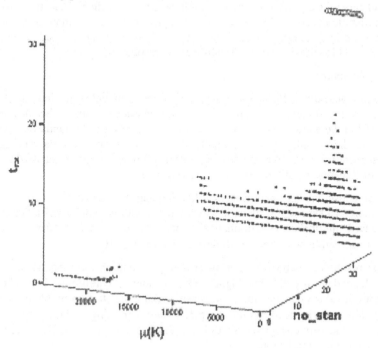

Figure 53: Stationary state period and total number of standardizing agents

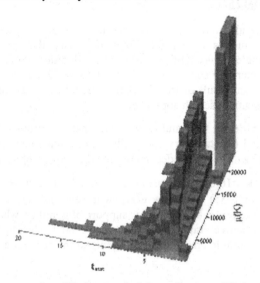

Figure 54: Histogram of equilibrium period depending on μ(K) (neglecting $t_{stat}>20$)

At lower costs, the correlation is in fact reversed. According to Figure 50 there is always one standard winning the whole market at intermediate prices. If "competitors" are cheaper the equilibrium process might take a longer time. Thus, the lower the standardization costs the longer the diffusion process towards a monopoly. Below a certain price, though, monopoly is not a feasible outcome. Instead, a static oligopoly or - in few cases - no stable stationary state turns up.

4.3.2.7 Summary

There are five possible diffusion patterns in the extended model with simultaneous reversible technology choice. Depending on the parameter values, besides no standardization there are mostly two results. Either at intermediate standardization costs one standard is adopted by all agents of the network or at low standardization costs a static multiple standards equilibrium emerges. Partly standardized networks or dynamic equilibria are comparatively rare.

Under these constellations, there is a twofold dilemma: if standardization costs are too high, there is a start-up problem, if they are too low there will be an inefficient multi-standard equilibrium with dramatically increased total costs (standardization costs plus information costs not saved) despite decreasing $\mu(K)$.

Analogous results are valid for the time reaching an equilibrium. Again, this is primarily dependent of $\mu(K)$. The higher $\mu(K)$ the later an equilibrium is reached because individual savings potentials decrease, making the start-up problem more important. The opposite accounts for low $\mu(K)$. With increasing savings potentials agents more frequently change technologies, leading in some cases to the extreme result of a dynamic equilibrium.

4.3.3 Sequential choice

Analyzing the extended model now once more leaves the adaptation of the decision model. Thus in this section the effect of altering the model premise that agents have a single choice within a sequential decision process is discussed. Simulation parameters are equivalent to those of Table 29. Disclosing these differences is an important result of the simulation model that was only possible because of the systematic research approach.

Figure 55 shows GEe for Q=1 and Q=4. Additionally, various GE graphs of the simultaneous model (at stationary state) allow for comparisons (GEiw is the simultaneous model with revisable decisions and GEi with a single decision).

To the right of $\mu(K)$=16,000, increasing Q shifts GEe to a lower level. It is also mostly below GEiw(t=35). Very low $\mu(K)$ (with reversible simultaneous choice) have a negative influence because they support oligopolies where GEiw(t=35) falls below the respective graph of the sequential model. The slightly smaller GE result from non reversible errors of some agents in the sequential model in early periods.

Still, GEe is mostly above GEi(t=35), since in both models decisions cannot be revised, although the sequential model allows for better information in the course of time.

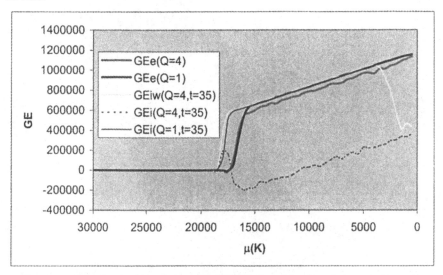

Figure 55: GE of the sequential model (GEe(Q=1 and Q=4) and the simultaneous model (thin: GEiw (reversible choice) and GEi (single choice))

A very interesting question within the sequential model is what is the chance of a particular technology if the first mover had chosen it instead of some other? For analyzing this, the adapted Herfindahl index can be used again (Figure 56).

For $\mu(K)<16,500$ there is a clear picture. At higher costs, the frequency of cases with no one standardizing increases. Since HKa cannot be determined in this case, its artificial value of zero disturbs the average. From $\mu(K)=16,500$ the Herfindahl index is 1 from the first period on (see figure). That means that the first agent always decides in favor of standardization. In t=2 the index decreases by 0.3 on average, by 0.09 in t=3. In later periods, it only marginally changes and continually increases from t=5 until HKa=0.85. In all periods, this is unrelated to $\mu(K)$.

Because the index can only be 0.5 or 1 in the second period (given a standardization) this means that the second agent often chooses a different technology than his predecessor. Looking closer into that phenomenon revealed that in 37.8% of all cases with standardization activities in the first period the second decider followed the first mover's decision. That is not too high a percentage when considering that the original probability is 25%. But even the remaining 12.8%-points make a difference and hint at the power of only one agent's (representing only 2,9% of the communication partners) decision influencing the available information set.

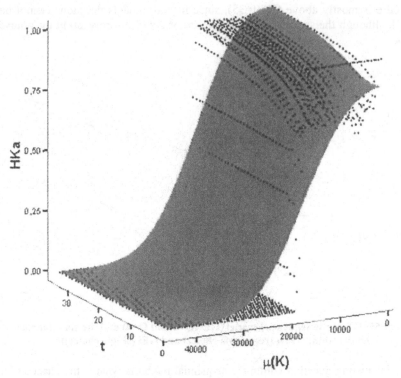

**Figure 56: Adapted Herfindahl index for the sequential model
depending on t and μ(K)**

Table 31 shows more data from that sample. All simulations with standardization activities in the first period are considered, showing agents' behavior in periods 2 to 4. Agents could not standardize (nst), chose a new standard not chosen yet (ast) or a standard already adopted by someone (gst). If the first three agents chose two standards then agent 4 could either "balance" the net (2:2) or chose the mostly adopted one more time (3:1). The table shows the number of occurrences relative to the whole sample. Relative frequencies to higher-ranking steps are in brackets.

The case of nst was of little importance because according to the assumptions on average all agents had to bear the same standardization costs as agent 1. When looking at the imitations it is a key factor to see how many standards have already been adopted. For instance, after the second period one standard (main row gst) or two (main row ast) can have been implemented. It is thus not surprising that in case gst|ast 40,9% and in case gst|gst only 20,5% resulted. The independent probabilities for these cases were 25% and 50% (given all standards yield net benefits). Underscored values show the centrally optimal strategy: Everyone chose the predecessor's standard. This probability strongly increased with every decision from 37,8% over 54% to 74%. "Market concentration", i.e. the degree of network monopolization was determined quite quickly.

Table 31: Relative frequency (%) of decisions in periods 2-4, sequential model ($x_1=1$)

t=2		nst (no standard)			gst (established standard)			ast (new standard)		
		2,6			37,8			59,6		
t=3		nst	gst	ast	nst	gst	ast	nst	gst	ast
		1,9 (73)	0,2 (8)	0,5 (19)	0,7 (2)	20,5 (54)	16,6 (44)	1,4 (2)	40,9 (69)	17,3 (29)
t=4	nst	1,5 (79)	0,1 (50)	0,1 (20)	0,5 (71)	0,1 (0)	0,3 (2)	1,0 (71)	0,2 (0)	0,0 (0)
	gst (2:2) (3:1)	0,1 (5)	0,1 (50)	0,4 (80)	0,2 (19)	15,1 (74)	4,8 (29) 7,8 (47)	0,4 (19)	11,4 (28) 20,6 (51)	14,7 (85)
	ast	0,3 (16)	0,0 (0)	0,0 (0)	0,0 (0)	5,3 (26)	3,7 (22)	0,0 (0)	8,7 (21)	2,6 (15)

4.3.4 Individual consequences

After looking into the multi-standard diffusion process from a network perspective we now turn to the individual agent again. First, individual decisions resulting from centralized and decentralized coordination are compared. The decentralized model is based on simultaneous reversible choice. 6,000 simulation runs (parameters as in Table 29) at different average standardization costs generated individual agents' savings that are visualized using box plots. As in Figure 26, the abscissa needed to have a reverse scale.

From the previous findings we know that the network does not have to be in a stationary state, per se. Total as well as individual savings vary only slightly in a dynamic equilibrium, though.

The development of the categories depicted by the box plots equals the aggregated GE graphs of section 4.2.4. In contrast to Figure 26 individual losses are significantly more severe. Here, in the first period at $\mu(K)=17,000$ almost 100% of the agents are worse off after their decision to standardize, compared to 25% earlier. In an intermediate area of $\mu(K)$ between 8,000 and 19,000, most solutions are monopolies. That is why the box plots showing individual savings for t=35 are for the most part identical with the centralized results. For smaller standardization costs ($\mu(K)<6,000$) centralized solution quality could not be achieved any more. As seen in section 4.3.1.3, there is no monopoly at low standardization costs. This implies that some agents make long term losses due to their standardization decisions even at standardization costs as low as $\mu(K)=250$.

136

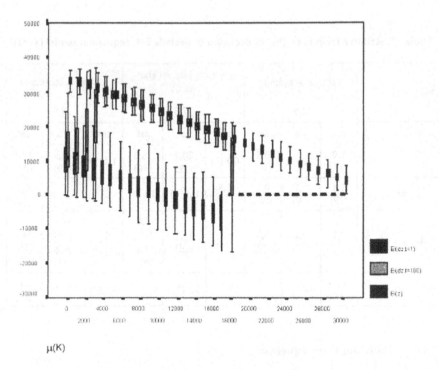

$\mu(K)$

Figure 57: Individual savings ($E_i(dz,t=1)$ and $E_i(dz,t=35)$)

The second category explored in section 4.2.4 was relative error frequency. i.e. relating the number of agents deciding wrongly to network size. There are positive (standardization; ex post $E_i<0$) and negative (no standardization; ex post $E_i>0$) errors. Due to the multi standard property of the extended model (Q>1), the definition of negative errors needs calibration. If an agent decides against standardization, for all possible standards potential savings are determined given the decisions of the relevant neighbors. If the highest of these values is greater than zero we call this a negative error. Clearly, another category of errors is not included: decisions for a particular standard while ex post savings resulting from using a different standard would have been greater. Omitting these secures comparability to the basic model, though. Figure 58 shows error occurrence f dependent of $\mu(K)$ and t and below differentiated between f_{pos} and f_{neg}. The f_{neg} scale in the bottom right figure is significantly more fine-grained than the others.

In the multi standard scenario, almost all errors are positive. At $\mu(K)=17,000$ there were cases with basically all agents deciding erroneously in the first period. Figure 57 shows monetary consequences at standardization costs so low that all agents standardized in t=1. But due to the heterogeneity of standards they could only save minimally on information costs. In the following periods these errors vanished quite soon.

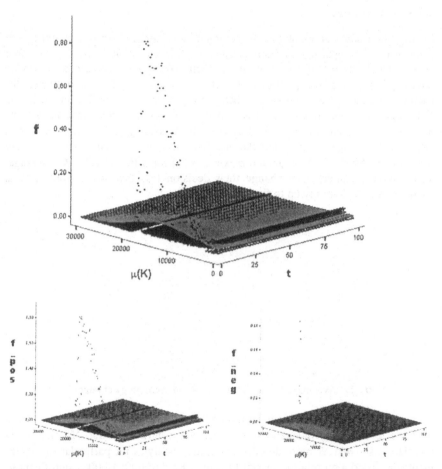

Figure 58: Relative occurrence of errors depending on μ(K) and t (f, f$_{pos}$, and f$_{neg}$)

Negative errors can mostly be witnessed in the first period at μ(K)=[20,500;19,000]. Here, some penguins lingered before jumping. The fraction of these errors is small, though, and could be corrected in the second period.

There were two parameter constellations that exposed errors which were not redeemable later. For μ(K)=[18,000;18,500] there is a persistent f=0.01. The explanation is that only 1 up to 6 agents standardized, but not the remaining agents in the network. For μ(K)=[2,000; 4,000] standard hopping resulted in a persistent error rate of 4%. Here considering the errors of not realized savings when using *an-*

138

other technology as well would increase f (but only slightly for on average savings are the same).

4.3.5 Agent size

Finally, the impact of agent size (as summed individual information costs) on the propensity to standardize is analyzed again. Now the main focus is how often agents change technology with respect to their size. Simulations are based on reducing $\mu(K)$ in steps of 1,000 from 26,000 to 0 with n=35, T=35 and 40 runs for each constellation. For each agent, change frequency w(n) was documented. The first implementation of a standard is a change, too, so that agents that did not implement any standard are described by w(n)=0. Accordingly, the sample per $\mu(K)$ step was 1,400 agents. Only simulations that ended with a stationary state were used. Figure 59 shows average and maximal w(n) for different $\mu(K)$. On average, agents having standardized change their decision less than once. Some agents changed their technology up to five times, though.

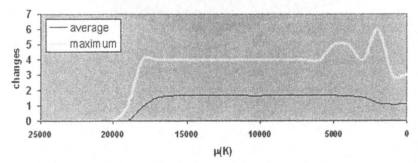

Figure 59: Average and maximal number of technology changes w(n)

To check the significance of the relation between w(n) and size(n) the correlation over the total sample independent of $\mu(K)$ was determined first. No significant correlation showed. A more detailed correlation analysis for particular $\mu(K)$ segments disclosed a correlation of r=0.137 for $\mu(K)$=[17,000; 18,000] significant to 0.01.

In this area agents having to bear higher communication costs changed their technologies slightly more often. One might have expected huge players to standardize less often because they standardize earlier (section 4.2.5) so that their first mover influence could determine the standards which would be victorious in the end. But four different "first movers" could for instance choose four different standards (e.g. due to their simultaneous decisions or because they are not direct neighbors or because their individual cost situation implies doing so) so that in a situation when monopoly is expected anyway the majority of those early decisions need revision. Especially when there are high standardization costs the penguin effect prolongs the diffusion process and induces more changes on part of the first movers.

For other cost values no significant correlation could be found. In summary, the empirical correlation between size and decision behavior is rather weak.

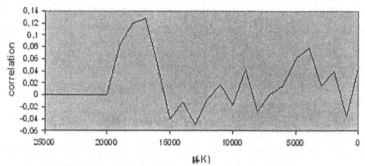

Figure 60: Correlation between size(n) and w(n) for different μ(K)

4.3.6 Variations of network structure

In this section, parameters determining network structure are varied for the extended standardization model (simultaneous reversible choice). First, decentralized total savings were determined when reducing the density parameter V from 1.0 to 0.0 at standardization costs of 14,000 and 2,000 in order to see system behavior for probable monopolies as well as oligopolies. Data was generated for both network structures as described in Table 32 (random topologies (structure 1) describe relationships between randomly selected agents while in close topologies (structure 2) neighbors are selected with regard to their geographical proximity). Results for t=1 and t=35 are shown in Figure 61.

Table 32: Simulation parameters

μ(C) = 1,000	σ(C) = 200	μ(K) = 2,000;14,000	σ(K) = 1,000	
n = 35	T = 100	V = *var.*	B = 0.0	Q = 4

Results for μ(K)=14,000 are structurally identical with those from section 4.2.6. Lowering density has similar effects to increasing μ(K), while curves are somewhat more stretched in close topologies. Deviations of the GE(t=1) graph from the basic model can again be explained by the heterogeneity of standards. Although many agents standardize in the first period they cannot save too much in information costs before the adaptation process migrates the network towards a single technology solution.

140

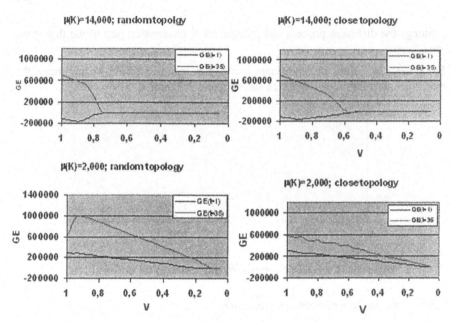

Figure 61: GE in t=1 and t=35 at different V

Low standardization costs entail different results compared to the basic model as well as between the different network structures. There are different diffusion pattern developments leading to the equilibria. This is shown in Figure 62 (that consists of a total of over 10 million decisions by agents in 2,100 simulation runs per scenario).

At high standardization costs, both network structures are in essence identical. If agents have stronger communication links with their geographically closer partners, communication islands (network clusters) can form making solutions more probable with only parts of the network standardizing. Consequently, Figure 62 shows standardization activities for smaller V in close topologies (top right) than in random topologies (top left).

If average standardization costs are so low that for V=1 oligopolies can be expected, reducing network density has different effects depending on the network structure. In random topologies, monopoly rapidly replaces oligopoly. The explanation is that reducing communication links does not substantially change the internal structure of the network: edges are still equally distributed and some of the edges are randomly removed from the set of communication links of some agents. Hence, for constant standardization costs the savings potential decreases. This is equivalent to increased standardization costs with constant information costs. The effect is accordingly equivalent to the results of varying $\mu(K)$ in complete networks (V=1; see section 4.3.1.3).

This is different for close topologies. First, the communication links representing the longest Euclidean distances are removed. This leads to more and more isolated parts (clusters) within the network. For that reason, oligopolies can persist better and the occurrence of monopoly declines. A single standard therefore has less power when penetrating those parts of a network where there are few communication links except when by chance events in early periods that technology has been established in the respective network islands. The phenomenon that in close topologies there is no inactivity when V is very low (as is the case in random topologies) is obviously explained by the equivalent results at μ(K)=14,000. Interestingly, the only case of a dynamic equilibrium shows in the bottom right diagram.

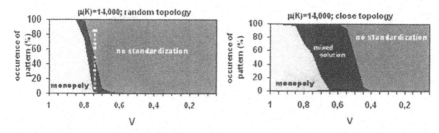

☐1 (no standardization) ■2 (mixed solution) ☐3 (monopoly) ☐4 (oligopoly) ■5 (dynmaic equilibrium)

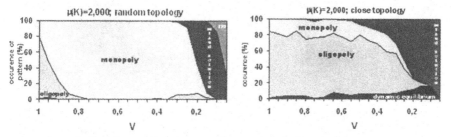

Figure 62: Distribution of diffusion processes at different V

The smaller the network density the fewer (and therefore closer) are the communication links between agents. Close topologies implicitly secure the bi-directionality of information relationships. This implies that p_{ijq} are positive more often. In random topologies, p_{ijq} often cannot be determined because although $c_{ij}>0$ there often is $c_{ji}=0$. The (bi- or) multilateral dynamics can more frequently show due to bilateral links and focusing on fewer partners (V=0.05 is equal to 1.7 communication partners).

Figure 61 and Figure 62 represent selected cross sections of overlays of the diagrams from Figure 63; thus, no further explanation is required. Figure 63 illustrates the distribution of the five diffusion processes while simultaneously varying μ(K) and V. Figure 64 shows the paths of total savings in t=1 and the period of reaching the stationary state (if there was no dynamic equilibrium).

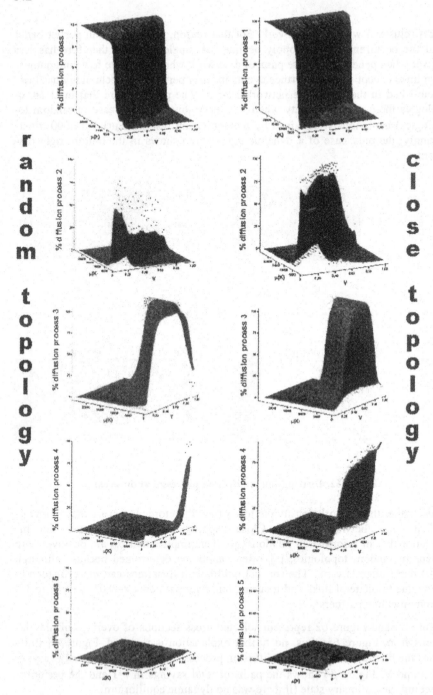

Figure 63: Occurrence of diffusion patterns
depending on μ(K), V, and network topology

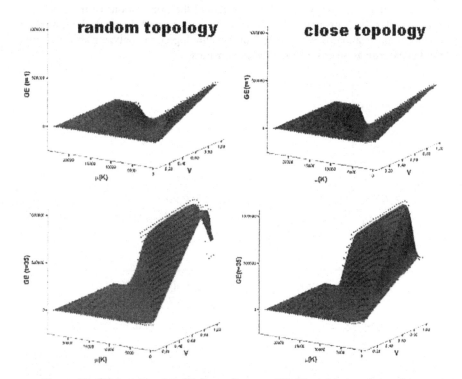

Figure 64: GE in t=1 and t= 35 depending on μ(K), V, and network topology

These findings support the conclusions of the diffusion model. There, density (called *connectivity*, used to model the *personal network exposure*) shows a higher correlation with monopoly in random topologies. Increasing connectivity implies higher concentration. As in the standardization model described above, this correlation weakens with increasing standardization costs (see Figure 62, Figure 63, Figure 64). Increasing the *heterogeneity of preferences* in the diffusion model is analogous to increasing the deviation of the standardization costs in the standardization model. Again, the overall findings in both models are similar in identifying less concentration at high prices (K), see Figure 51. In contrast to the diffusion model that reveals a higher diversity of standards the higher the standardization costs are, the standardization model does not necessarily start with a complete installed base that is randomly generated. As a consequence, when standardization costs are so high that no standardization activity would occur in the standardization model, those ("switching") costs preserve the heterogeneity of the installed base [Weitzel/Wendt/Westarp 2002, 21-25; Westarp 2003; Wendt/Westarp/König 2000].

4.3.7 Installed base effects

Exploring installed base effects for the extended standardization model is done in two parts. First, in analogy with the basic model the implications of the existence of an installed base on network behavior are investigated. Second, the complete network is pre-standardized with 1, 2 or 4 technologies to analyze stability at different standardization costs and network densities.

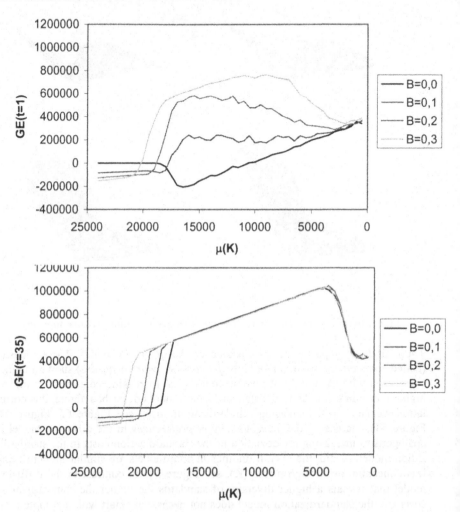

Figure 65: GE at different B(1) in t=1 and t=35

To compare results with those of the basic model, 10%, 20%, and 30% of all agents are pre-standardized with the first technology. Agents forming the installed base were randomly selected and could certainly change their standard from the first period on. Another simulation with the assumption that installed base agents have to stick to their pre-standards showed no relevant differences for Figure 64 and Figure 65. The only figure in this work affected would be Figure 69.

Table 33: Simulation parameters

$\mu(C) = 1,000$	$\sigma(C) = 200$	$\mu(K) = var.$	$\sigma(K) = 1,000$	
$n = 35$	$T = 35$	$V = 1.0$	$B = 0.1; 0.2; 0.3$	$Q = 4$

Figure 65 does not show any differences to the total savings in the stationary state of section 4.2.7. In t=1 the direction of the development of GE switches for $\mu(K)=[16,500;18,500]$ when there is an installed base. The reason is that a monopoly can emerge faster while for B(1)=0.0 there is an oligopoly in the first period starting the monopolization process later. The stationary state (t=35) shows identical total savings, though. One dissimilarity is that when increasing B activities start - as in the basic model - at higher costs. Consequently, increasing the number of available technologies will not yield any further findings concerning total savings.

It is interesting that the sudden decrease of GE while increasing B(1) remains untouched for very low standardization costs. This means that although the installed base had set a standard this cost area can produce oligopolies similar to a diffusion process without any installed base. To look more deeply into this the adapted Herfindahl index and the process distributions for B(1)=0.0 and B(1)=0.3 are compared (Figure 66 and Figure 67).

Figure 66 does not explicitly show t=0 because here HKa is 0 for B(1)=0.0 and HKa is 1 for B(1)=0.3 which would make the figures more difficult to compare.

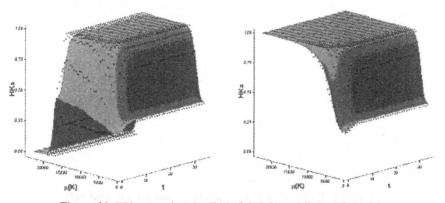

Figure 66: HKa over time for B(1)=0.0 (left) and B(1)=0.3 (right)

146

The development of HKa reveals that the maximal HKa=1 is reached significantly faster. That means that the battling out process towards a monopoly is substantially weaker. This corresponds to the findings above indicating a switch of the direction of GE at μ(K)=[16,500;18,500] (the graphs are different at high μ(K) because the installed base alone induces HKa=1).

There are no other new findings in this scenario except that activities of agents not part of the installed base at higher μ(K) begin earlier as was the case in the basic model.

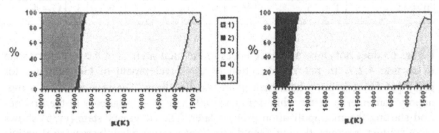

Figure 67: Distribution of diffusion patterns for B(1)=0.0 (left) and B(1)=0.3 (right)

Figure 68 reveals the average period of reaching a stationary state for different B(1). Again it shows that the existence of an installed base accelerates arrival at an equilibrium. For cost ranges implying monopolies, an installed base of no more than 10% of the network shortens the equilibrium process by one period. Nonetheless, for low standardization costs regularly resulting in oligopolies there are no changes.

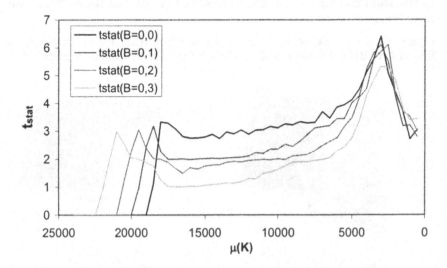

Figure 68: Period of reaching stationary state for different B(1)

One important question remains to be answered: In monopoly situations, does the first standard always win the race? The answer is no.

There are cases of networks where the eventual monopoly technology was not part of the installed base. See Figure 70 for an example. With decreasing $\mu(K)$ and $B(1)=0.1$ the fraction of monopolies in standards 2 to 4 increases to up to 64% (Figure 69). For $B(1)=0.0$ this would be 75%. Consequently, installed base effects do not wane as late as at $\mu(K)<4,000$ when most solutions are oligopolies. Instead, it is significantly earlier that agents are hardly influenced in their technology choice by installed base standards. Figure 70 exemplifies the development of "market shares" over time for the scenario described.

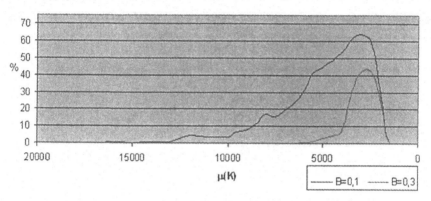

Figure 69: Fraction of monopolies of standards q=2 to q=4

To analyze the robustness of decisions under installed base effects the scenario is now slightly changed. The next simulations are based upon completely pre-standardized networks (in t=0) with different standards: $\sum_{q=1}^{Q} B(q) = 1$

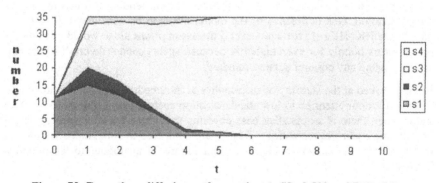

Figure 70: Exemplary diffusion path over time ($\mu(K)$=3,500 and B(1)=0.3)

148

Table 34: Simulation parameters

n = T = 40	Q = 4	V = 1.0	μ(C) = 1,000	σ(C) = 200	σ(K) = 1,000
Scenario 1	B(1) = 0.5	B(2) = 0.5	B(3) = 0.0	B(4) = 0.0	μ(K) = [0;30,000]
Scenario 2	B(1) = 0.25	B(2) = 0.25	B(3) = 0.25	B(4) = 0.25	μ(K) = [0;30,000]
Scenario 3	B(1) = 1.0	B(2) = 0.0	B(3) = 0.0	B(4) = 0.0	μ(K) = [0;6,000]

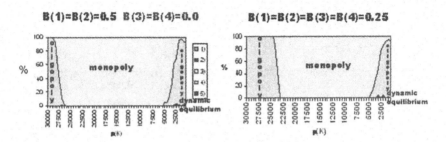

Figure 71: Process distribution with installed base (scenario 1 (left) and 2 (right))

For scenarios 1 and 2 Figure 71 shows resulting process distributions and Figure 72 examples of diffusion processes over time.

Monopoly appears to be completely stable for the intermediate cost range. The higher the market concentration of the installed base (scenario 1: HK=HKa=0.5; scenario 2: HK=HKa=0.25), the higher the standardization costs that cause agents to become active and make an advantageous decision tending towards monopoly standardization. One deficiency of the model needs to be considered: for B(q)=1 (and hence HK=HKa=1) for whichever q the assumptions alone would guarantee a persistent monopoly for even higher K because agents cannot deinstall a standard and stop using any communication standard.

Having looked at the stability of monopolies at intermediate standardization costs, we now turn our attention to low standardization costs to see if oligopolies remain stable when there is an installed base covering the whole network and consisting of only one particular technology. Results are compared to simulations without an installed base and shown in Figure 73 and Figure 74 analogous to the previous figures.

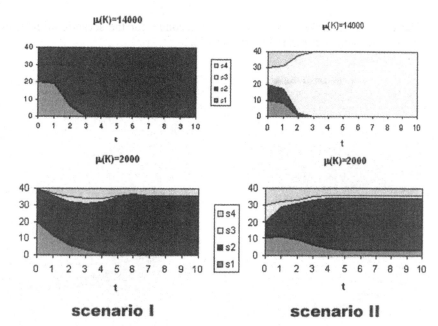

Figure 72: Typical examples of diffusion processes at medium and low standardization costs and a complete installed base (left: scenario I; right: scenario II)

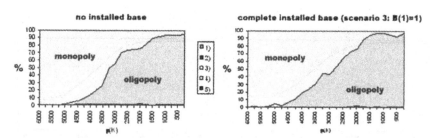

Figure 73: Distribution of diffusion patterns depending on installed base

Figure 73 reveals that there are no substantial installed base effects on the process distribution. For very low μ(K) oligopoly is still the most probable outcome. This implies that from a central perspective agents not only move out of a local optimum but also "consciously" worsen their situation. Figure 74 clearly shows this. In Figure 73, too, there is no certainty that a monopoly consists of an installed base technology. An example of this is shown in Figure 74 (top right). A possible hypothesis is that oligopolies exhibit higher market concentration at B(1)=1, i.e. standards q=2 to 4 would find only few installations. But the development of the Herfindahl index when lowering μ(K) is predominantly independent of the existence of an installed base (Figure 75). The average HK of 0.4 at μ(K)<1,500 coinciding with very few monopolies discloses that most oligopolies consist of incom-

150

pletely balanced market shares. The same accounts for the scenario without installed base as can be seen in Figure 74 (left).

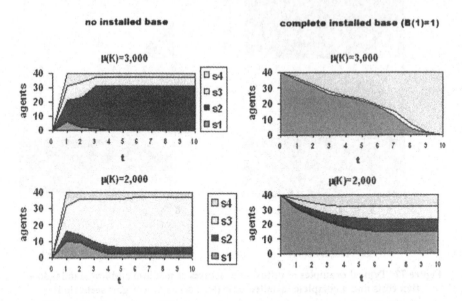

Figure 74: Exemplary diffusion paths over time depending on installed base

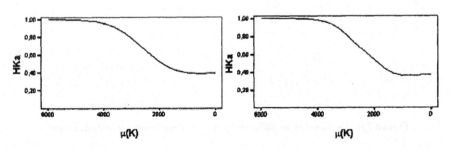

Figure 75: HKa for different $\mu(K)$ without installed base (left) and B(1)=1 (right)

These observations lead to the conclusion that the decision model used might bear
some problems for low standardization costs. Looking at the formula for determining p_{ijq} reveals the reason. At low $\mu(K)$ probability p_{ijq} converges towards 1.0 and
thereby almost equals the probability "estimating" standardization decisions of
agents who have formed the installed base. Since standardization costs are then
the main variable which leads an agent to anticipate the partner's technology
choice (all other parameters are independent of q) an installed base can only play a
smaller role. Thus, while in most cases the decentralized model proved to be a
very instructive and efficient tool for describing agents' standardization behavior,

results in multi-standard cases with very low standardization costs can possibly be more shady. On the other hand, standardization costs can only be evaluated in relation to relevant information costs. The problematic parameter range discussed here represents quite extreme cost benefit relations. At $\mu(K)=1,000$ potential savings would be 39 times those costs (per period). Although there might be situations like this in reality, they are most probably relatively rare. In addition, in the next section a completely different calculus for determining and describing an agent's anticipatory decision behavior is developed and evaluated, serving as a benchmark solution.

4.4 A different decentralized anticipation calculus

As in the previous chapters, a reformulation of the decentralized model helps to get a better awareness of the remaining danger that results might owe their particularities partly to some implicit model properties rather than the scenarios analyzed. The adaptation is also a major step towards integrating the standardization model with the diffusion model of Westarp/Wendt, which was developed as part of the research project Economics of Standards, too. The diffusion model is explicitly introduced in Westarp (2003), see section 4.5 for a brief overview. A first integration is presented in Weitzel/Wendt/Westarp (2001).

Individual utility in the diffusion model is not dependent on information costs. Thus, there is no equivalent or analogy to c_{ij} which is a crucial concept in the standardization model for considering the agents' individuality. The basic problem of anticipating the communication partners' behavior remains, though.

The question is thus how to model a probability estimation

- that does not require information about individual information costs

- that can be used within the standardization model's decision function

- that works with the limited information availability of the diffusion model.

The idea is to use observable states of network agents. An agent state describes - by analogy with the state of a network - if and what standard is implemented by an agent.

An agent tries to anticipate his partners' standardization decisions by aggregating what standards have been implemented by the particular neighbor's neighbors (analogous to the *locally relevant* or visible subset of the network state as a binary 1*n-vector consisting of all agents' x_{iq} from section 4.2.2.1). The agent's hypothesis is that his neighbor is most likely to implement the standard that enjoyed the widest diffusion in the neighbor's neighborhood which will be called his 2nd degree neighborhood in the following.

$$p_{ijq} = \frac{\sum_{k=1}^{n} x_{ijq} \cdot sign(c_{jk})}{n(j)}$$

Equation 25: p_{ijq} for the 2nd degree neighborhood

$$E_{iq} = \sum_{j=1}^{n} p_{ijq} \cdot sign(c_{ij})$$

Equation 26: Decision function (2nd degree neighborhood)

sign() returns the algebraic sign of the original value. If there is a communication link between agents i and j, then sign(c_{ij})=1 or 0 otherwise. p_{ijq} expresses the part of the 2nd degree neighborhood of j that uses standard q. The relevant parameter E_{iq} is no longer the expected information cost savings, and the individual standardization costs of agent i are not used for the decision function. The basic decision rule remains the same: Agent i implements the standard q with maximal expected value E_{iq} given that at least one expected value is positive.

Another problem is how to start. In the diffusion model, all agents have already implemented some standard. This is the special case of $\sum B(q)=1.0$ in the standardization model. Consequently, in the first period the original decision function from Equation 16 is applied and then for t=2,...,T replaced by the new decision function in Equation 26. At the end of this section, simulation results will be presented showing diffusion results in networks with an installed base of all agents, too. Of course, in that particular case a sequential application of both models is unnecessary.

First, development of total savings (Figure 76) and market concentration (Figure 77) at V=1 depending on $\mu(K)$ are determined. Parameter data are summarized in Table 35.

Table 35: Simulation parameters

$\mu(C) = 1,000$	$\sigma(C) = 200$	$\mu(K) = var.$	$\sigma(K) = 1,000$	
n = 35	T = 35	V = 1.0	B = 0.0	Q = 4

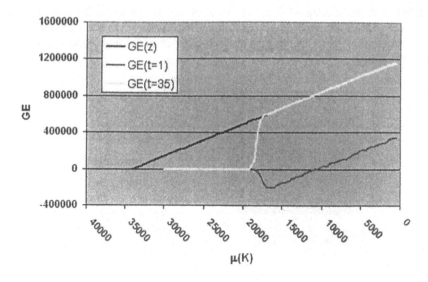

Figure 76: GE in adapted model in T=1 and in t_stat

The development of total savings is for the most part identical with the original model except for very low μ(K). There is a slightly higher responsiveness in that the network is fully standardized at μ(K) that are 500 higher (if there had been first movers which are determined by the original model, though).

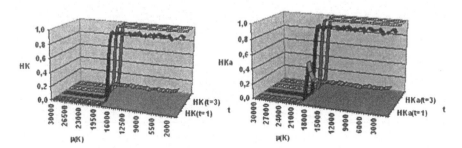

**Figure 77: HK (left) and HKa (right) in adapted model
from t=1 to t=4 (stationary state)**

In the adapted decision model, there is no emerging of inefficient oligopolies because total savings increase strictly monotonously. This finding is supported by the Herfindahl index.

Figure 77 only shows the first four periods since using the 2nd degree neighborhood concept has equilibria established no later than in the third period, in most cases as early as t=2.

154

Implications of the adapted decision model to the occurrence of the different diffusion processes are apparent. In maximum density networks there are only monopolies (Figure 78). This can also be seen in terms of the high concentration coefficient HK.

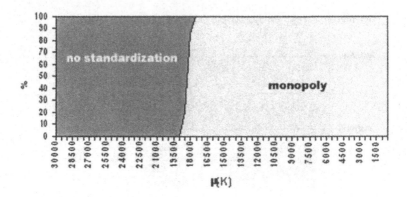

Figure 78: Process distribution in adapted decision model

Due to this efficient agent behavior, the proportion of monopolies implementing that particular standard in a centralized network (centralized heuristic) is shown in Figure 79. It is 74% on average.

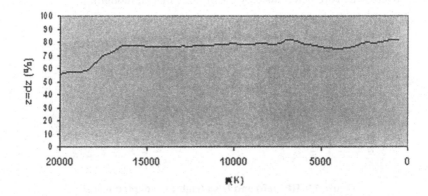

Figure 79: Fraction of monopolies with centrally optimal standard (%)

It is surprising that although neglecting costs after t=1 in the adapted model the results are that efficient. If there were no dependencies, one could expect this percentage to be around 25%. When using only the original model, about 30% resulted. But we must not fail to be aware that the adapted decision model also implies an extension to the information set available to the individual agent: they can "look further", as will be discussed later in section 4.5.1.2.

In t=1 agents implemented the most advantageous technologies. The adapted model favored a very fast adoption of the standard with the biggest market share in the first period. In contrast, in the original model mutual reactions were stronger and took more periods.

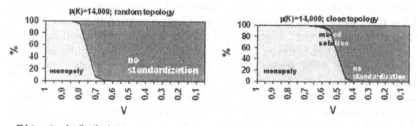

□1 (no standardization) ■2 (mixed solution) □3 (monopoly) □4 (oligopoly) ■5 (dynamaic equilibrium)

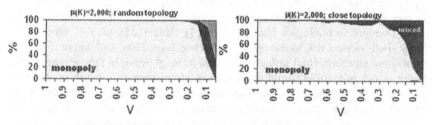

Figure 80: Diffusion paths at different V, K and topologies

For exploring the implications of the adapted model, for various network densities the procedures of the former sections are applied again. The density parameter V is altered in both structures from 1.0 to 0.0 while μ(K) are held constant at 14,000 and 2,000. Figure 80 shows the distribution of the diffusion processes for each of the four scenarios. In contrast to the former findings, in the adapted model there is no oligopoly among the completely standardized networks. Especially in close topologies there are many partly standardized networks (even with different standards) at smaller densities as a result of clustering. But monopoly is appreciably stable.

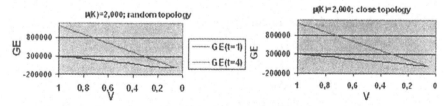

Figure 81: GE at μ(K)=2,000 in different topologies

Only at small μ(K) is there a difference in total savings compared to section 4.3.6 (Figure 61). This is why Figure 81 only shows diagrams for μ(K)=2,000. The development is steeper than in the original model since the inefficient oligopolies do not occur.

Concerning the period of reaching an equilibrium there are no differences to V=1.

We now turn to installed base effects again, and discuss whether the adapted model is more suitable for addressing the problems identified in section 4.3.7. If agents use the concept of 2nd degree neighborhood when deciding about standards, then ex post inefficient behavior at small standardization costs can be excluded. But there are then more severe problems. When considering that the adapted model does not consider costs at all (due to the installed base not even in the first period the original decision function is used) it becomes evident that the parameters GE and variations of $\mu(K)$ that have been used throughout this work are not an appropriate means of representing and evaluating simulation results. A high density network (V=1; n=35) will definitely standardize completely and independently of the value of the standardization costs if only there is an installed base of only one agent. Going back to n=40 and a complete installed base consisting of equally frequent technologies (B(1)=B(2)=B(3)=B(4)=0,25), at V=1 there is no activity at all because due to the symmetric network structure each agent is subject to equivalent environmental influences (states of neighbors). In fact, arranging the network actors in a circle would draw a completely symmetric graph of that network. Even slight reductions of network density destroy that symmetry and leave room only for monopolies. A further decrease of V allows more and more oligopolies that again are significantly more frequent in close topologies. It is noteworthy that allowing for de-installing standards without getting a new one all those areas belonging to process 4 in Figure 82 would actually be mixed equilibria (process 2). As a result, complete oligopolies are highly unstable in this model and can only emerge in the extreme case described by the conditions of Equation 27.

$$B(q)=1/Q \qquad \forall q$$

$$V=1.0$$

$$n \bmod Q = 0$$

Equation 27: Conditions for complete oligopolies in adapted standardization model

Applied to a 4 standards scenario this implies:

$$B(1) = B(2) = B(3) = B(4)$$
$$B(1) + B(2) + B(3) + B(4) = 1$$
$$V=1.0$$
$$n \bmod 4 = 0$$

Equation 28: Complete oligopolies in adapted standardization model (Q=4)

No differences are observable concerning the duration of the activity phases. The average period of reaching a stationary state is (with only smaller deviations) t=2.

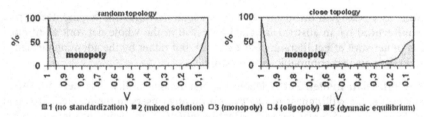

Figure 82: Process distribution in adapted model
(complete installed base; different V)

Summary:

The adaptation of the decision calculus of the diffusion model to the conditions of the decentralized standardization model implies significantly more stable (decentralized) monopolies and faster adoption processes. The results are difficult to compare to those of the original model, though, for both are based on quite different parameters. After all, especially for modeling problems with a heterogeneous cost structure, the adaptation is not likely to deliver a more precise description of decentralized standardization processes.

4.5 Adapting the diffusion model

> "The scientific theory I like best
> is that the rings of Saturn are composed entirely of lost airline luggage."
> *Mark Russell*

In the previous section, parts of the diffusion model have been adapted to be used within the scope of the standardization model and to look into effects caused by altering the method behind estimating partners' standardization behavior. We now switch perspectives and develop a more inclusive integration between the two models by adapting the anticipatory decision concept of the standardization model for use within the diffusion model. This will complete our effort to achieve a unified standardization framework bringing together all the research contributions of the project *Economics of Standards* and providing a building block for further research. A comparison of the main findings of the diffusion model with those of the standardization model has been presented in section 4.3.6.

4.5.1 From standardization to diffusion

4.5.1.1 The diffusion model

The diffusion model is elaborated in Westarp (2003). Its basis is a simple model of the buying decision in network effect markets. The terminology is similar to the model of Katz/Shapiro (1985), but the terms are interpreted differently. The basic idea of the diffusion model is to conduct simulations by modeling the software

158

market as a relational diffusion network. In such networks the buying decision is not influenced by an abstract installed base within the whole network as in most parts of network effect literature (section 2.2), but rather by the adoption decisions within the personal communication network.

Basic diffusion model. Let r denote the stand-alone utility of a network effect product (i.e. the willingness to pay even if no other users in the market exist) and $f(x)$ denote the additional network effect benefits (i.e. the value of the externality when x is the number of other adopters). For reasons of simplification all network participants are assumed to have the same function $f(x)$, i.e. their evaluation of network benefits is identical. Also, network effects are assumed to increase linearly, i.e. $f(x)$ increases by a certain amount with every new user. The willingness to pay for a software product can then be described by the term $r+f(x)$. Let p be the price or the cost of a certain software product/solution, then a consumer buys the solution if $r+f(x)-p>0$. In case of v competing products in a market, the consumer buys the product with the maximum surplus in cases where this exceeds 0:

$$\max_{q \in \{1,...,v\}} \left\{ r_q + f(x_q) - p_q \right\}$$

Equation 29: Objective function for the network diffusion model

If the surplus is negative for all q then no product is bought. Equation 29 implies that only one product is used at the same time. This is a common assumption in many network effect models (e.g. Wiese 1990; Arthur 1989; see section 4.3).

Network Structure. First, the n consumers are distributed randomly on the unit square, i.e. their x- and y-coordinates are sampled from a uniform distribution over [0; 1]. In a second step, the network's structure is generated by either choosing the c closest neighbors measured by Euclidean distance (*close* topology, section 4.2.6) or selecting c neighbors randomly from all n-1 possible neighbors (*random* topology). This distinction is made to support the central hypothesis of the diffusion model, namely: ceteris paribus (e.g. for the same network *size* and *connectivity*) the *specific* neighborhood structure of the network strongly influences the diffusion processes.

Preferences, Prices, and Network Effects. Regardless of topology, every consumer can choose from all existing software products and knows all their prices. Initially, all consumers are (randomly) equipped with one software product, which may be considered to be their "legacy software" that is already installed and does not incur any further cost.

The direct utility that each consumer draws from the functionality of the v different products is then sampled from a uniform random distribution over the interval [0;*util*]. For each consumer and every software product the same interval is used. Thus a value of *util*=0 leads to homogeneous direct preferences (of zero) while the higher the exogenously given value of *util*, the more heterogeneous the preferences of the consumers become (with respect to the different software products as well as with respect to the neighbors they communicate with).

The weight of the positive network externalities deriving from each neighbor using the same software has been set to an arbitrary (but constant) value of 10,000 (for every consumer and every run).

In order to isolate the network externalities and heterogeneity of consumer preferences from other effects, all prices for the software products are fixed to a constant value and all marketing expenditures to zero for the simulations presented here, i.e. consumers decide solely upon potential differences of *direct utility* and the *adoption choices of their neighbors*.

Dynamics of the decision process. In each iteration of the diffusion, every consumer decides whether to keep his old software or whether to buy a new one based on the decision rationale described above. The old software is assumed to be discarded once a new product is bought, i.e. it can neither provide the deciding consumer with direct utility nor the neighbors with positive externalities anymore. The adoption decisions are made in a sequential order, i.e. all consumers may always be assumed to have correct knowledge about the software their neighbors are currently running. Although we have not yet established a formal proof, for our simulations this decision process always converged towards an equilibrium in which no actor wanted to revise his decision anymore. We did not experience any oscillation.

4.5.1.2 An integration

Although using a different notation, the strong similarities of the standardization model and the diffusion model are obvious: The stand-alone utility r_q of the consumer's utility function $\max_{q\in\{1,\dots,v\}}\{r_q + f(x_q) - p_q\}$ may directly be deducted from the price which then corresponds to the individual standardization cost:

$$\underbrace{-(p_q - r_q) + f(x_q)}_{\text{Diffusion}} = \underbrace{x_q\left[\sum_{q=1}^{v}K_q - \sum_{j=1}^{n}c_{ij}\,prob_{ijq}\right]}_{\text{Standardization}} \to \max_q$$

Equation 30: Decision functions of the standardization and diffusion models

The network benefits of the network diffusion model, however, are modeled as a function of the number of partners using the same product, which is furthermore restricted to being linear and homogeneous for all consumers. In contrast to that,

the standardization model allows for differentiating these benefits c_{ij} (while naming them "cost savings") to be a function of the individual link from agent i to a specific partner j.

Although whenever there is empirical data available representing the bilateral real-world network benefits, the diffusion model should account for this data, we did not experience any significant changes in the diffusion processes when we decided to sample the bilateral benefits derived from a uniform distribution [5,000; 15,000] instead of taking a fixed value of 10,000 units (see above).

A complication in the integration of both models arises from the different designs of the decision functions. Let us recall the informational assumptions:

Agent i only knows his own cost and benefits and all bilateral cost savings/benefits relating to his direct neighbors (c_{ij} and c_{ji}) as well as their K (section 3.1). Data about other agents' costs and benefits are considered to be unknown since gathering them is too expensive and estimating them is too imprecise. Decision making by other agents is unknown *ex ante* but observable on an *ex post* basis (incomplete but perfect information). Up to now, the second assumption of ex post observability has furthermore been restricted to the actors' direct neighbors. If we relax this restriction, i.e. assume that each agent i also knows the identity and the product used by the direct neighbors of his own neighbors (called his 2nd degree neighbors, see section 4.4), we may use their current endowment for a more precise forecast of actor i's direct neighbors' decisions.

One possible way to do this is to replace actor i's decision criterion "installed number of product q used in my direct neighborhood" by "expected number of product q used in my direct neighborhood" and trying to approximate this number indirectly by the observable "installed number of product q used in my 2nd degree neighborhood", of course normalized to the number of direct neighbors, since we will not receive ten times the positive network gains, even when each of our ten neighbors has ten distinct neighbors himself. Formally, we may express this expected "installed base" of an agent i by

$$E_i(base_q) = \sum_{j \in neighbors(i)} prob_{ijq}$$

Equation 31: Expected "installed base" of agent i

with

$$prob_{ijq} = \frac{\sum_{k \in neighbors(j)} x_{kq}}{|neighbors(j)|}$$

Equation 32: Probability approximation

with x_{kq} being the boolean variable indicating whether actor k currently uses product q.

The decision of each actor is then made as before according to the decision function used in the diffusion model.

The following figure shows that this anticipative behavior (**anticip=true**) from the adapted decentralized standardization model leads to a significantly higher expected market concentration than in the original network diffusion model. This effect is of course stronger in close topology networks, since random topology networks already exhibited a strong tendency towards market concentration with the non-anticipative decision criterion. This observation is not very surprising if we consider the question of choosing an operating system for your new PC: Although you may run into some trouble by installing a Windows 2000 workstation if your company still runs NT 4.0 servers, it may be wise to do so if you observe your company's suppliers and customers switching to Windows 2000 and thus expect your system administrator to be urged to follow them soon.

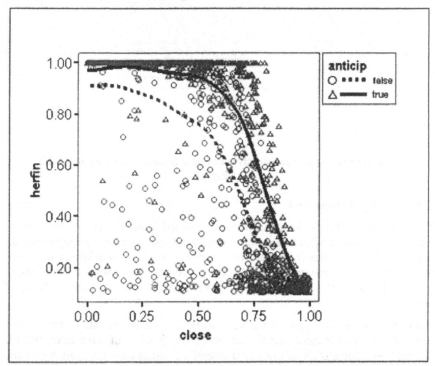

Figure 83: The effect of anticipative consumer behavior on market concentration

Figure 84 also illustrates that this anticipative behavior really pays off compared to the ex-post observation of direct neighbors: the figure shows the difference in the cumulative benefit to all consumers measured by the aggregated utility (direct and external effects) minus the total cost of buying the products and maybe buying a new product in the next period, since we have to revise the decision made in the last period.

162

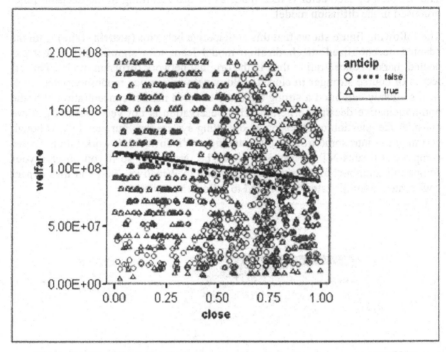

Figure 84: The effect of anticipative consumer behavior on consumer welfare (GE(dz))

4.5.1.3   Further research

With the integration of the standardization and diffusion models, more sophisticated analysis of coordination problems subject to network effects might contribute to achieving a deeper insight into the determinants of standardization problems. Given the importance of IT standards, software, and communication architectures, the diversity and ubiquity of network effects requires a sound theory of networks.

Promising future extensions of the framework include an analysis of anticipative behavior of a higher order and the efficiency implications of other informational assumptions. Some mechanisms could extend the information set available to any network agent to contribute to individual as well as collective welfare gains, provided information and agency costs are taken into account. In this context, using the models as a "sparring ground", bi-, tri- and multilateral (collaborative) optimization behavior and adequate mechanism designs enabling advantageous behavior can be developed, implemented and tested. Application domains suitable for testing the results are, for example, business networks such as EDI networks in different industries, corporate intra- or extranets, supply chains etc.

One of the most frequently discussed questions still remains open: does the supposed ubiquity of network effects and their particular presence in IT markets imply more regulation in these markets, since markets are said to fail under network effects? As will be discussed in section 6.2, a sophisticated theory of networks explaining real world phenomena (among others, equilibria transitions) still needs to be established.

Some theoretical requirements for a unified theory of network effects derived from the findings of this work are presented in section 6.

5 Solution mechanisms and empirical data

"However beautiful the strategy,
you should occasionally look at the results"
Sir Winston Churchill

In the previous sections, the implications of the existence of network effects on the decision quality of interdependent agents have been extensively elaborated. For understanding general principles behind standardization processes the framework proposed two extreme institutional settings; one being centralized coordination as a hypothetical benchmark of coordination quality at no agency costs, the other being decentralized coordination with agents acting and reacting according to the ever changing information sets available to them but without engaging in bi- or multilateral deals with their partners so as to accomplish concerted efforts. This gives rise to the question how such activities could contribute to enhancing agents' decision quality: how can (groups of) agents internalize otherwise unexploited network gains? How to close the standardization gap?

In sections 3 and 4 we assumed that the "rules", i.e. the institutional settings determining the standardization games are set. It became evident that these settings (centralized vs. decentralized, sequential vs. simultaneous choice etc.) greatly influence the outcome. A comparison of the results of different settings helped us to understand the implications of different institutional mechanisms. Thus, based on the framework presented, different mechanisms can be designed and evaluated with regard to their capacity for achieving optimality (welfare) goals to be defined. As could be seen in the simulations and the game theoretical analysis prior to that, non cooperative games are rarely suitable when overall (aggregate) efficiency is sought. This leads to a very interesting area of further research: How do equilibria change under alternate institutional environments? What is, then, the optimal institutional design for network interaction [Holler/Illing 2000, 28-29]? First steps towards a mechanism design for networks are proposed in the following sections.

To find some preliminary answers to these questions and to identify interesting areas of further research, empirical data collected during the course of the research project "Economics of Standards in Information Networks" will be used. This helps to evaluate real-life standardization problems and to propose possible solutions.

5.1 Empirical data for the standardization problem

> "Information technology so far has been a producer of data
> rather than a producer of information"
> *Peter Drucker*

There are at least as many studies trying to quantify the economic effects of standardization as there are definitions of the term standard. Consequently, one has to be very careful when studying data on standardization benefits for they depend heavily on a large number of assumptions and are sampled from the most diverse application domains.

One famous study of national standardization gains was undertaken in the 1950s by the Indian Standards Institution about production and utilization of structural steel and revealed savings of about 25%, adding to a national economy benefit for a ten-year period (1966-1976) of the equivalent of US $820 million (in 1973!) as opposed to $100,000 of direct expenditure for that project, which is a substantial benefit for a developing country [Verman 1973, 335-340].

Other researchers stress the negative effects of standards, mostly as a threat to innovation dynamics by saying that standards hamper fundamental innovations in exchanging inter- for intratechnological competition, see the discussion in section 2.2.7.

In corporate environments the outstanding importance of business-to-business communication has EDI appear to be a highly relevant example of standardization issues. Forrester Research estimates that the B2B market will reach $1.3 trillion by 2003, up from $43 billion in 1998, which is ten times the online retailing market and amounting to possibly 12% of GDP (see [Fronfield 2000]; similar figures are presented by Gartner Group [Gartner 2000] or Goldman, Sachs & Co [Goldmann 1999]; for a regional comparison see [Weitzel/Harder/Buxmann 2001, 4-5]). Indeed, the case of EDI provides an interesting application domain for the discussion of standardization problems. The history of EDI and reasons for the problems associated with it are presented in Weitzel/Harder/Buxmann (2001). In the next sections, empirical data especially from EDI networks but also from other domains such as X.500 directory services are presented. They demonstrate that the data sets used in the previous sections are in fact retrievable and they will provide the foundation for a discussion of managerial and policy implications in section 7.

5.1.1 Standardization problems in corporate networks

As mentioned in the previous sections, there are a variety of standardization problems in corporate environments. Our Fortune 1,000 study shows the perceived relevance in the categories office and business software and communication. Figure 85 shows the heterogeneity of software solutions in use as the percentage of the responding companies using different products in each of the listed software categories. The upper and lower bars of each category show the results in Germany and in the US respectively. Overall, results for Germany and the U.S. are quite similar with standard software being an exception that can be explained by the dominant market position of SAP in Germany.

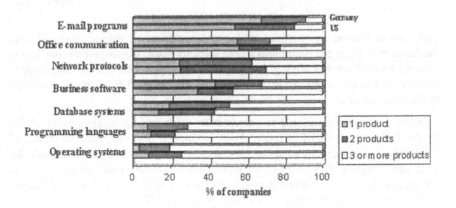

Figure 85: Heterogeneity of software products in Fortune 1,000 enterprises

The largest variety of standards is found in the area of "programming languages" and "operating systems". Only 29% of the largest companies in Germany use fewer than three programming languages (23% in the US) and only 20% (26% in the US) use fewer than three operating systems. By contrast, we find less variety in the categories "e-mail programs" and "office communication".

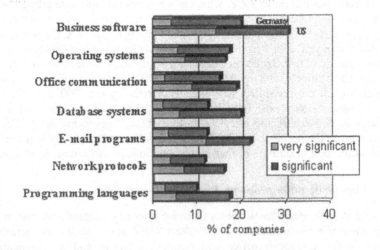

Figure 86: The problem of incompatibility

The extent to which MIS managers associate "significant" or "very significant" incompatibility problems (drawn from a five category Likert scale with the extremes "very significant" and "very insignificant") with the described heterogeneity is depicted in Figure 86. For reasons of simplification, the figure does not show the answers in the other categories.

MIS managers of both countries report their largest problems of incompatibility in the area of "business software". This is likely to be a result of the strategic importance of such systems in enterprises, as business software has an impact on basically all key processes. For case studies on business software in German enterprises (Deutsche Bank, Heraeus, Deutscher Fachverlag, Bosch Telecom, Balzers und Leybold see Westarp/Weitzel/Klug/Buxmann/König (2000).

Also, there seems to be no stringent strategy as to whether decisions concerning standards should be made centrally (e.g. top-down by a centralized IS unit) or decentrally (bottom-up). For business standard software, respondents to the Fortune 1,000 survey said that in most of the cases decisions (concerning the selection of business software) are made within teams, i.e. both central IT departments and decentralized departments are involved in the decision process. An interesting result in this context is that in Germany decision-making is currently more often centrally organized. Table 36 shows the proportion (in percent) of how decisions concerning business software are currently made.

Table 36: Decisions about business software

% of companies	decentralized	team	centralized
Germany	3.3	56.7	40
US	8.5	61.7	29.8

One of the reasons for the large proportion of mixed (i.e. team) decisions especially in large enterprises is the attempt to leverage the advantages of a centralized information management with the advantages of decentralized decision-making (see section 5.2.3). However, these structures often lead to disputes over particular areas of responsibility and sometimes to extremely long decision-making processes (leading to the implementation problem discussed in section 5.2.2). These problems have recently become even more important due to the increasing number of mergers and acquisitions [e.g. Windfuhr 1993].

5.1.2 The importance of network effects

Despite many efforts aimed at quantifying standardization benefits by and large, difficulties in operationalizing network effects like separating the network effect influence from others in particular (stand-alone functionality etc.) result in the existence of only surprisingly few empirical cases proving their existence (for problems of famous empirical cases trying to prove market failure due to network effects see section 2.3.7). Among the most notable exceptions are Cabral/Leite (1992) who present a survey of the Portuguese Telex-network from 1962 to 1987 to prove the major role of network effects in the diffusion of technology. They show that an increase of network size by 10% induces an increase in average network traffic by 1.6%, i.e. network traffic does not only increase proportionally to the number of users but on an additional level. At the same time, a short term (exogenous) increase in installed base size by 10% resulted in long-term increase of users by 15.9%. Gandal (1994) compares the prices of different spread sheet software programs from 1986 to 1991 and shows that buyers were ready to pay a significant premium (of sometimes over 100%) for programs compatible with the de facto standard (which was Lotus 1-2-3) interpreting these as network effects. In fact, the average price of the Lotus product between 1986 and 1988 was $365 while non-compatible products average $80. In an interesting study based on observations of the Web server market (Windows and Unix products, monthly from August 1995 to February 1997) Gallaugher/Wang (1999) prove a positive relation between price and market share in markets without free products. At the same time, they could find no relationship in markets where free products dominate.

The perceived incompatibility problems described in the previous section could also be interpreted as a (qualitative) evaluation of the relevance of standardization problems (it should be noted, though, that the study was mostly aiming at past decisions, i.e. there is only secondary consideration of the opportunity cost). See also Figure 101 on page 184 for an indicator of the relevance of network effects and the standardization problem from our Fortune 1,000 survey.

5.1.3   Diffusion of EDI-Standards

Ever since the first EDI implementations in the middle of the 20th century ([Parfett 1992, 5] cites the LACES communication system at London's Heathrow airport as the pioneer application; Germany's MAN (internally) has used EDI since the early 1960s [Niggl 1994, 6]) EDI standards have often tended to emerge from around individual major users and dispersed from there to become industry standards. Accordingly, the content of the transmitted documents and therefore the respective EDI standards vary with regard to the industry. As a result, a variety of industry specific EDI standards have emerged over the years. Examples are VDA in the automotive industry, SWIFT in the banking sector, SEDAS in the consumer goods industry or DAKOSY in the transportation industry. In addition, national standardization efforts led to national EDI standards like TRADACOMS in the UK or ANSI ASC X12 in the USA. See Weitzel/Harder/Buxmann (2001, 65-75) for a more detailed overview of EDI standards and consortia.

Overcoming compatibility problems caused by the variety of standards was the motivation for the United Nations (UN), the European Community and the worldwide standardization organization ISO to develop a globally effective, industry-neutral standard. This effort resulted in UN/EDIFACT (EDI for Administration, Commerce and Transport, ISO 9735). The complexity of EDIFACT (because it was claimed that it would meet all possible message requirements) led to so-called - again mostly industry specific - subsets. These subsets are a 'small solution' or an 'EDIFACT light' application, a fraction of the usable message types, data elements, codes and qualifiers of the extensive set supported by EDIFACT. Subsets only employ the small part of the large amount of EDIFACT messages that the particular user really utilizes. Therefore, from a user's perspective, subsets are often more efficient, since their implementation is considerably more cost-effective. This led to industry-specific EDIFACT subsets like ODETTE (Organization for Data Exchange by Teletransmission in Europe) in the automotive industry, CEFIC (Conseil Européen des Fédérations de l'Industrie Chemique) in the chemical industry, EDIFICE (EDI Forum for Companies with Interests in Computing and Electronics) in the electronics industry, EDICON (EDI Construction) in the construction industry or RINET (Reinsurance and Insurance Network) in the insurance industry.

A famous EDI study with 115 German enterprises from 1990 to 1993 found that 63.4% used or planned to use EDI [Kilian et al. 1994, 235-239]. They showed that larger enterprises (above 500 employees) adopted EDI earlier and more often, and that EDI use was dependent on the particular industry, with the automobile industry being the sector with the highest EDI diffusion. Deutsch (1994, 5-6) estimates that in 1992 there were 40,000 EDI users worldwide, 25,000 of them in North America.

The results of our empirical study with the Fortune 1,000 enterprises show that about 52% of the responding enterprises in Germany and about 75% in the US use EDI in 1998/99. On average, German enterprises use EDI with 21% of their business partners, while it is 30% in the US. 38% of the revenue is realized with these business partners in Germany and 40% in the US. This confirms the hypothesis that EDI is primarily applied with important customers. It also seems that EDI plays a more important role in the United States than in Germany.

The respondents of the questionnaire were asked which particular standards are in use in their companies. Figure 87 depicts the diffusion of the particular standards.

EDIFACT is by far the most popular EDI standard in Germany. It is used by nearly 40% of the responding enterprises. Other common standards follow at a large distance: about 11% of the responding German companies use VDA, 6% use SEDAS, 5% use SWIFT, 3% use ODETTE, only 2% use ANSI X12, and about 1% use DAKOSY. Despite the strong position of EDIFACT, the survey reveals a rather strong heterogeneity in the use of EDI with many different industry-specific standards.[6] An explanation for the bigger diversity in Germany is its more developed organization in associations resulting in various clusters of internally organized players. This heterogeneity of EDI standards cannot be found in the United

---

[6] Some confusion results from the frequent imprecise use of EDI terminology (EDI vs. EDIFACT vs. EDIFACT subset).

States. The leading US EDI standard is ANSI X12 (more than 48%) followed by EDIFACT (24%). Only two of the responding enterprises in the US use SWIFT or TRADACOMS respectively.

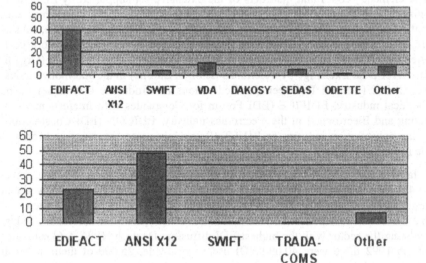

Figure 87: The use of EDI standards in Germany (top) and the US (bottom) (%)

These numbers offer a snapshot of the use of different EDI standards in 1998/9. To show the diffusion process over the past 14 years we also asked the respondents when they implemented their EDI solutions and if they plan changes in the future.

Figure 88 shows the diffusion process of the two most common standards in Germany. The number of new implementations and the cumulated percentage of users are shown for every year since 1984. The (*) symbol shows the number of respondents who plan to use the standard in the near future. The success story of EDIFACT is obvious. Taking into account those enterprises which plan to use EDIFACT, this standard will soon reach a diffusion of nearly 44% among large companies in Germany.

When focusing on the EDIFACT and ANSI X12 curves at the bottom of Figure 88 *without* those enterprises which are only planning to implement an EDI solution it appears that the diffusion process of ANSI X12 is slowing down significantly. While we observe rather high rates of increase between 1989 and 1995, the rates have decreased in recent years. The curve remains stable at a high level of about 48%. In contrast, EDIFACT does not seem to have reached its peak yet. The rates of increase in 1996 and 1998 are higher (and equal in 1997) than the ones of ANSI X12. This might be explained by agreements in the relevant years to migrate (future) X12 to EDIFACT (and adapt to it). Yet again, actual deployment seems to

171

take significantly more time than merely to commit to it and at the time of writing there has not been any real conversion success or progress yet.

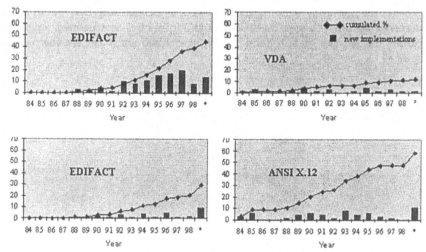

Figure 88: Diffusion of EDI standards in Germany (top) and the US (bottom)

5.1.4   EDI data: costs and benefits

Electronic Data Interchange (EDI) is the business-to-business exchange of electronic documents in a standardized machine-processable format. EDI enables partners to electronically exchange structured business documents, such as purchase orders and invoices, between their computer systems. EDI is a means of reducing the costs of document processing and, in general, to achieve the strategic business advantages made possible by shorter business process cycle times.

In general, the direct benefits of using EDI result from decreased information costs due to cheaper and faster communication. Costs for paper document handling and processing include paper, mailing and, most of all, personnel. The costs associated with document processing are estimated to amount to about 10% of all business expenditure or $300 billion in Europe alone [Jonas 1992, 234; Neuburger 1994, 31; Schumann 1990]. In addition, avoiding media discontinuities eliminates errors due to re-keying of data. It is estimated that even professional data entry produces error rates of 2% [Emmelhainz 1993, 8-11]. And the immediate availability of data allows the automation and coordination of different business processes, e. g. enabling just in time production.

Another reason discussed in the literature on EDI for why EDI is implemented in enterprises is that it offers better service to the customers [Emmelhainz 1993; Marcella/Chan 1993, 5-6]. It is also common that smaller companies in particular are forced to implement the EDI standard of a big partner by threat of giving up

172

the business partnership otherwise, sometimes described as "gun-to-the-head-EDI" or "EDI or die" [Tucker 1997]. Some studies find 55% of all EDI systems to have been "requested" by suppliers or customers [Marcella/Chan 1993, 7]. Interestingly, as EDI veterans often say, the original intention behind "EDI or die" was the belief that not using the efficiency potential associated with EDI would make enterprises uncompetitive or that they would not find business partners anymore. Reasons for the use of EDI from the Fortune 1,000 study are summarized in Figure 89

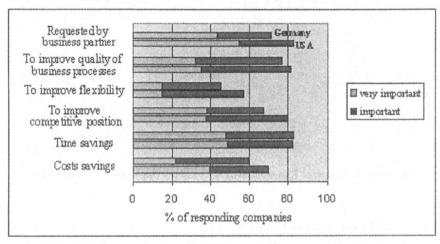

Figure 89: Reasons for the use of EDI among Fortune 1,000 enterprises

Implementation costs for EDI systems consist of costs for hard- and software, possibly for an adaptation of in-house software, external consultancy and the reengineering of business processes. The costs for restructuring internal processes are difficult to quantify and are often underestimated when anticipating the implementation costs of an EDI system. In addition, these systems are often only compatible with one EDI standard. If an EDI connection is to be established with another business partner, and this potential partner uses a different EDI standard, it becomes necessary either to implement a new EDI system or to expand the existing system to this new standard. Both measures incur significant costs. In order to enable communication between the EDI systems of companies, so-called Value Added Networks (VANs) are used, which cause additional expenses. The charges for using the VAN depend on the size and the frequency of the data transfers as well as the transfer time [Emmelhainz 1993, 113-116].

5.1.4.1   Empirical EDI benefits in the literature

There are many cost and benefit examples from EDI networks, of which some are summarized in this section. Unless otherwise noted data is taken from Emmelhainz (1993, 17-29). See Neuburger (1994, 34) for more empirical examples.

Traditional EDI is estimated to enable **overall cost savings** of about 5-6% of total revenue independent of industry. American automobile manufacturers save $200 per car; the US air force can economize 2% on all electronic purchases, amounting to $50 million per year. An EDI expert of (former) Price Waterhouse expects EDI savings to amount to up to 5% of annual revenues [Marcella/Chan 1993, 5].

For **document processing**, there is a rule of thumb that EDI reduces document processing costs by a 10:1 ratio, e.g. reducing document handling costs from $49 to below $5 per document. DEC (Digital Equipment Corporation) is reported to cut down per document costs from $125 to $32. See our own surveys below with similar findings.

Personnel costs can also be cut back: DEC estimates that processing 80% of all orders electronically could save 30% of all purchasing personnel.

Stock reductions are among the most significant savings. Navister International Corporation was enabled to reduce its stocks by 1/3 within the first 18 months of using EDI which resulted in cost savings of $167 million. Bergen Brunswig was able to reduce its stocks from a 10 day to a 4 day supply.

More **consistent data** is another beneficial source. It is estimated that correcting incorrect purchase orders costs five times as much as avoiding the errors. Beyond that, the availability of more and more timely customer data (for market research, profiling etc.) can enhance other processes such as invoicing. The U. S. Treasury Department saves more than $60 million per year using electronic invoicing. Others used EDI to reduce invoice processing personnel by 200 [Kimberley 1991, 179], to "write" up to 10,000 invoices per day fewer [Butler Cox Foundation 1987, 10] or save $10 per invoice or 85% per purchase order.

5.1.4.2 *Empirical EDI costs in the literature*

The costs associated with implementing EDI are easier to identify. They generally consist of costs for software, hardware, personnel and services and heavily depend on solution size, integration depths (the difference between a deep end-to-end integration and some superficial solution can be a factor of 50 to 100) and legacy systems.

In the first half of the 1990s, costs for software have been estimated to average between $1,000 and $20,000 with annual costs between $200 and $2,000. Additionally, training of old or new personnel might be required. Depending on existing hardware, upgrades or additional investments can be necessary. Finally, there are communication costs for networks, VANs or other services. Emmelhainz (1993) estimates average EDI set-up costs (not considering process reengineering etc.) to amount annually to:

▸ Hardware $13.567

▸ Software $16.438

▸ VANs/communication $12.689

Others estimate an overall EDI implementation to cost about 1% of annual revenue over 3-5 years or at least $1 million [Marcella/Chan 1993, 5]. According to the U.S. Chamber of Commerce, the costs for a typical initial installation of an EDI system average at least $50,000 [Waltner 1997]. Figures for VAN costs vary strongly but they used to be one of the major obstacles for smaller enterprises. Internet based communication has recently contributed greatly to cutting down communication costs. A company with about 25,000 EDI messages would pay its VAN-Provider something between 14,000 and 25,000 US Dollars a month [Curtis 1996].

5.1.5 EDI data from large enterprises

As part of our Fortune 1,000 study, we asked the MIS managers of the 1,000 largest enterprises in Germany and the U.S. about their use of EDI. Additionally, particular case studies were made to get a precise picture of EDI standardization problems. Whenever there were figures based on German DEM in this work they were transformed to US $, a consistent rate of $1 = DM 1.7 being used to ensure the comparability of the data sets. Thus if needed, data from Karstadt, Woolworth, Lufthansa, and the SME study can easily be recalculated to DEM. The full report including the 3Com case study can be found in Westarp/Buxmann/Weitzel/König (1999). For the Lufthansa data see Westarp/Weitzel/Putzke/Buxmann/König (2000). The other case studies, showing among others a trend towards more Web and less partners (that are more deeply integrated), are described in Westarp/Weitzel/Buxmann/König (1999). For analogous data and implementation studies concerning standard software like SAP R/3 see Westarp/Weitzel/Klug/Buxmann/König (2000). For the SME data in the right-hand column see section 5.1.6 below. Overall, the findings support the figures above; some deviations always result from different use of EDI vocabulary (e.g. EDI vs. EDIFACT vs. EDI standards vs. EDIFACT subset).

The cost and savings differences between Germany and the U.S. in the Fortune 1,000 study are remarkable. Part of the discrepancy can be explained by the fact that on average the U.S. companies in the sample are significantly larger. In addition, the sample may be too small; the individual differences of reported costs and benefits are substantial and are a reflection of the various particular networks, partners, legacy systems etc. For instance, the overall savings in the US range from $ 100,000 to $ 20,000,000, while at the same time between 100 and 250,000 person-hours were needed to implement the solution.

Table 37: Costs and benefits of EDI systems

		Fortune 1,000		case studies			SME
		Germany	US	3Com	Karstadt	Wool-worth	(produc-ers)
costs of company-wide EDI implementation	**set-up costs (K_i)**						
	internal personnel hours (months)	2400 (15)	20350 (127)		(24)	(50)	
	software and hardware ($)	167,000	201,000		88,200	47,000	21,200
	training ($)	13,000	33,000				15,300
	external consulting ($)	71,000	54,000		29,400	147,000	34,100
	other costs ($)	39,000	-				
	(new partner set up)			2-3 PD (program.)	2-3 days		
	K_i (set up)	290,000	288,000	125,000	117,600	194,000	
annual costs to run the EDI solution company wide	**operating costs (K_i)**						
	internal personnel ($)	68,000	224,000	350,000	35,300	117,700	29,250
	comm. costs (phone, network, etc.) ($)	59,000	75,000	36,000			8,500
	external (EDI service provider) ($)	48,000	158,000	17,000	58,800 (VAN)	42,400	25,900
	K_i (operations)	175,000	457,000	403,000	94,100	160,100	134,250
annual savings	**savings (Σc_{ij})**						
	cost savings per year in $ (Σc_{ij})	208,000	3,218,000	1,300,000	20,590,000 - 24,118,000	294,100	

176

Table 37: Continuation

		Fortune 1,000		case studies			SME
		Germany	US	3Com	Karstadt	Wool-worth	(produc-ers)
variable savings				36.65 /document	7/document + 2.5% to-tal stock value		
EDI since				1995 (X12), 1998 (EDI-FACT)	1984 (SE-DAS), 1993 (EAN-COM)	1994 (EAN-COM)	
EDI traffic with partners in % (total): revenue share		21% (38%)	30% (40%)	with 15% (30)	with 30% (600); generating 52.2% of revenues	3% (105)	

5.1.6   EDI data from SMEs

Adding to our empirical data basis in order to gather figures for SMEs as compared to the Fortune 1,000 data, we conducted an empirical survey in 1999 and 2000 with the German office supply industry that consists of up to 95% of SMEs (i.e. revenues below € 1 million). Due to its structure – the large majority of players are small and medium sized enterprises (SMEs) – and comparably early and innovative efforts in EDI standardization it is especially appropriate for gathering figures and learning about the experiences of small enterprise standardization.

The German office supply industry is a relatively small part of the retail/trade industry in Germany. Size and market structure make the industry an unattractive target for traditional EDI. Most market participants are small retailers and quite typical SMEs. 88.7 of all enterprises in that industry (i.e. 8,079 out of 9,104) have annual revenue below € 0.5 million. Market volume in 1999 was about € 7.9 billion. In the industrial sector there are more than 9,000 retailers and approx. 180 suppliers.

The survey was sent to 223 retailers (2.5% of the industry in Germany). 34 answered (15.25%). A similar survey was sent to 66 producers and wholesalers (40% of German industry) 11 (16.18%) of whom answered. The office supply industry has long been trying to integrate its members. Most notably, an industry consortium called PBS Networks offered a traditional EDI solution ("PBSeasy direct") and a Web-based EDI solution ("PBSeasy online") to address the SME integration problem. All responding retailers therefore use some form of EDI ("EDI" or "WebEDI") with some partners but 50% do not even have automated tracking of outgoing materials. For an elaborate description of the particular solutions, including industry bonus programs etc. see Beck/Weitzel/König (2001).

In all it turned out that the three main obstacles to SME participation in the EDI networks in the industry are personnel costs (and know-how), operations costs (converter, usage fees, ILN numbers and communications costs) and the set-up of the EDI converter. A profitability analysis of the use of traditional EDI and Internet-based EDI for SME based upon the survey revealed that for an average frequency of 4 orders per day a breakeven cannot be achieved for either EDI solution. The most efficient alternative to EDI that is actually in use is ordering by FAX. Even using rebates on electronic orders could not help make the solutions efficient for the SMEs. As elaborated in Beck/Weitzel/König (2001) solutions include better compatibility between material management systems (MMS) e.g. via certification, lower usage fees, offline-capabilities (e.g. SMIME for orders), and open XML-based converter interfaces.

5.1.6.1 Results of the retailers survey

The heterogeneity of materiel management systems in use is shown in Figure 90. This heterogeneity is one of the major obstacles to a common EDI solution (or an underlying unique data model). Most of the WebEDI users do not employ any MMS at all.

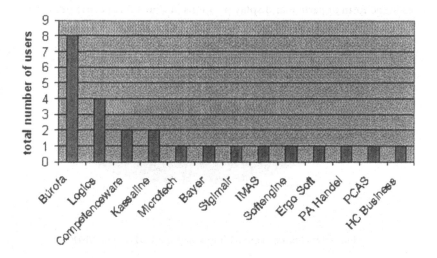

Figure 90: Heterogeneity of materiel management systems

As in the Fortune 1,000 study, we also asked the respondent about the reasons for implementing EDI. The most interesting result is that pressure from business partners is comparatively irrelevant. The reason is that fewer partners use EDI them-

178

selves. Later it will be shown that the important goal of cost savings in particular
could not be achieved by using EDI.

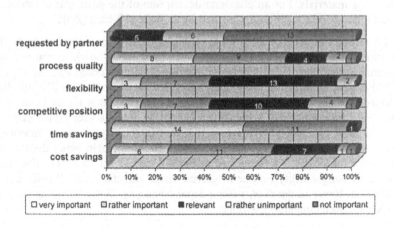

Figure 91: Reasons for implementing EDI among SMEs

In addition, we asked for possible reasons *against* using EDI. A third responded
that deals made by sales personnel are not describable using EDI: the reasons
range from individual pricing negotiations through negotiations not representable
in prices at all to contracts outside the scope of EDI as like for example natural rebates in the form of particular display positions in stores for specific products.

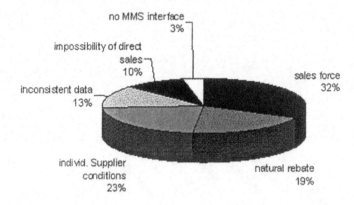

Figure 92: Reasons against implementing EDI among SMEs

To a large extent, business process improvements and cost savings depend on the
number of partners (and the associated share of EDI messages) also using EDI. At
the same time, the number of business documents limits the potential savings. The
SMEs that responded to the survey generate on average 3.56 purchase orders per
day.

More than a third use EDI for less than 10% of their purchase orders. In all, both the total number of orders and the fraction of electronic orders appear to be too small to benefit from using EDI. As a consequence, those already using EDI stand little chance of increasing the fraction of electronic orders. This becomes obvious when looking at the relation between the number of suppliers and the fraction of EDI capable partners. On average, retailers in our survey have 146.5 communication partners. Out of those, only 9.18% use EDI.

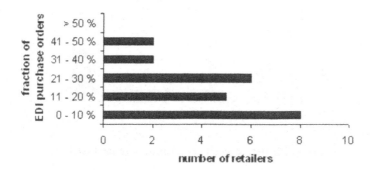

Figure 93: Fraction of EDI orders (excluding WebEDI users)

When asked about Internet-based EDI, 30% of the respondents see advantages compared to X.400 (Figure 94).

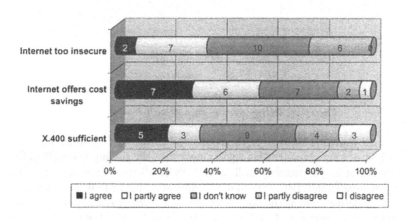

Figure 94: EDI over the Internet from small retailers' perspective

5.1.6.2 Results from the producers and wholesalers survey

Producers and wholesalers were also asked about their use of EDI and MMS standards. Since this group consists of larger players, some used standard ERP systems (more than half SAP R/3), as shown in Figure 95. Using SAP systems has the advantage of being able to use certified EDI converters making implementation and maintenance of EDI systems easier and improving internal data quality.

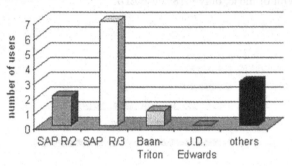

Figure 95: Heterogeneity of business standard software

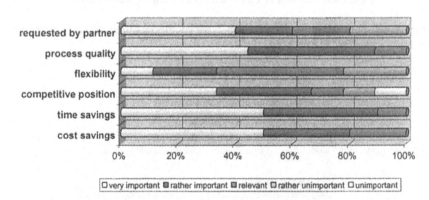

Figure 96: EDI in the German office industry

The producers claim that 0.94% of all listed retailers are EDI capable. They account for 9.54 of total revenue. This again emphasizes the finding that EDI traffic is found between larger partners. Still, over 80% of all revenue is generated by business with small enterprises that do not employ and kind of EDI. Revenue generated by EDI derive from an average of 26 electronic orders per day. For 40% of the respondents, the fraction of EDI orders is less than 1% of all orders. Only one out of five of the producers execute more than 5% of all orders via EDI. It is this group that could most probably in fact benefit from the use of EDI.

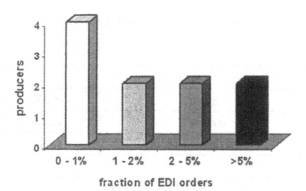

Figure 97: Few producers extensively use EDI

Since the cost side is regularly easier to quantify than the benefits of standards, only few enterprises made explicit statements about the cost/benefit-ratio. But 2 out of 3 considered EDI too expensive to use now although that might change in the future.

When asked about reasons for a particular EDI solution the overall picture was that a solution that will also be used in the future is highly valued. Over 50% considered the future availability and use of a solution "very important".

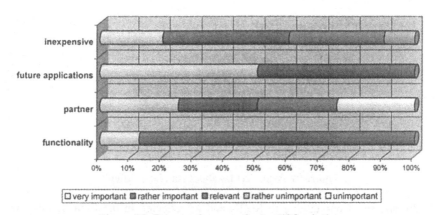

☐ very important ☒ rather important ☒ relevant ☐ rather unimportant ☐ unimportant

Figure 98: Reasons for a particular EDI solution

EDI set-up and operations costs are expectedly higher than for the - smaller - retailers and are summarized in Table 38.

Since an investment in an EDI infrastructure is strategic the question arises of who decides about that standardization problem. In 30% of the cases EDI decisions are made by the management, in 30% the IT department is also involved, another 10% also integrate the sales department and in 20% it is only the IT and sales department.

Table 38: EDI set-up and operations costs for producers

	DEM
set-up costs	
converter	36,500
training	26,000
external services	58,000
annual operating costs	
personnel	49,750
communication costs	14,500
EDI service providers	44,000

The producers also have positive expectations about future Internet-based EDI. In contrast to the retailers, opinions on the suitability of X.400 telebox solutions differ and there is less fear of security threats. This can be explained by a higher level of experience with firewalls.

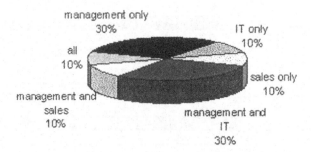

Figure 99: Who decides about standardization?

In the course of our talking to SMEs and as reflected in the figures above we found a higher willingness to standardize among SMEs in the German office supply retail industry than expected but at the same time a lack of human resources and a small actual number of EDI capable messages like orders. On the other hand, participating in automated business processes requires using MMS to gain net profits from EDI standardization. In this context, the heterogeneity of systems, often individually built, adds to the list of obstacles to standardized message exchange.

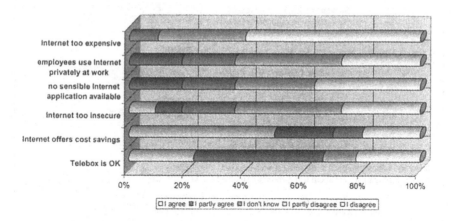

Figure 100: EDI over the Internet from producers' perspective

Switching to an individual view of the standardization problem from the perspective of an SME reveals that the most common form of ordering - i.e. by FAX - is the most inexpensive way for the small players. A full analysis of the cost structures associated with FAX ordering vs. WebEDI vs. EDI also considering various bonus models and expected growth of EDI traffic is presented in Beck/Weitzel/König (2001). It turns out that for an average frequency of 4 orders per day a breakeven cannot be achieved for either EDI solution; using the bonus models EDI becomes advantageous if there are more than 1,475 orders per year (from 1,068 messages upwards EDI is also superior to - always the least attractive - WebEDI). Of course these findings are only valid for the particular cost constellations and compensation mechanisms established in that particular industry. For premises and solution proposals (such as ASP-EDI, i.e. using the print spool (ASCII) as common denominator) see Beck/Weitzel/König (2001).

5.1.7 MIS managers opinion on general standardization issues

It is also instructive to see what standards' users opinion on questions as to who will set the standards might be. A summary of the answers of the respondents to our Fortune 1,000 survey is presented in Figure 101.

Interestingly, only very few respondents see standards and "smooth" processes as separable issues: Only fewer than 17% of the German MIS managers and about 25% of their US colleagues do not care about which standards others use as long as everything runs smoothly in their own company. This is another indicator of the practical relevance of standardization problems. A strong majority of the respondents thinks that national boundaries will no longer influence standards in general. This implies new challenges for the global coordination of standards.

184

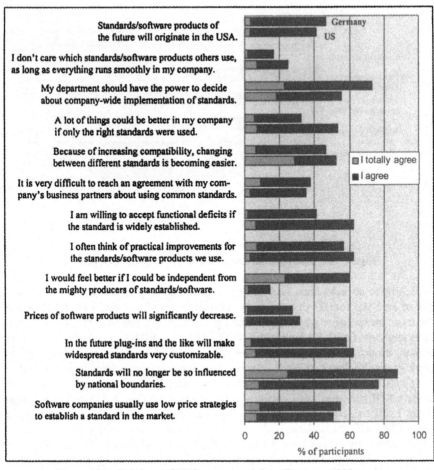

Figure 101: Opinions of MIS managers of the Fortune 1,000 study

5.2 Closing the standardization gap

> "A new scientific truth does not triumph by convincing its opponents
> and making them see the light, but rather because its opponents
> eventually die, and a new generation grows up that is familiar with it."
>
> *Max Planck*

5.2.1 Solution designs for standardization problems

Inefficiencies in standardization problems (i.e. a standardization gap) can result from insufficient local information about the partners' standardization behavior, or from the fact that standardization is not desirable from an individual but only from a centralized perspective. In the latter case, from the perspective of a central entity such as the management of a huge firm where the "agents" are autonomous business units, the agency problem arises of how to synchronize individual and aggregate objective functions. One classic solution is *profit sharing*, so that each business unit does not have to pay K_i and save c_{ij} but rather gets a share α of the centralized net solution so that the individual objective function changes from $\sum_{\substack{j=1 \\ j \neq i}}^{n} \frac{c_{ji}(n-1) - K_j}{c_{ji}(n-1)} c_{ij} - K_i$ to $\alpha \cdot \left(\sum_{i=1}^{n} \sum_{i=1}^{n} c_{ij}^{p} - \sum_{i=1}^{n} K_i^{p} \right)$. Analogous to the conditions

in Equation 12 on page 78 the index p represents those business units i that participate in the solution (and their respective communication relations). Incentive compatibility now results from the virtual identity of the individual and collective objective functions given that agents are well informed about their situation in the network. Rooted in this principle, in section 5.3 a network ROI is proposed that has already proved to be a useful tool in realistic standardization problems. One general problem of the profit sharing concept is that it relies on agents reporting honestly. And true reporting is one, but not a unique Nash equilibrium [Ewert/Wagenhofer 1993, 480]. A famous mechanism to establish true reporting as a unique Nash equilibrium regardless of how others report is the Groves scheme. A Groves mechanism adapted to the standardization problem is developed in section 5.4. In a true reporting equilibrium with no uncertainty both concepts are factually identical [Ewert/Wagenhofer 1993, 485]. A third proposal for solving standardization problems is developed in section 5.5. The principal idea is that agents use parts of their standardization gains to "bid" for others participating in a solution deemed favorable by the bidding agents. Although side payments might actually be executed, this mechanism works quite successfully due to its ability to reduce uncertainty because agents can communicate about the importance of their individual relations and because accordingly the ex post situation is synchronized with the agents anticipated behavior.

5.2.2 Problems of centralized coordination

Coordination of standardization decisions among "all" agents to ensure the mutually advantageous adoption of standards throughout the entire network certainly seems to be desirable, as agents thereby realize the maximum benefits of the network [Katz/Shapiro 1986, 824]. The costs of coordination, however, hinder such efforts. The existence of such costs (actually in both the design and diffusion phases of a standard) can generate a free-rider problem because there is a positive incentive to avoid the costs of development of and agreement on a given standard by implementing these results free of charge after their evolution. Another negative result of coordination costs is the start-up problem, in which all agents perceive an incentive to wait and see which standard prevails in order to avoid the risk of a premature and possibly unfavorable selection.

Centralized coordination as modeled in this work ensures that an optimum solution is achieved, as all relevant data are considered in the calculation and the means of enforcing implementation of these results exist and induce no costs. However, in real life application the central manager might encounter significant coordination problems. Generally speaking, coordination costs can result from the following problems.

5.2.2.1 Data problem

Given the realistic assumption of asymmetric information distribution and opportunistic behavior on the part of the agents, it is questionable whether accurate and complete information can be retrieved from all network nodes at acceptable costs considering that the nodes' reporting might incur resource allocation. Thus, a "regulator" responsible for determining favorable allocations needs to come up with a mechanism so that agents have proper incentives to provide information known to them that is relevant for the regulator's task and that might even be used to achieve additional distributional goals like, for instance, compensating particular agents harmed by externalities [Varian 1994] or granting a fair distribution of benefits.

Famous approaches aiming at solving the data problem (or more generally speaking aiming at implementing efficient solutions in decentralized games) are found in the literature on public goods, see Varian (1994) for a literature review, and include demand revealing mechanisms [Clarke 1971; Groves 1976], mechanisms based on punishment payments in cases of wrong reporting [Hurwicz 1979], individual offerings in terms of a collective investment (see the bidding mechanism proposed in section 5.5) [Bagnoli/Lipman 1989] or cost sharing [Jackson/Moulin 1992]. Based upon these principal solution possibilities, in the following sections of this chapter, mechanisms for coordinating decentralized networks are proposed.

5.2.2.2 Complexity problem

The computational complexity of the standardization problem makes a determination of the centralized solution intricate. Even solutions to simple centralized coordination problems are difficult. Yet, despite the binary variables x_i and y_{ij} at least the basic standardization problem is solvable in polynomial time using a simplex algorithm as has recently been proven by Konstroffer (2001). See Kettani/Oral (1990) and Domschke/Mayer/Wagner (2002) for an alternative formulation of the centralized problem, see Schober (1994) for an application.

Generally, we know from graph theory, if value relations assigned to nodes and edges of a network are linear (additive and proportional) then network problems are solvable as linear programs, see e.g. Neumann/Morlock (1993, 176-188; computational complexity 189-191; integer and dynamic optimization 380-535). Thus, a graph can be represented by a matrix if every matrix element is 1 in cases where the respective element of the graph exists or otherwise 0. Since any edge is always associated with 2 nodes the incidency matrix consists of two times the number of edges ones. For a digraph, the source of an edge can be denoted +1 and the sink -1 so that the following is true for the incidency matrix:

$$m_{ei}^I = \begin{cases} +1 \text{ if edge e has its source in i} \\ -1 \text{ if edge e has its sink in i} \\ 0 \text{ else} \end{cases}$$

Or utilizing the symmetry properties for the adjacency matrix:

$$m_{ij}^A = \begin{cases} 1 \text{ if edge} < \text{ij} > \text{is part of the graph} \\ 0 \text{ else} \end{cases}$$

In the LP representation of a network, the coefficient matrix is generally an incidency matrix with +1 and -1 in each column (or both elements 1 if the graph is not directed). Those matrices are called (totally) unimodular. The unimodularity property requires that the determinant of each quadratic submatrix is +1 or -1 or 0, or more precisely a square integer matrix B is called unimodular if det B = +1 or if det B = -1. An integer matrix A is called totally unimodular if each non-singular square submatrix has a determinant in 1, -1, hence if every square submatrix of A has a determinant in {0, 1, -1}. Every element of a totally unimodular matrix is in {0, 1, -1}. For example, the incidency matrix of every digraph is totally unimodular [Konstroffer 2001, 34]. Unimodularity is the condition for relaxing the integer conditions in the formulation of the centralized standardization problem; for integer optimization problems with totally unimodular coefficient matrices see Neumann/Morlock (1993, 384-386). Thus, if unimodularity can be proven a relaxation of the centralized (basic) standardization problem can be solved using a simplex algorithm because due to the unimodularity property a solution to the relaxed formulation will also be the solution to the integer problem [Neumann/Morlock 1993, 384-385]. A proof of the unimodularity [e.g. Schrijver 1986] of the basic standardization problem has recently been presented by Konstroffer (2001, 35-39). In addition, Domschke/Mayer/Wagner (2001; 2002) show that the extended model with Q=2 can also be solved in polynomial time. For Q≥3 they show that the warehouse location problem (n customers, m warehouses) can be interpreted as a special instance of an extended standardization problem (m standards, n+1 agents). Since the warehouse location problem is known to be np-complete [Mirchandani/Francis 1990, 127] the extended standardization problem can be expected to be at least as complex.

As has been shown in section 4.1.2, the LP used to solve the basic centralized standardization problem consists of $(n^2+n)/2$ variables and $2n^2-n$ restrictions. Thus, for larger size problems (a network consisting of e.g. 1,000 agents implies a linear program with almost 2 million restrictions) heuristic approaches can offer reasonable trade-offs between solution time and quality. COSA (cooperative simulated annealing) proved to be especially valuable for the standardization problem [Wendt 1995] and was able to reduce solution determination time for a centralized standardization problem with n=10 and Q=7 from 350 hours to 5 minutes, missing the optimum in only about 1% of all cases [Buxmann 1996, 49-57].

188

5.2.2.3 Implementation problem

A centralized coordination system is no guarantee that a given, preordained solution will be implemented by all agents. Limits on authority exist even within a hierarchy. The existence of agreements and contracts does not automatically ensure their acceptance. Systems of control and incentives for bridging this problem also involve costs. The railway gauge example or the French change to a metric system described in section 2.1.1 illustrate the difference between "ordering" a standard and seeing it accomplished. Here, French peasants used the old measures as late as 1870, and the change from old to new Franc as decreed by President de Gaulle in 1958 (at a 100:1 ratio) has been ignored by considerable parts of the population until the late 20th century [Kindleberger 1983, 390]. A more recent and still developing example is the United State's slow momentum in applying decimal standards. See also Mertens/Knolmayer (1998, 75) for disincentives leading to acceptance problems under a centralized information management. Since discrepancies between a possible centralized solution and local agents' preferences will probably grow with company size, this problem will intuitively be most prevalent in larger enterprises.

The implementation problem is closely related to the data problem, of course, since agents who favor a centralized solution will have an incentive to report their costs and benefits honestly in a relevant scenario.

5.2.3 Excursion: A word on centralization and decentralization

> "Two roads diverged in a wood, and I -
> I took the one less traveled by,
> And that has made all the difference."
> *Robert Frost, The Road Not Taken*

Besides the definitions of *centralized* and *decentralized* environments in the standardization model, there are many advantages to both, centralized and decentralized decision structures for corporate decisions in the traditional literature on organizational aspects of information management. Many of them draw on the argument of different physical and logical locations of knowledge or information influencing the decision quality and different managerial challenges and possibilities in various forms of hierarchies or teams. Thus, a frequent argument in favor of decentralization is more and/or better relevant information on the part of decentralized units, i.e. those agents the closest to the standard in dispute [Heinzl 1996, 36]. This, among others, is an important part of the literature on information systems, controlling, and organizational theory. Interestingly though, only 13% of the respondents to our Fortune 1,000 study in Germany and only 15% in the US agree that this is a very important or important problem of centralization (see Figure 103 below). It is interesting that in the context of business process reengineering team decisions in the sense of consensus (or participatory) management are seen as a prime cause of failure in organizational change due the discrepancies between local and global efficiency especially in times of crises leading to burden sharing rather than complete restructuring [Bashein/Markus/Riley 1994].

For decisions concerning the (centralized and decentralized) structuring of organizations see Mintzberg (1979). Empirical benefits of centrally and decentrally deciding on IT standards are presented in the Fortune 1,000 study. In the models developed in this work the information set is exogenously given (i.e. the problem described above is not a generic *standardization* problem) but incorporating these considerations could be valuable future extensions, e.g. in the form of an increasingly misinformed central principal (higher probability of ex post disadvantageous decisions) versus lower coordination costs, i.e. finding spots within the standardization gap that have a beneficial balance of coordination costs and quality.

In a slightly broader understanding of the term standard, there also are benefits from reduced learning time for new employees or a better chance of finding skilled people. Another advantage of centralized information management is economies of scale in terms of costs for IT solutions [Mertens/Knolmayer 1998, 51; section 5.3].

In our Fortune 1,000 survey we also asked MIS managers about advantages and disadvantages of centrally deciding on the use of certain software products in their companies. The respondents were asked to give their evaluation, using a five category scale with the extremes "very important" and "unimportant". Figure 102 and Figure 103 show how often the respondents have chosen the categories "very important" and "important". For reasons of simplification, the figure does not show the answers in the other categories.

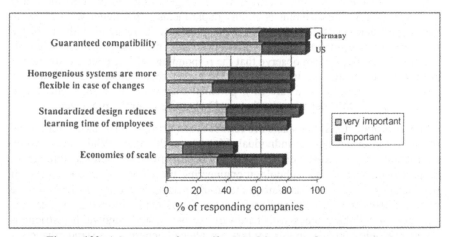

Figure 102: Advantages of centralized decisions on software standards

Almost all of the responding MIS managers (92% in Germany and in the US) see the improvement of compatibility as the main advantage of centralization. About 82% of the responding German enterprises (82% in US) think that flexibility in

190

case of changes is very important or important in this context, very close to the evaluation of the reduction of learning time of employees (88% in Germany and 80% in the US). Comparing the two countries, there is a remarkable difference concerning the evaluation of potential economies of scale. While 77% of the US respondents consider this a very important or important advantage of central decisions on software standards, it is only 45% in Germany.

After learning that all the advantages considered get very high ratings in terms of importance, we want to take a closer look at potential disadvantages.

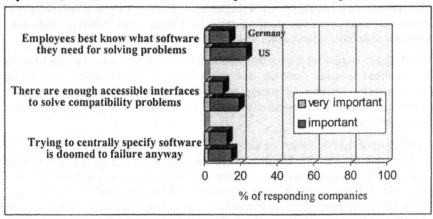

Figure 103: Reasons against centralized decisions on software standards

Only 14% of the responding German MIS managers (24% in the US) think that the employees in the different operating departments know better what software best serves their needs. It is clear that the respondents do not agree with one of the most important arguments against central decisions in the organization theory literature. Generally, we can observe that the responding MIS managers evaluate the advantages of central decision making far higher than potential disadvantages. However, we have to be aware of a potential bias since the respondents themselves belong to MIS departments that are likely to be centrally organized.

Often, corporate decision makers are torn between using standardized solutions on the one hand or developing individual solutions on the other. While this question from a software solution vendor's side has been explicitly discussed throughout both, network effect and technology engineering literature, e.g. in the context of proprietary versus open standards, the user's perspective often focuses on the trade-off between simplicity and performance for particular problems (e.g. service delivery on cellular phones with hardware, software, and bandwidth restrictions [Weitzel/König 2001b]). In this context, the alleged benefits of a standardized solution are network effects (smaller danger of stranding and being the only 'loser' among competitors), utilizing the technological experience of many others, cheaper to develop (fewer local resources), easier to find trained personnel and complementary tools, fewer media discontinuities, and also bigger potential market. On the other hand, there are disadvantages to standards in this context. Particularly, individual solutions are customizable to individual needs and thus often provide technologically superior solution quality (at least in the short run). In addition, adapting standards to fit individual needs is often not possible or bears substantial costs. In this context, it is interesting that about 82% of the responding MIS managers of our Fortune 1,000 survey in Germany and 90% in the US agree (or totally agree) that their companies will use more standardized business software in the future. At the same time a majority of the respondents (77.2% in Germany and 71.4% in the US) believes that the standard software will be easier to customize.

Again, these important considerations have been discussed at length in the context of standards. But they address a very different topic from the centralized and decentralized coordination of standardization decisions in this work. In this context, centralized and decentralized networks are two extreme poles of institutional settings for agents subject to interdependencies brought about by the existence of network effects. Of course, a total model of the whole enterprise incorporating its complete embeddedness and its economic and social environment is desirable (i.e. an analysis of a closed system incorporating all dependencies with any other institution or agent). But as yet its complexity would destroy all particular relevance. Thus, we try to focus on those effects endemic to standardization problems as laid out in the previous sections.

Also, the assumption that centralized planning ensures first-best results only holds if there are no learning dynamics in the technology development. In the case modeled in sections 3 and 4 this is not problematic, since the technology at choice is assumed to be given. But in real life, technologies are faced with improvements over time that add to their use value. Habermeier (1989, 1297) has shown that "even in the presence of centralized planning, path-dependencies and their attendant suboptimalities may arise". This brings us back to the conceptual problems of optimality concepts. Even though ex post (with hindsight), diffusion results might appear to be sub optimal, ex ante the decisions were optimal "given the initial condition of the decision maker". And even then, one will hardly know the path not taken.

5.3   The implementation problem

> „Infrastructure is a necessary investment
> that business units of functional areas are unlikely to make"
> *[Taudes/Feurstein/Mild 1999]*

As discussed earlier, due to interdependency (or commonality) properties associated with standards interoperability problems are often infrastructural problems [Perine 1995]. A good example is the case of deciding on what directory infrastructure to use within or between enterprises. For similar examples see section

5.1. Typically, in standardization problems there are significant uncertainties concerning factual costs and benefits as well as adequate planning and controlling strategies that can be centrally (top down by a centralized authority) or decentrally (bottom up, e.g. by business units with autonomous IT budgets) organized. Due to the asymmetry of costs and benefits between the mostly heterogeneous participants (or affected agents) these phenomena often result in considerable underestimations of network potential, leading to observable behaviors like "aggressive awaiting". There are many structurally similar examples, among them EDI networks and most corporate intra- and extranet decisions (e.g. document, knowledge, and security management systems or office software).

There are many approaches trying to support decisions concerning these problems, e.g. in the controlling literature [e.g. Kargl 2000; Krcmar 2000; Mayer/Liessmann/Freidank 1999; Pietsch 1999], TCO models (total cost of ownership) as proposed by Gartner Group in 1986 [Berg/Kirwin/Redman 1998; Emigh 2001; Herges/Wild 2000; Riepl 1998], scoring models or qualitative models such as Balanced Score Cards [Wiese 2000]. While contributions to network effect theory suffer from the drawbacks identified in section 2, these approaches are incapable of incorporating interdependencies given rise to by network effects.

Another uncertainty endemic to (typically long-term) infrastructure decisions is the scope of future (usually shorter-term) applications utilizing that infrastructure. Application software is significantly more subject to changes in functionality (and thereby utility) over time than is the underlying infrastructure which is typically very hard to change, politically as well as financially. This has the infrastructure's flexibility regarding future applicability appear an important aspect that has not been dealt with so far. While budgeting models like the NPV method (discounted cash flow/net present value) only determine lower utility bounds for unchanged software applications, future changes might be considered using option price models [Taudes/Feurstein/Mild 2000] [Weitzel/Gellings/Beimborn/König 2003]. An online bibliography of "Software Investment Analysis – Real Options and related Topics" is provided at http://wwwsel.iit.nrc.ca/~erdogmus/SIA/SIA-Biblio.html.

5.3.1 A case of X.500 Directory Services

The case study described below deals with the decision to use a common X.500-based directory service as an electronic phone directory among six German bank and insurance companies in cooperation with Siemens AG. As part of a profitability analysis, costs and benefits are qualified. To guarantee anonymity, the six enterprises are called E1 to E6 in order of decreasing size (number of employees). Unfortunately, no records concerning data traffic *between* the enterprises has been available so far so that the benefits cannot precisely be assigned to the networks' edges as in the model of section 3. To distinguish technological and network benefits anyway, we discriminate between a centralized (cooperative solution that allows reaping 'central' coordination benefits) and decentralized (individual) decision. As will become obvious, due to the particularities in this case, this distinction is possible since it is not the determination of the optimal set of participating agents but rather the determination of costs and benefits *given that all enterprises participate* that is focused on. In doing so, cooperation benefits on the cost side that are often neglected become visible. A sensitivity analysis will demonstrate the influence of particular parameters and their variations on the outcome. This study helped the participating enterprises identify synergies and plan the introduction of a common directory.

Empirical data was collected using a questionnaire that was presented to the respective IT managers in personal interviews. In particular, additional cost data information was provided by Siemens managers due to their experience with DirX. Necessary assumptions were based on the experience of Siemens employees and the six enterprises and are, compared to similar studies, largely conservative.

5.3.1.1 *Directory Services*

A Ferris study from November 1998 shows the importance of a common infrastructure for sharing data from different sources: 50 Fortune 1,000 IT managers are responsible for 9,000 directories which makes an average of 180 directories per enterprise [Ferris 1998b, 45ff.]. Since 1988, the OSI standard X.500 has been the foundation for distributed directory services aiming at integrating computer systems of different vendors and platforms [ISO 1988]. An X.500-Directory (meta directory) can be considered a virtual data pool residing on top of (and synchronizing) all underlying directories ("all directories in one"). The benefits of using X.500 directory services and associated interface standards like LDAP in particular (making data easily available using TCP/IP [Eichler 1998, 78ff.]), are the following:

▶ Enhanced data availability: There is only one directory for all global objects (objects can be employees, access rights, printers...) improving search time and accuracy as well as data consistency. Examples are telephone directories or call center applications. Since data objects need not be textual, a directory can be the foundation for knowledge management systems.

▶ More reliable and real time data: using a *Single Point of Administration & Access* concept, data changes are easily and readily available throughout the entire network.

▶ Security and single sign on/single log on (SSO/SLO): X.500 supports data protection mechanisms by definition of access classes (*Access Control Information – ACI*) and authentication mechanisms [Meyer zu Nautrup 1991, 13ff.]. Additionally, using X.509 public key infrastructures (PKI) and key management for cryptographic applications can be defined [Fumy 1995, 115ff.].

▶ Efficient administration: Compared to traditional phone books, data retrieval time is decreased, data is more reliable and up to date, and all costs of printing and paper can be avoided. Data maintenance is more efficient since there are no multiple sets and storage points of identical data, automated data synchronization is possible [Schmidt 1995, 4ff]. User management, software updates etc. are easier, routine tasks like installation, support, synchronization and data backup become more efficient.

The benefits ("information cost savings" of sections 3 and 4) consist of short term and long term benefits [Lewis/Blum/Rowe 1999, 13ff.]. Short term benefits describe improved communication between network participants and are composed of reduced communication costs, long term benefits describe strategic effects that are very difficult to estimate. The costs associated with directory services are these:

▶ product costs: hardware, software, licenses: These costs typically amount to 50% of total costs.

▶ professional services: especially during system integration, these costs derive from namespace design, development of a directory schema, integration with legacy data and testing. There can also be (administrator and user) skilling costs.

5.3.1.2 Empirical data

5.3.1.2.1 Standardization costs

Product costs ($C_P^{X.500}$) contain start-up costs and operational ongoing costs (support etc.) [Lewis/Blum/Rowe 1999, 25]. Each enterprise must buy a server (DEM 25,000), client licenses (DEM 100 per user, rebates are described later) and support (2,8% of total costs for three years). In cases of centralized coordination, rebates of up to 30% are possible for user licenses but a seventh server would also be required [Siemens 1999, 6ff.].

Professional services ($C_{PS}^{X.500}$) include personnel (especially status quo analysis, directory design, and implementation). Burton Group estimates that the costs of a directory for a Global 1,000 enterprise average $ 1-2 Mio. [Lewis/Blum/Rowe 1999, 5]. The average personnel service costs of the analyzed enterprises (decentralized coordination) were DEM 350,000 (gross costs of 1 person, 1 year) per enterprise which was weighted relative to the complexity of the respective task (measured by administration overhead as time per data change operation) using a multiplier of the interval [0.6; 1.3] with 0.6 describing low complexity. The complexity key is used to assign professional service costs according to their origin:

$$\text{complexity key for } C_{PS}^{X.500} = \frac{\text{administration (hour/month)}}{\text{fluctuation} * \text{employees}}$$

Equation 33: Complexity key

With centralized coordination, professional services ($C_{PS}^{central}$) amount to two man years (DEM 700.000,-) because collectively implementing the standard offers great savings potential especially when planning the directory. Again, these costs are assigned using the complexity key.

5.3.1.2.2 Standardization benefits

Short-term benefits ($C_i^{X.500}$) of the meta directory comprise communication cost savings consisting of user costs ($C_{User}^{X.500}$), administration costs ($C_{Admin}^{X.500}$), printing costs ($C_{Print}^{X.500}$) and possibly of reduced friction costs ($w_i^{X.500}$) although those are often considered to be long-term benefits due to their strategic nature and problems of measuring them.

Long-term benefits are not quantified because of their vague nature. Yet these benefits are probably the most important, especially considering tendencies towards growing system complexity due to mergers, acquisitions and generally the increasing significance of integrating partners into common networks. Examples of strategic aspects are security management (PKI), knowledge management, customer care (CRM), directory-enabled computing (applications are provided by a directory or use a centralized information pool) or new collaboration forms like virtual teams. The short-term benefits are based upon these premises:

End user cost savings ($C_{User}^{X.500}$) quantify accelerated searches and improvements qua single sign on [Radicati 1997, 5ff.]. These improvements are estimated to be 5 minutes per user and day with a user productivity of 80% and tariff wages of DEM 80,000 p.a. (210 working days, 38.5 hours per week). Social costs etc. to determine gross employee costs are considered by multiplying the annual gross wage by 1.8. Variations of the 5 minute assumption are discussed in the sensitivity analysis in section 5.3.1.3.2.

Administration cost savings ($C_{Admin}^{X.500}$) come about due to easier data management (bi-directional synchronization, single point of access & administration [Schmidt 1995, 15ff.], consistent data, integrated HR systems with globally working set-up, change and delete operations etc.). Time savings are estimated to be 25% (average wage DEM 100,000; 40 hours per week)

Print cost savings ($C_{Print}^{X.500}$) consist of hard costs (materials) and distribution costs. The Canadian government was able to save $ 1.5 million within two years using a directory because the number of phone books printed twice a year could be reduced from 250,000 to 7,000 [Ferris 1998a, 16ff.]. Print costs are estimated to amount to DEM 10-20 per employee and are assigned based upon the number of employees and their dispersion (number of locations).

Friction cost savings ($w_i^{X.500}$) are often considererd to be long-term benefits and describe increases in the information value (section 3.1) due to higher consistency and timeliness of data, fewer transfer errors and increased interoperationability.

5.3.1.3 Profitability analysis

E1 is the largest of the participating enterprises, accounting for more than half of network size (58.1%) and therefore being responsible for the majority of costs and benefits.

Table 39: Basic data

	E 1	E 2	E 3	E 4	E 5	E 6
employees/ locations	11500 / 88	4580 / 22	1200 / 5	1000 / 9	800 / 73	700 / 3
fluctuation (in %)	1.5%	8.6%	30%	> 100%	18.75%	30%
administration (h/month)	88	24	24	1,5	16	16
phone books used (p)aper, (e)lectronic	p e	p e	p e	p	p e	p e
issued	biannually	biannually	biannually	biannually	biannually	biannually
synchronization	manually	manually	manually	manually	manually	manually
complexity key professional services	$\dfrac{88}{0.015 \times 11500} \approx 0.51$	0.061	0.067	0.0015	0.107	0.076

Table 40: C$_{PS}$-multiplier and professional service costs

	E 1	E 2	E 3	E 4	E 5	E 6	Σ
C$_{PS}$- multiplier	1.3	0.68	0.69	0.6	0.74	0.7	
C$_{PS}$ (de-central)	455,000	238,000	241,500	210,000	259,000	245,000	1,648,500
C$_{PS}$ (central)	193,206	101,062	102,547	89,172	109,979	104,034	700,000

After determining the complexity keys according to Equation 33, within the interval multipliers are determined for all enterprises with E1 having the highest complexity grade (0.51) and therefore the largest multiplier (1.3) as shown in Table 40: Table 40 shows a centralized professional service savings potential when implementing the directory of DEM 948,500. In addition, there are decentralized product costs.

Table 41: Calculation for product costs of E6

server DEM	25,000	
user licenses (700 x 100.- DEM)	70,000	
support (2,8% of total costs for 3 years) DEM	(0.028 x 95,000)/3= 887	= 95,887 DEM

Centralized coordination allows for license rebates of 30% resulting in centralized standardization costs of DEM 2,273,924. Decentralized coordination amounts to DEM 3,796,362 (+ DEM 1,522,438).

Table 42: Product costs (DEM)

	E 1	E 2	E 3	E 4	E 5	E 6	Σ
DECENTRAL							
server	25,000	25,000	25,000	25,000	25,000	25,000	150,000
client licenses	1,150,000	458,000	120,000	100,000	80,000	70,000	1,978,000
support	10967	4508	1353	1167	980	887	19,862
total costs	1,185,967	487,508	146,353	126,167	105,980	95,887	2,147,862
CENTRAL							
server	25,000	25,000	25,000	25,000	25,000	25,000	150,000
client licenses	805,000	320,600	84,000	70,000	56,000	49,000	1,384,600
support	7,747	3,226	1,017	887	756	691	14,324
total costs	837,747	348,826	110,017	95,887	81,756	74,691	1,548,924 + 25,000 1,573,924
DIFFERENCE							
$C_p^{dec} - C$	348,220	138,682	36,336	30,280	24,224	21,196	Δ 573,938

Increased user productivity is achieved by accelerated information search and single sign on. Based on an estimated 5 minutes per user and day, benefits ($C_{User}^{X.500}$) of $((80{,}000.\text{- DEM} \cdot 1.8)/(210 \cdot 7.7 \cdot 60 \text{ min})) \cdot 5 \text{ min} = 7.40$ DEM/day or DEM 1,554.- p.a. can be achieved. At 80% productivity, this results in DEM 1,243.20 per user and year. Institutional savings are summarized in Table 43.

Table 43: Annual user cost savings

	E 1	E 2	E 3	E 4	E 5	E 6	Σ
users	11,500	4,580	1,200	1,000	800	700	19,780
$C_{User}^{X.500}$ (DEM/year)	14,296,800	5,693,856	1,491,840	1,243,200	994,560	870,240	24,590,496

Besides reducing user costs, a directory can improve upon administration costs as described in Table 44.

Table 46 summarizes overall standardization benefits. Print cost savings are easily and definitely measurable. Table 45 shows the results for administration cost savings while

Table 44: Administration cost savings

	E 1	E 2	E 3	E 4	E 5	E 6	Σ
administration (min/year) data management	5,280	1,440	1,440	90	960	960	10,170
$C_{Admin}^{X.500}$ (DEM/year)	28,195	7,690	7,690	481	5,126	5,126	54,308

Table 45: Print cost savings

	E 1	E 2	E 3	E 4	E 5	E 6	Σ
employees/phone users	11,500	4,580	1,200	1,000	800	700	19,780
total costs phonebooks (DEM)	20	16	14	14	12	10	∅
print cost savings p.a. ($C_{Print}^{X.500}$)	460,000	146,560	33,600	28,000	19,200	14,000	701,360

Table 46: Determinants of standardization benefits

	E 1	E 2	E 3	E 4	E 5	E 6	Σ
$C_{User}^{X.500\ DEM}/year$	14,296,800	5,693,856	1,491,840	1,243,200	994,560	870,240	24,590,496
$C_{Admin}^{X.500\ DEM}/year$	28,195	7,690	7,690	481	5,126	5,126	54,308
$C_{Print}^{X.500\ DEM}/year$	460,000	146,560	33,600	28,000	19,200	14,000	701,360
$\Sigma C_i^{X.500\ DEM}/year$	14,784,995	5,848,106	1,533,130	1,271,681	1,018,886	889,366	25,346,164

5.3.1.3.1 A network ROI

The empirical data can now be aggregated as a profitability measure. An often used measure is the return on investment (ROI) describing the profitability of invested capital (of firms, units, products etc.) that serves as a strategic yield return rate that is usually supposed to cover the costs of capital and that should be above the industry's average [Franke/Hax 1995, 177-179]. The concept became famous as early as 1910 when DuPont company used it for finance allocation [Kaplan 1984]. A basic presupposition is a clear definition of input and output [Horvath 1988] so that a ROI can be determined as $\frac{output}{input} - 1$. Break-even analysis analogously determines the period of ROI=1 (or a similar minimum success) and was called the "dead point" in 1923 by Johann Friedrich Schär [Schär 1923]. A return on investment for directory services (ROI$_{DS}$) [Radicati 1997, 5] can now be determined as

$$ROI_{DS}^{central} = \frac{C_{User}^{X.500} + C_{Admin}^{X.500} + C_{Print}^{X.500}}{C_P^{X.500} + C_{PS}^{X.500}} = \left[\left(\frac{24,590,496 + 54,308 + 701,360}{1,573,924 + 700,000} \right) = \left(\frac{25,346,164}{2,273,924} \right) \right] \approx 11.15$$

Equation 34: Return on investment (directory services)

Ultimately, implementing the directory enables to help realize savings amounting to DEM 25 million. The benefits exceed the costs by 11 in the centralized scenario, by 6.7 in the decentralized case. The break-even point is reached within 8 months. Figure 104 summarizes the findings and shows the relations between enterprise size and costs and benefits.

200

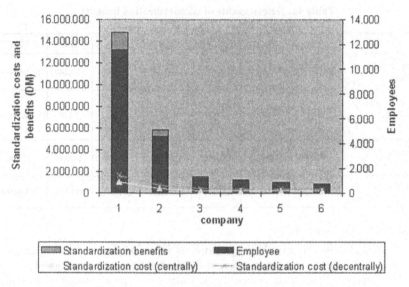

Figure 104: Costs and benefits of the participating enterprises

See section 5.3.4 for warnings of misapplying the concept.

5.3.1.3.2   Sensitivity analysis

Results of the profitability analysis depend on parameter values like the assumption that a directory infrastructure can save five user minutes per day. The sensitivity analysis in this section shows the responsiveness of important parameter values (and changes thereof) on the overall results. Other studies about directory efficiency show structurally similar results. Although the overall impression is analogous, individual results vary along with particular cost and benefit developments depending on the application domain (phonebook, SSO, knowledge management). Independent of vendor (e.g. Novell NDS, MS Active Directory, Notes Directory, Netscape Directory Service, Siemens DirX), Radicati Group found directory costs for larger enterprises to be around $ 2,5-3 million for the first three years resulting in an ROI of 3 (average number of employees 50,000) [Radicati 1997]. Burton Group reports costs of $ 1-2 million [Lewis/Blum/Rowe 1999, 10]. For a large multinational enterprise they found short-term administration cost savings of $ 10 million. Gartner Group introduced a methodology for identifying applications (benefits) beyond phonebooks that is based on clustering enterprises in terms of their number of servers and their server management. Within these groups, the number of information units and their interrelatedness determine the importance of a meta directory. Intuitively, it is low for small decentralized units who have few common information objects and high for all centralized information management systems employing more than 30 servers or 3,000 users [Silver 1997].

The assumptions of the case study presented are also comparable. While other researchers often estimate time savings at up to 30 minutes daily, depending on application of the directory, Radicati Groups assumes the advantages just from SSO to be 5 minutes/day. Information retrieval, in addition, is 25% faster [Radicati 1997].

Implications of variations of some of the important parameters can ceteris paribus be seen for individual enterprises as well as for the entire network using a sensitivity analysis. For instance, fluctuation in the enterprises analyzed varied between 1.5% and 100% but has no significant influence on profitability: the central (decentral) ROI decreased when cutting the fluctuation rate in half from 11.15 (6.68) only to 11.12% (6.65%) or increases to 11.17 (6.69) when doubling fluctuation. Since standardization cost and benefits are dependent on the number of employees, a more subtle analysis is necessary. Due to rebates, client license costs are DEM 75 if more than 10,000 are bought, DEM 70 for more than 15,000 and DEM 65 for more than 20.000. Professional service costs are unaffected by that, because using the complexity key they are (relatively) assigned to the enterprises. All benefits vary with number of employees, with user costs being the most important component. With decentralized coordination, a directory service is profitable at as early as 3.68% of network size (727 user). The key findings of the sensitivity analysis are summarized in Table 47, variations of the 5-minute-assumption in Table 48.

Table 47: Variations of number of employees

Δ employees to	product costs (DEM)			savings				ROI	
	central	decentral	difference	print	admin.	user	Σ	central	decentral
3.68%	224,869	224,869	0%	25,810	1,999	904,930	932,739	1.00	0.50
50%	1,149,631	1,149,631	0%	350,680	27,154	12,295,248	12,673,082	4.68	2.76
100%	1,548,922	1,857,678	19.93%	701,360	54,308	24,590,496	25,346,164	11.15	6.68
200%	2,746,800	3,331,809	21.30%	1,402,720	108,618	49,180,992	50,692,328	14.69	10.18

Table 48: Variations of user minutes saved by a directory

user savings	ROI							
	E1	E2	E3	E4	E5	E6	central	decentral
18.5 sec	0.83	0.69	0.34	0.31	0.23	0.21	1.00	0.59
24.3 sec	1.00	0.85	0.42	0.38	0.29	0.26	1.22	0.72
1 min	2.04	1.78	0.88	0.82	0.61	0.57	2.52	1.49
5 min	9.01	8.06	3.95	3.78	2.79	2.61	11.2	6.68

With centralized coordination, the directory is advantageous if the savings per user and day are at least 18.5 seconds, with decentralized coordination approximately one minute. Network size and coordination form have a significant influence on the efficiency of the solution. Not surprisingly, in all cases a centralized solution quality is at least as good as a decentralized. But the strongest influence is exerted by the users' communication behavior; if user savings are below 18.5 seconds per day, the electronic phone directory is not profitable in any scenario.

5.3.1.3.3   A virtual principal as solution

The enterprises participating in the study had searched for ways of building a common IT infrastructure (i.e. of closing a standardization gap). Like business units in one large enterprise, E1-E6 have been working together closely for years and plan doing so in the future. Thus, the partners already knew each other and building a common infrastructure was basically already agreed upon. The situation is therefore similar to the early stages of airline alliances such as the Star Alliance with huge enterprises and voluminous internal data traffic with an increasing fraction of cross enterprise communication.

For planning and maintaining their common infrastructure they founded in common a firm (which we will call F subsequently) (in late 2000) that was intended to take care of planning, development and operations of telecommunications technology and applications. Other duties include controlling quality and security standards and the integration of new partners. Among the anticipated benefits, collaborative procurement, learning effects (later adopters can learn from the earlier experience of others), and network convergence are considered the most important.

Since E1-E6 autonomously decide on how to spend their individual IT budgets, a major responsibility of F is offering cooperation designs to the six enterprises that promise greater utility than individual, decentralized activities. From the interviews it was obvious that the enterprises considered substantial long-term collaboration to be essential. Thus reflecting the fact that especially investments in infrastructure yield some "hard" benefits but mostly serve as an enabler for a variety of other applications the benefit of which are only very tough to anticipate, participants exhibited a satisfactory rather than maximization decision behavior during an early planning stage: investments in a common infrastructure are made as long as there is a substantial expectation that costs will at least be covered. In this context this implies that short-term benefits should suffice to accommodate the cost, enabling the long-term benefits to accrue. Thus, F generally has to come up with a cost and compensation plan, making sure that no participant suffers from net losses. In addition, it was able to implement IT solutions and control costs. In a next step, traffic records (based on so-called CDRs (call detail records)) will be used to quantify data transfers between the enterprises to get a detailed picture of communication flows and to allow integration in a network simulation model as presented in section 4. Based upon this, different coordination designs can be proposed for the enterprises to evaluate in terms of perceived fairness and efficiency.

5.3.2   A network ROI

We now try to generalize the approach depicted above. It was shown how (qualitative and quantitative) data can be gathered for real life standardization problems that can be used for determining a network ROI or that might be used for determining the optimal set of actors of a solution using the centralized model (section 3.1). Infrastructure decisions like that described above, in particular, can only profit from the adaptive dynamics of standardization processes as shown in section 4 to a very limited extent; the situation is rather comparable to a simultaneous one period single choice scenario so that solution designs need to be known ex ante.

5.3.2.1   A two player solution

Since not all decision situations are as easy as the one above when all participants are supposed to standardize and also profit from it, first we analyze the situation, that in a 2-player scenario with complete information agent 2 favors standardization, but not agent 1 ($c_{12}<K_1$ und $c_{21}>K_2$) while from a central perspective standardization is advantageous ($c_{12}+c_{21}>K_1+K_2$) (see section 3.3 and Figure 9 on page 55). Without redistribution, bilaterally no standardization is an equilibrium. Let A_{21} be the compensation paid by agent 2 in case of bilateral standardization, then the standardization equilibrium (s_{12},s_{22}) is realized when the standardization costs of 1 reduced by the side payment are smaller than information costs:

$$K_1-A_{21}<c_{12}$$

Equation 35: Condition for side payment from the perspective of agent 1

Table 49: Infrastructure decision with side payments[7]

	agent 2	
agent 1	s_{21}	s_{22}
s_{11}	(c_{12},c_{21})	$(c_{12},c_{21}+K_2)$
s_{12}	$(c_{12}+K_1-A_{21},c_{21}+A_{21})$	(K_1-A_{21},K_2+A_{21})

Agent 2 agrees to the side payment design if his savings exceed his standardization costs including the compensation.

$$K_2+A_{21}<c_{21}$$

Equation 36: Condition for side payment from the perspective of agent 2

---

[7] Note that in the X.500 case the sum of all K_i also decreases due to the rebates. Thus, in some cases A could be implicitly provided by a large partner opening his superior prices to the smaller firms, too.

204

The lower and upper bounds for the side payment can now be determined as in Equation 37.

$$K_1\text{-}c_{12} < A_{21} < c_{21}\text{-}K_2$$

Equation 37: Lower and upper bounds of side payment

Still, standardization is not a unique equilibrium and the eventual amount of the side payment remains open. It will be determined by factors like the negotiation skills of the partners. Especially in the context of decisions like the X.500 case, developing mechanisms for determining side payments that are considered to be *fair* by all affected agents is crucial for finding solutions to standardization problems. In the following, we will propose a possible method of determining "fair" compensation payments that is based on the idea of redistributing a network ROI such that all participants in the solution reap similar network benefits. Ultimately, a higher degree of standardization will be achieved at the cost of the biggest profiters. It is important to remember that an investment's return in this definition is not necessarily associated with a direct cash flow, making all calculations somewhat soft, of course.

In a two player network the ROI can be determined analogously to Equation 34:

$$ROI = \frac{c_{12} + c_{21}}{K_1 + K_2} - 1$$

Equation 38: Network ROI for a two player network

If the ROI is negative, standardization will not pay off. In cases where it is positive, standardization can possibly be advantageous for all agents. The side payment for overcoming a possible coordination problem can be determined according to Equation 39.

$$ROI_i = \frac{c_{ij} + A}{K_i} - 1 \overset{!}{=} \frac{c_{12} + c_{21}}{K_1 + K_2} - 1 = ROI_{(network)}$$

Equation 39: Individual ROI$_i$

A positive side payment A implies transfers from j to i and vice versa. For two player networks, possible side payments are alike and can be determined according to Equation 40. Although fairness is a concept that is often disputed, the proposition of guaranteeing positive payoffs for all participants could meet a basic understanding.

How can the equilibrium achieved by the network ROI be evaluated according to the discussion in section 3? Using side payments the strategic situation of the players changes as shown in Table 50.

$$A* = \frac{c_{12} + c_{21}}{K_1 + K_2} K_i - c$$

Equation 40: Side payment in a two player network

Table 50: Infrastructure decision with side payments

agent 1	agent 2	
	s_{21}	s_{22}
s_{11}	(c_{12}, c_{21})	$(c_{12}, c_{21}+K_2)$
s_{12}	$(c_{12} + K_1 - A^*, c_{21} + A^*)$	$(K_1 - A^*, K_2 + A^*)$

Algebraic signs of equilibrium side payments A* are determined according to Table 49.

$$A* = \left| \frac{c_{12} + c_{21}}{K_1 + K_2} K_1 - c_{12} \right|$$

Equation 41: Side payment in two player network

The ROI-based compensation is within the interval $(K_1 - c_{12}) < A < (c_{21} - K_2)$:

$$K_1 - c_{12} < \left| \underbrace{\frac{c_{12} + c_{21}}{K_1 + K_2}}_{>1} K_1 - c_{12} \right| = A*$$

$$c_{21} - K_2 > \left| c_{21} - \underbrace{\frac{c_{12} + c_{21}}{K_1 + K_2}}_{>1} K_2 \right| = A*$$

difference exchangable
since only algebraic sign
is relevant

s.t.: $c_{12} < K_1$

$c_{21} > K_2$

$c_{12} + c_{21} > K_1 + K_2$

Equation 42.1-5: Side payments within the bounds described in Equation 37

In summary, ROI-based compensations can establish a unique (Nash) standardization equilibrium that is Pareto-efficient as well as Kaldor-Hicks-efficient. It is not strictly trembling hand perfect, though: The error probability of agent 1 concerning the standardization strategy (s_{12}, s_{22}) is determined by Equation 43.

$$E(s_{11}) = \varepsilon_2 c_{12} + (1 - \varepsilon_2) c_{12} < \varepsilon_2 (c_{12} + K_1 - A^*) + (1 - \varepsilon_2)(K_1 - A^*) = E(s_{12})$$

$$\Rightarrow \varepsilon_2 > 1 - \frac{K_1 - A^*}{c_{12}}$$

Equation 43: Critical error probability of agent 1

If agent 1 estimates error probability ε_2 of agent 2 erroneously choosing strategy 1 (no standardization) to be greater than expressed in Equation 43 he will choose strategy 1, too. Accordingly, agent 2 chooses s_1 if he considers the tremble of 2's hand to be greater than expressed in Equation 44.

$$E(s_{21}) = \varepsilon_1 c_{21} + (1 - \varepsilon_1)(c_{21} + A^*) < \varepsilon_1 (c_{21} + K_2) + (1 - \varepsilon_1)(K_2 + A^*) = E(s_{22}) \Rightarrow \varepsilon_1 > 1 - \frac{K_2}{c_{21}}$$

Equation 44: Critical error probability of agent 2

5.3.2.2 An n-player solution

The network wide ROI for n-player networks can be determined using Equation 45.

$$ROI_{network} = \frac{\displaystyle\sum_{\substack{i=1 \\ }}^{n} \sum_{\substack{j=1 \\ i \neq j}}^{n} c_{ij}}{\displaystyle\sum_{i=1}^{n} K_i} - 1$$

Equation 45: Network ROI for n agents

The numerator sums all c_{ij} since it is assumed that no optimal solution with regard to the optimum set of participating players in a network has been determined yet. If a network ROI for a particular constellation of agents is to be determined the c_{ij} of course only denote the relevant edges. See section 5.3.4 for deficiencies of the ROI concept when applied to decide between alternative network constellations.

The individual decision functions have to consider the proposed side payments A_{ij} (given or received by i) as in Equation 46 (it is possible that payments can be received as well as paid).

$$ROI_i = \frac{\sum_{\substack{j=1 \\ i \neq j}}^{n} c_{ij} + \sum_{\substack{j=1 \\ i \neq j}}^{n} A_{ij}}{K_i} - 1$$

Equation 46: Individual ROI of agent i

$$ROI = \frac{\sum_{i=1}^{n} \sum_{\substack{j=1 \\ i \neq j}}^{n} c_{ij}}{\sum_{i=1}^{n} K_i} - 1 = \frac{\sum_{\substack{j=1 \\ i \neq j}}^{n} c_{ij} + \sum_{\substack{j=1 \\ i \neq j}}^{n} A_{ij}}{K_i} - 1 = ROI_i \;\Rightarrow\; \sum_{\substack{j=1 \\ i \neq j}}^{n} A_{ij} = \frac{\sum_{i=1}^{n} \sum_{\substack{j=1 \\ i \neq j}}^{n} c_{ij}}{\sum_{i=1}^{n} K_i} K_i - \sum_{\substack{j=1 \\ i \neq j}}^{n} c_{ij}$$

Equation 47: Determination of side payment for agent i

This proposed solution to the implementation problem requires that the set of agents participating in the standardization solution is already determined as for instance in the X.500 case. Generally, this approach might be considered within somewhat established and stable user groups (such as large companies with many business units, supply chains, etc.) but hardly supports 'adhocracies', i.e. spontaneous agent clusters that do not yet know about their interdependencies in terms of having determined their optimal set of partners. But considering the satisfying hypothesis for infrastructure decisions it could also be used to heuristically evaluate or compare possible cooperations.

5.3.3   A network ROI for a virtual principal

> "Trying to defend an (...) allocation is like clapping one's hand,
> then trying to defend how much of the sound is attributable to each hand"
> Y. Ijiri [Ewert/Wagenhofer 1993, 542]

Using a virtual principal, agents in a decentrally coordinated network could try to internalize some of their network effects. Among others, the principal can reduce the number of communication acts between the agents for coming up with a solution or provide a trusted service of using reported local information for controlling mutual network infrastructures but keeping them secret so as to protect individual information from being seen by others. Electronic marketplaces might serve as an example as well.

In controlling theory centralized (administrative) services are described by subadditive cost functions (due to economies of scale) which has the question arise what part of the associated costs should be covered by the business units receiving the services. Here the concept of fairness is discussed with regard to the different allocation schemes. See Ewert/Wagenhofer (1993, 540-552) for an overview.

208

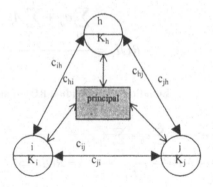

Figure 105: Network with three agents and a principal

Abstractly speaking and given that all agents report truthfully (see next section), the (virtual) principal described can transform a decentralized standardization problem under uncertainty to a centralized scenario. These services will require some compensation that can in this context be interpreted as agency costs [Schmidt/Terberger 1997, 405] that reduce the network wide ROI but might still yield better results than a decentralized scenario without any multilateral coordination. These principal's costs (K_P) increase aggregate standardization costs.

$$ROI_{network} = \frac{\sum_{\substack{i=1}}^{n}\sum_{\substack{j=1 \\ i\neq j}}^{n} c_{ij}}{\sum_{i=1}^{n} K_i + \underbrace{K_P}_{\substack{coordination \\ costs}}} - 1$$

Equation 48: Network ROI in n-player network with principal

$$ROI_i = \frac{\sum_{\substack{j=1 \\ i\neq j}}^{n} c_{ij} + \sum_{\substack{j=1 \\ i\neq j}}^{n} A_{ij}}{K_i + \frac{1}{n}K_P} - 1$$

Equation 49: Individual ROI of agent i in n-player network with a principal

Side payments can be determined by equaling ROI_i and $ROI_{network}$.

$$ROI_{network} = \frac{\sum\limits_{i=1}^{n}\sum\limits_{\substack{j=1 \\ i\neq j}}^{n} c_{ij}}{\sum\limits_{i=1}^{n} K_i + K_P} - 1 \stackrel{!}{=} \frac{\sum\limits_{\substack{j=1 \\ i\neq j}}^{n} c_{ij} + \sum\limits_{\substack{j=1 \\ i\neq j}}^{n} A_{ij}}{K_i + \frac{1}{n} K_P} - 1 = ROI_i \Rightarrow \sum\limits_{\substack{j=1 \\ i\neq j}}^{n} A_{ij} = \frac{\sum\limits_{i=1}^{n}\sum\limits_{\substack{j=1 \\ i\neq j}}^{n} c_{ij}}{\sum\limits_{i=1}^{n} K_i + K_P}(K_i + \frac{1}{n} K_P) - \sum\limits_{\substack{j=1 \\ i\neq j}}^{n} c_{ij}$$

Equation 50: Side payments for agent i considering principal's costs

The concept of the network ROI has been developed to propose a general way of solving the implementation problem. Still, for a particular problem a determination of individual side payments deemed fair by everyone involved remains a difficult task and is, among others, depending on individual negotiating skills and probably additional goals. The simple proposition to use a homogeneous ROI as a *fair* redistribution concept is certainly nothing more but a practical and supposedly controllable approximation. See Güth/Königstein/Kovács/Zala-Mezõ (2001) for an experimental analysis of fairness within firms (one principal, many agents).

5.3.4 Problems associated with the ROI

The determination of target costs, earnings, or revenues is a prominent problem in corporate accounting and planning [Sakurai 1989, 43; Ewert/Wagenhofer 1993, 289]. The ROI is a measure frequently used to describe the cost effectiveness of investments. In contrast to the more frequently used ROS (return on sales) the ROI requires the difficult assignment of invested capital to products. What is often surprising, is that the biggest problem is the interpretation of the ROI in dynamic problems. As emphasized above, the network ROI is not suitable for determining the optimal set of network participants. The reason is that an ROI measures average capital efficiency. As a result, maximizing the ROI regularly yields results very different from the (centrally) optimal strategy. Under-investing is an especially frequent result when mistaking the ROI for determining the optimum investment policy because any additional investment besides the single most profitable - in this case new agents - has *average* profitability decrease. Thus using an ROI to configure an investment program would result in the investment manager choosing only one project which is the one with the highest profitability. See Ewert/Wagenhofer (1993, 460-465) for an example. In the context of the standardization problem this implies that for any given constellation of network participants an ROI needs to be positive to make it possible for the solution at choice to be centrally advantageous. But since the ROI measures average profitability it is not adequate for choosing between different solutions. The problem becomes obvious in the network of Figure 106. Evidently, all three agents should standardize. But the highest ROI is achievable if only agents 1 and 2 standardize (33% versus 20% if all standardize). This is, of course, only a very rudimentary consideration (or a 'capital productivity') since the capital stock is quasi endogenized: what happens to the remaining capital not invested? For a more subtle analysis capital costs need to be considered in order to discuss an ROI in the context of investment problems in managerial accounting.

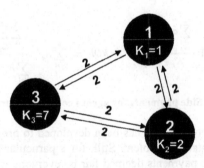

Figure 106: Example of discrepancy between maximum ROI and centralized solution

In contrast to traditional investment problems subject to budget restrictions, due to the existence of network effects potential benefits of an investment (i.e. another agent adopting a standard) are more dependent on previous decisions. As a consequence, in a network the proposition that only the smallest number of "investments" (in this case 2 standardizing agents) is chosen does not hold. Applying the network ROI to the example of Figure 8 on page 54 shows the problem. Given no solution is known yet, for the five agent example the network ROI generates these values the sum of which is 0, of course:

$A_1 = -10,86$ $A_2 = 22,23$ $A_3 = -30,83$ $A_4 = 19,88$

The network wide ROI for all players then is 0.46%. In contrast, the ROI of the optimum solution (agents 1, 3, 5) is 10%.

Despite the problems, for traditional investment and internal controlling decisions an empirical survey among 620 of the biggest U.S. enterprises revealed that 65% of all managers use the ROI as their only profitability measure, another 28% used the ROI and residual earnings (which avoids most of the problems) [Reece/Cool 1978 in Ewert/Wagenhofer 1993].

5.4 The data problem

> "One possible solution to the public goods problem
> is a Groves-Clarke mechanism [...] which enables 'truth telling'
> with respect to the agents' private information"
> *[Alsytne 1997, 18]*

One solution to the problem of sub optimal equilibria in decentralized networks is to use a virtual principal to plan and control standardization decisions and to redistribute costs and benefits among network agents in order to achieve Kaldor-Hicks (central) optima. Determining a centralized, i.e. network wide aggregate best solution, requires access to all relevant data of all network participants. Agents might have an incentive to give manipulated information for they anticipate allocative implications from their reporting [Ewert/Wagenhofer 1993, 407-408, 471-486]. Any incentive system as such might incur costs, though. Thus, closing the standardization gap makes deciders face the trade-off between solution cost and solution quality.

In this section, an incentive and control system based on a Groves scheme adapted to networks is developed that enables a neutral principal to determine relevant decision data to implement a centralized solution while at the same time redistributing costs in such a way that for each individual agent it is a dominant strategy to provide that principal with true local cost and benefit information.

The principle is based on the idea that the ("lump sum") distribution of an agent's surplus (or deficit) he induces in the network is independent of the agent's (technology) choice [Groves 1973; Groves 1976; Groves/Ledyard 1977; Groves/Loeb 1979; Groves 1979].

5.4.1 An adapted Groves mechanism for the decentralized standardization model

First, the demand revealing Groves mechanism that "implements the efficient amount of a public good via a dominant strategy equilibrium" is briefly introduced and later adapted for use within the standardization framework [Varian 1994].

5.4.1.1 *The Groves mechanism*

The Groves mechanism is based on the following premise [Laux 1995, 532-3]:

▶ risk-neutral principal decides about investment in a resource usable by various agents

▶ there are no capacity restraints to using the resource

▶ resource costs (K) are known to the principal. Business units $(1,...,n)$ using that resource report their expected benefit $(E(G_i))$ from using the resource. Their reported expected benefit is $rE(G_i)$

▶ If the sum of all reported expected benefits exceeds the resource's costs,

the principal buys it: $\sum_{i=1}^{n} rE(G_i) - K > 0$

Thus, the principal's decision quality depends upon how close the reported benefits are to the real benefits.

▶ The agents' individual benefits from using the resource ex post are determined by a premium P_i that depends upon a bonus base BG_i that is determined by his earnings and the resource cost: $BG_i=G_i-K_i$. The premium is deducted from a bonus rate (f_i) multiplied by BG_i: $P_i=f_i \times BG_i$ while

$f_i > 0$ and $\sum_{i=1}^{n} f_i < 1$. If $\sum_{i=1}^{n} G_i > 0$ every agent is better off if the principal

buys the resource, the principal would be worse off if $\sum_{i=1}^{n} f_i > 1$. That is

why the aggregate bonus rate needs to be below 1 from the perspective of the principal.

The idea behind the Groves scheme is to retrieve true expected values from the individual agents by making manipulated cost reports disadvantageous qua cost redistribution. This can be achieved by having each agent bear the costs of the resource that are not yet covered by the other agents' reported expected benefits

(K_i): $$K_i = K - \sum_{\substack{j=1 \\ i \neq j}}^{n} rG_j$$

The costs any agent has to bear (K_i) are therefore independent of his reported benefits (rG_i) resulting to a bonus base of:

$$BG_i = G_i - (K - \sum_{\substack{j=1 \\ i \neq j}}^{n} rG_j)$$

This way, true cost reports are a dominant strategy for all individual agents. Manipulated reports cannot improve an agent's situation for his bonus is independent of his report. If an agent reports benefits that are too high he risks the principal buying the resource although it won't pay off. In this case, a negative bonus base means the agent would have to pay the additional money to the principal. Analogously, the reverse case of reporting too little benefits could prevent the principal from buying the resource and the agent from profiting from the resource (in the amount of his bonus). A brief example will demonstrate the individual incentive situations when manipulating reports.

5.4.1.2   A Groves example

Let K=1,000 and n=3.

Table 51: True reporting (in brackets: agent 3 manipulates)

N	G_i	rG_i	K_i	BG_i
1	300	300	100 (200)	200 (100)
2	400	400	200 (300)	200 (100)
3	500	500 (400)	300 (300)	200 (200)
enterprise (principal)	1200	1200 (1100)	600 (800)	

If everyone reports truthfully $rG_i = G_i$ and $\sum_{i=1}^{3} rG_i = 300 + 400 + 500 = 1200 > 1000$.

The principal buys the resource and gets net profits of 200. But not all costs are covered by the cost assignment scheme; thus, the enterprise has to cover the remaining 400 itself.

If agent 3 reports $gG_n = 400$ instead, the results are as shown in brackets in Table 51. The principal buys the resource, costs assigned to 1 and 2 decrease decreasing the bonus base. 3 is unaffected so far but risks that the principal does not buy the resource at all since he does not know what the others report. And if 1 knows of 3's manipulation and tries to counterbalance it by reporting 600 instead of 300, the situation changes as described in Table 52. Agent 1 suffers a disadvantage. It becomes clear that true reporting is dominant.

Table 52: Counterbalancing the manipulation of Table 51

N	G_i	rG_i	K_i	BG_i
1	300	600	400	-100
2	400	400	200	200
3	500	200	0	500
enterprise (principal)	1200	1200	600	

5.4.1.3 A Groves mechanism for decentralized standardization problems

The basic principle behind the Groves scheme is providing a mechanism for a principal so that his agents report truthfully as a dominant strategy by offering payoffs independent of the agents' reports. Accordingly, in order to be used within the standardization framework, some adaptations are necessary that are described below. General problems of the Groves mechanism as well as of the proposed adaptation are discussed later in section 5.4.2. The network incentive and control scheme consists of eight steps:

1) Premises: As in the Groves scheme, the principal knows all standardization costs $K = \Sigma K_i$.

2) Reporting of information cost savings rc_{ij}: The agents report their information costs to the principal.

3) Determination of the optimal solution: The principal determines the optimal solution according to centralized model. Aggregate standardization costs now increase by the costs necessary for paying the principal K_p as in the previous section.

4) Control and sanctions function: Those agents who are part of the optimal solution, report their partners' information costs rc_{ji} to the principal who compares them with the respective rc_{ij} of the partners. If one partner's re-

214

port deviates from the other's report about the same information relation, the principal checks that set of data; the additional costs of this action are to be paid for by the manipulating agent (sanction).

5) Determination of individual savings rG_i: Based upon the optimal solution and the reported – and possibly corrected – savings the principal determines the individual savings.

6) Determination of the Groves costs: Based upon the individual savings the principal determines the Groves costs for those agents standardizing. The costs consist of that part of aggregate standardization costs not covered by the reported savings of the other agents. For agents not participating in the optimal solution, standardization costs are zero, of course.

7) Determination of relative costs: Costs not covered are assigned to standardized agents, according to their relative participation.

8) Determining total costs: The principal determines all agents' total costs by adding Groves costs and relative costs.

5.4.1.4   Example of dominant strategies for the adapted Groves mechanism

In this section, the five-node-network from Figure 8 is used to determine decentralized network behavior using the network incentive and control scheme described above. In addition, the effects of data manipulation using the scheme are demonstrated.

1) Premises: The principal knows all standardization costs

   $K_1=30$ $K_2=50$ $K_3=36$ $K_4=75$ $K_5=25$

2) Reporting of information cost savings rc_{ij}: The agents report their information costs to the principal. Let us first presume they report truthfully.

Table 53: Edge values of Figure 8

$rc_{12}=4$	$rc_{21}=4$	$rc_{31}=15$	$rc_{41}=7$	$rc_{51}=10$
$rc_{13}=20$	$rc_{23}=10$	$rc_{32}=12$	$rc_{42}=7$	$rc_{52}=7$
$rc_{14}=7$	$rc_{24}=7$	$rc_{34}=15$	$rc_{43}=15$	$rc_{53}=20$
$rc_{15}=10$	$rc_{25}=7$	$rc_{35}=25$	$rc_{45}=7$	$rc_{54}=8$

3) Determination of the optimal solution: The principal determines the optimal solution. Aggregate standardization costs now increase by the costs necessary for paying the principal. For the example, let the principal costs be 5 MU ($K_p=5$). The optimal solution is equivalent to that in 3.1.1. Agents 1, 3, and 5 standardize resulting in total standardization costs of 91+5=96.

4) Control and sanctions function: Agents 1, 3, and 5 report rc_{ji} respectively.

Table 54: Participating agents

Agent 1	Agent 3	Agent 4
$rc_{31}=15$	$rc_{13}=20$	$rc_{15}=10$
$rc_{51}=10$	$rc_{53}=20$	$rc_{35}=25$

The principal compares data from step 2 and 4. In this case agents have reported truthfully and thus no additional control on behalf the principal is required and therefore there are no additional costs.

5) Determination of individual savings rG_i: The principal determines the individual savings.

agent 1: $rG_1 = rc_{13} + rc_{15}$ $\Rightarrow$ $rG_1 = 20+10=30$
agent 2: no standardization $\Rightarrow$ $rG_2 = 0$
agent 3: $rG_3 = rc_31 + rc_{35}$ $\Rightarrow$ $rG_3 = 15+25=40$
agent 4: no standardization $\Rightarrow$ $rG_4 = 0$
agent 5: $rG_5 = rc_{51} + rc_{53}$ $\Rightarrow$ $rG_5 = 10+20=30$

6) Determination of the Groves costs: Groves costs are that part of the standardization costs not yet covered by rG_i.

agent 1: $GK_1 = (K+K_P) - rG_2 - rG_5$ $\Rightarrow$ $GK_1 = 96-40-30=26$
agent 2: no standardization $\Rightarrow$ $GK_2 = 0$
agent 3: $GK_3 = (K+K_P) - rG_1 - rG_5$ $\Rightarrow$ $GK_3 = 96-30-30=36$
agent 4: no standardization $\Rightarrow$ $GK_4 = 0$
agent 5: $GK_5 = (K+K_P) - rG_1 - rG_3$ $\Rightarrow$ $GK_5 = 96-30-40=26$

7) Determination of relative costs: Costs not covered by Groves costs yet assigned to standardized nodes.

agent 1:
$$RK_1 = \frac{(K+K_P) - \sum_{i=1}^{n} GK_i}{3} \Rightarrow$$

$$RK_1 = \frac{96-88}{3} = 2,\overline{6}$$

agent 2: $\Rightarrow$ $RK_3 = 2,\overline{6}$

agent 3: $\Rightarrow$ $RK_5 = 2,\overline{6}$

8) Determining total costs by summing up Groves costs and relative costs:

agent 1: $K1 = GK_1 + RK_1$ $\Rightarrow$ $K_1 = 26+2,67=28,67$
agent 2: no standardization $\Rightarrow$ $K_2 = 0$
agent 3: $K_3 = GK_3 + RK_3$ $\Rightarrow$ $K3 = 36+2,67=38,67$

agent 4: no standardization $\Rightarrow$ $K_4=0$
agent 5: $K_5=GK_5+RK_5$ $\Rightarrow$ $K_5=26+2,67=28,67$

All data as well as the agents' gross (G_i) and ex post benefits or losses (π) are summarized in Table 55.

Table 55: Incentive and control system: Default situation as in Figure 8

agent i	G_i	rG_i	GK_i	RK_i	K_i	π_i
1	30	30	26	2,67	28,67	1,33
2	0	0	0	0	0	0
3	40	40	36	2,67	38,67	1,33
4	0	0	0	0	0	0
5	30	30	26	2,67	28,67	1,33
principal	100	100	88	8	96	4

In the following, the implications of possible manipulations are described using analogous tables. There are eleven different ways of manipulation to be considered:

1. An agent who is part of the optimal solution reports savings that are too high to another optimum solution participant.

2. A relation between two participating agents is "strongly" manipulated to be lower.

3. A relation between two participating agents is "slightly" manipulated to be lower.

4. A relation between one agent participating and the other not is reported too high.

5. A relation between one agent participating and the other not is reported too low.

6. Reverse situation of 4.

7. Reverse situation of 5.

8. A relation between two agents not in the optimal solution is reported too high so that at least one would standardize.

9. A relation between two agents not in the optimal solution is reported too low.

10. An agent knows about another's manipulation and tries to counterbalance it

11. Agents collaboratively manipulate.

Case 1: Agent 1 wrongly reports his savings potential c_{13} to be 30: $c_{13}=20$; $rc_{13}=30$.

The optimal solution remains unchanged for both agents standardize anyway, standardization cost, too. But there are impacts on the other agents:

Table 56: Incentive and control system: case 1

agent i	G_i	rG_i	GK_i	RK_i	K_i	π_i
1	30	40	26	9,33	35,33	-5,3
2	0	0	0	0	0	0
3	40	40	26	9,33	35,33	4,67
4	0	0	0	0	0	0
5	30	30	16	9,33	25,33	4,67
principal	100	110	68	28	96	4

The reported savings of agent 1 increase, reducing the Groves costs of the partners (but not his own). Thereby, all agents' relative costs increase, adding 1 MU to agent 1's total costs. Thus, an agent standardizing anyway has no incentive to report too high information costs with other agents standardizing, too, for he will only increase the costs assigned to him.

Case 2: Agent 1 strongly underestimates: $c_{13}=20$; $rc_{13}=10$.

If an agent who is part of the optimal solution strongly understates his information costs with another standardizing agent according to the optimal solution, the optimal solution itself can be affected. In this case, no agent would standardize at all. Agent 1 loses 1,33 MU he could have achieved plus the principal's cost that would be paid for by all agents. Thus, there is no incentive to underestimate potential benefits bearing the risk that a central solution that is not advantageous is determined.

Case 3: Agent 1 slightly understates: $c_{13}=20$; $rc_{13}=18$.

As in the first case, the optimal solution is unchanged but there are effects on the other agents.

Table 57: Incentive and control system: case 3

agent i	G_i	rG_i	GK_i	RK_i	K_i	π_i
1	30	28	26	9,33	27,33	2,67
2	0	0	0	0	0	0
3	40	40	38	9,33	39,33	0,67
4	0	0	0	0	0	0
5	30	30	16	28	28,33	0,67
principal	100	108	68	92	96	4

Agent 1's underestimating increases the others' Groves costs, thereby decreasing the relative costs resulting in smaller total costs for himself. Obviously, in this case the incentive system fails and the sanction mechanisms (step 4) must be applied. In this case, agent 3 has reported $rc_{13}=20$ to the principal, differing from agent 1 saying $rc_{13}=18$ and agent 3 $rc_{13}=20$ and having the principal validate the data at costs to be covered by the agent having reported wrong data. This weak manipulation allows an agent to reap profits at the cost of others who have an incentive reporting in such a way that the manipulation won't work. For the same reason there is no reason to report wrong data about the partners' information costs. Thus, in this case the incentives derived from the system described are not a sufficient means of solving the date problem; but the additional sanction mechanism covers this special case.

Case 4: Agent overstates rc_{12}: $c_{12}=4$; $rc_{12}=14$

In doing so, agent 1 risks changing the optimal solution. In fact, agent 2 would also be told to standardize, resulting in the costs and benefits of Table 58.

Table 58: Incentive and control system: case 4

agent i	G_i	rG_i	GK_i	RK_i	K_i	π_i
1	34	44	36	6	42	-8
2	21	21	13	6	19	2
3	52	52	44	6	50	2
4	0	0	0	0	0	0
5	37	37	29	6	35	2
principal	144	154	122	24	146	-2

Agent 1 is worse off. Had he only slightly overestimated the information costs, the overall solution might not have changed but he could not improve his situation anyway.

Case 5: Agent understates rc_{12}: Here, there is no impact to the overall solution. This manipulation cannot offer agent 1 any advantage and no disadvantage, either.

Case 6: Agent 2 manipulates rc_{25} so much that he would standardize: $c_{25}=7$; $gc_{25}=14$.

By doing so, agent 2 would become part of the optimal solution together with 1, 3, and 5. He suffers an ultimate loss of 5.75 MU due to this manipulation. In general, agents originally not part of the optimal solution cannot profit from reporting too high information costs to take part in the solution. If the manipulation is not strong enough to join the standardizing agents, his solution does not change at all.

Table 59: Incentive and control system: case 6

agent i	G_i	rG_i	GK_i	RK_i	K_i	π_i
1	34	34	29	3,75	32.75	1.25
2	21	28	23	3.75	26.75	-5.75
3	52	52	47	3.75	50.75	1.25
4	0	0	0	0	0	0
5	37	37	32	3.75	35.75	1.25
principal	144	151	131	15	146	-2

Case 7: Agents 2 underestimates rc_{21}.

The implications are equivalent to those in case 5.

Case 8: Agents 2 manipulates rc_{24}: $c_{24}=7$; $rc_{24}=16$.

Here, the principal tells all nodes to standardize. Agent 2 standardizes, too, but is worse off ex post. Again, a manipulation results in disadvantages.

Table 60: Incentive and control system: case 8

agent i	G_i	rG_i	GK_i	RK_i	K_i	π_i
1	41	41	36	4	40	1
2	28	37	32	4	36	-8
3	67	67	62	4	66	1
4	36	36	31	4	35	1
5	45	45	40	4	44	1
principal	217	226	201	20	221	-4

Case 9: Agent 2 understates rc_{24}.

Even with true reports, agent 2 is not part of the optimal solution. The implications are equivalent to those in case 5.

Case 10: Agent 1 strongly understates rc_{13} and agent 3 knowing this will counterbalance the manipulation $\Rightarrow c_{13}=20$; $rc_{13}=10$ and $c_{31}=15$; $rc_{31}=25$.

Both manipulations balance each other with respect to the optimal solution that remains unchanged. Let agent 3 know of the manipulation by agent 2 and cover it during step 4. This results in the situation described in Table 61.

Table 61: Incentive and control system: case 10

agent i	G_i	rG_i	GK_i	RK_i	K_i	π_i
1	30	20	16	2.67	18.67	11.33
2	0	0	0	0	0	0
3	40	50	46	2.67	48.67	-8.67
4	0	0	0	0	0	0
5	03	30	26	2.67	28.67	1.33
principal	100	100	22	8	96	4

Agent 3's covering is disadvantageous for him. Thus, true reporting is the superior strategy even when knowing about others' manipulation.

Case 11: Agent 1 and 3 form a coalition to commonly cheat.

Agent 1 and 3 agree that agent 1 slightly understates his information costs (<13>) and that they share the resulting profit. The results are described in Table 57 of case 3. Both agents now get 2.67+0.67=3.33 MU. Evenly divided they each get a benefit of 1.67 which makes them each 0.33 better off than in the original solution. As in the traditional Groves schema, collaborative manipulation can work.

5.4.1.5 Summary

In the previous section, a possibility of solving the data problem associated with the centralized standardization model was developed based upon the Groves mechanism.

Out of the eleven identified cases, only when an agent who is part of the optimal solution understates his information costs in such a way that the overall solution is not affected is true reporting not a dominant strategy and manipulation is advantageous. In exactly this case, the sanction mechanism comes into effect. See Alstyne (1997, Appendix A), Eccles/Crane (1987) for an analogous formal representation of a Groves-Clarke mechanism. A very interesting similar approach, implementing a compensation mechanism providing efficient subgame perfect equilibria in a two-stage game, is presented in Varian (1994).

5.4.2   Problems associated with the Groves mechanism

All problems associated with the original Groves mechanism positively also account for the network scheme and it only works given the assumed premises. Especially when there are differences between ex ante and post costs outside the control of the agents (e.g. stochastic benefits) or if all agents orchestrate their manipulations, the mechanism will fail. A theoretical drawback is the mechanism's dependence on (quasi-)linear utility and its unbalanced property.

A problem of the Groves mechanism for practical application is that most people do not really understand the elegant idea. See Waller/Bishop (1990) for an empirical experiment.

5.5 A bidding mechanism

"Most of what we call management consists of making it difficult for people to get their work done"
Peter Drucker

While the decentralized standardization model as proposed in section 3.1.2 allows to model the anticipative standardization behavior of agents without any communication or cooperation, one possibility of improving individual as well as overall decision quality is communication among the agents in such a way that they inform their partners about the value they assign to their standardizing and using this evaluation as a basis for possible (individually designed) side payments.

Corresponding to the information assumption of the decentralized model and relaxing the assumption that K_j is known, each agent first determines his maximum possible benefit from standardization U_i as the difference between information cost savings if all others standardize and individual standardization costs according to Equation 51 and weighs this value using his c_{ij} resulting in an edge utility u_{ij} (i.e. a relative individual valuation of the communications relations to i given a network wide standardization) according to Equation 52.

$$U_i = \left(\sum_{\substack{j=1 \\ j \neq i}}^{n} c_{ij} \right) - K_i$$

Equation 51: Maximum possible benefit from standardization for agent i

$$u_{ij} = U_i \cdot \frac{c_{ij}}{\sum_{\substack{j=1 \\ j \neq i}}^{n} c_{ij}} = \left[\left(\sum_{\substack{j=1 \\ j \neq i}}^{n} c_{ij} \right) - K_i \right] \cdot \frac{c_{ij}}{\sum_{\substack{j=1 \\ j \neq i}}^{n} c_{ij}} = c_{ij} - K_i \left(\frac{c_{ij}}{\sum_{j} c_{ij}} \right)$$

Equation 52: Individual valuation of i's communication partners ("bidding" for standardization)

The agents then publicize their u_{ij}. Comparing u_{ij} and u_{ji} can help us to get a better vision of the partners' decisions: whenever u_{ij} *and* $u_{ji} > 0$ (both standardize) or < 0

(none standardizes) is NOT true and at the same time the positive u_{ij} is sufficient to at least compensate the negative u_{ji}, side payments are determined. The possible situations are summarized in Table 62.

Table 62: Bilateral cost situations

1) both edge utilities u_{ij} and u_{ji} are positive	→ bilateral standardization expected
1) both edge utilities u_{ij} and u_{ji} are negative	→ bilateral non-standardization expected
3) Pos. edge utilities u_{ij} is greater than neg. edge utilities u_{ji}	→ side payment tr_{ij} of $|u_{ji}|$ from i to j (then, bilateral standardization) with $tr_{ij} \geq |u_{ji}|$
4) Pos. edge utilities u_{ij} is smaller than neg. edge utilities u_{ji}	→ bilateral non-standardization expected

If an agent decides different than this "public" expectation he has to pay for the losses caused by this to others ($st_{ij}=c_{ji}$). Thus, positive and negative side payments are known ex ante.

$$tr_{ij} = |u_{ji}|$$

Equation 53: Determination of tr_{ij} (A)

$$tr_{ij} = u_{ij}$$

Equation 54: Determination of tr_{ij} (B)

Table 63: Transfer payments for the situations of Table 62

case	expected standardization	side payment	possible standardization constellation ex post	punishment payment
I.	$exp_{ij} = 1$	$tr_{ij}=0$	a) $x_i = 1 \wedge x_j = 0$ b) $x_i = 0 \wedge x_j = 1$	a) $st_{ji} = c_{ij}$ b) $st_{ij} = c_{ji}$
II.	$exp_{ij} = 0$	$tr_{ij}=0$	--	$st_{ij}=0$
III.	$exp_{ij} = 1$	$tr_{ij} \geq |u_{ji}|$	a) $x_i = 1 \wedge x_j = 0$ b) $x_i = 0 \wedge x_j = 1$	a) $st_{ji} = c_{ij} - tr_{ij}$ b) $st_{ij} = c_{ji} + tr_{ij}$
IV.	$exp_{ij} = 0$	$tr_{ij}=0$	--	$st_{ij}=0$

Now, standardization rules can be determined using Z_i as utility of agent i using the rules described above:

$$Z_i = \left(\sum_{\substack{j=1 \\ j \neq i}}^{n} c_{ij} \cdot exp_{ij} \right) - \left(\sum_{\substack{j=1 \\ j \neq i}}^{n} tr_{ij} \cdot exp_{ij} \right) - K_i \qquad \text{(for } U_i > 0)$$

$$Z_i = \left(\sum c_{ij} \cdot exp_{ij} \right) - K_i \qquad \text{(for } U_i = 0)$$

$$Z_i = \left(\sum_{\substack{j=1 \\ j \neq i}}^{n} c_{ij} \cdot exp_{ij} \right) + \left(\sum_{\substack{j=1 \\ j \neq i}}^{n} tr_{ji} \cdot exp_{ij} \right) - K_i \qquad \text{(for } U_i < 0)$$

Equation 55.1-3: Benefit of agent I

Table 64: Standardization rules

if	then (standardization decision)
$Z_i \geq 0$	agent i standardizes ($x_i = 1$)
$Z_i < 0 \ \wedge \ |Z_i| \leq \sum_{\substack{j=1 \\ j \neq i}}^{n} st_{ij} \cdot exp_{ij}$	agent i standardizes ($x_i = 1$)
$Z_i < 0 \ \wedge \ |Z_i| > \sum_{\substack{j=1 \\ j \neq i}}^{n} st_{ij} \cdot exp_{ij}$	agent i does not standardize ($x_i = 0$)

5.5.1 Two examples

A simple three node instance (Figure 107) can exemplify the mechanism. In a first step, U_i (Equation 51) and u_{ij} are determined (Equation 52):

$$U_1 = (10+15)-20 = 5 \qquad u_{12} = 5 \cdot \frac{10}{10+15}$$

$$U_2 = (2+2)-6 = -2$$

$$U_3 = (12+15)-18 = 9 \qquad u_{13} = 5 \cdot \frac{15}{10+15}$$

...

Then, the standardization expectations are formed and Z_i are computed.

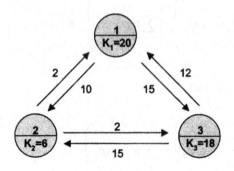

Figure 107: Example of "bidding" for standardization

Table 65: Results from communication

agent	edge utility		expectation	transfers to	
				model A (Equation 53)	model B (Equation 54)
1	$u_{12}= 2$ $u_{13}= 3$	$u_{21}= -1$ $u_{31}= 4$	$\exp_{12}= 1$ $\exp_{13}= 1$	$tr_{12}= 1$	$tr_{12}= 2$
2	$u_{21}= -1$ $u_{23}= -1$	$u_{12}= 2$ $u_{32}= 5$	$\exp_{21}= 1$ $\exp_{23}= 1$	$tr_{12}= 1$ $tr_{32}= 1$	$tr_{12}= 2$ $tr_{32}= 5$
3	$u_{31}= 4$ $u_{32}= 5$	$u_{13}= 3$ $u_{23}= -1$	$\exp_{31}= 1$ $\exp_{32}= 1$	$tr_{32}= 1$	$tr_{32}= 5$

Table 66: Benefits in the example

	model A ($tr_{ij} = \lvert u_{ji} \rvert$)	model B ($tr_{ij} = u_{ij}$)
agent 1	$Z_1 = (10+15) - (1) - 20 = 4$	$Z_1 = (10+15) - (2) - 20 = 3$
agent 2	$Z_2 = (2+2) + (1+1) - 6 = 0$	$Z_2 = (2+2) + (2+5) - 6 = 5$
agent 3	$Z_3 = (12+15) - (1) - 18 = 8$	$Z_3 = (12+15) - (5) - 18 = 4$

Here, for all agents $Z_i \geq 0$ is true, so that all standardize, which is also the centralized solution. Deviations would result in punishment payments making deviators worse off. In contrast, decentralized coordination would lead to no standardization ($E[U_{(1)}]=-16,25$; $E[U_{(2)}]=-4,67$; $E[U_{(3)}]=-14$).

It is interesting to note that once expectations have been formed determination (and validity) of Z_i are independent of others standardizing ex post as long as possible transfer payments are guaranteed.

Table 67: Compensations when deviating from expected behavior

case	situation ex ante	expected standardization savings for i	for j	situation ex post	punishment payment when deviating ex post (from j to i)	(from i to j)
I.	$exp_{ij}=1$	a) c_{ij}	a) c_{ji}	a) $x_i=1 \wedge x_j=0$	a) $st_{ji}=c_{ij}$	---
		b) c_{ij}	b) c_{ji}	b) $x_i=0 \wedge x_j=1$	---	b) $st_{ij}=c_{ji}$
III.	$exp_{ij}=1$	a) c_{ij}-tr_{ij}	a) c_{ji}+tr_{ij}	a) $x_i=1 \wedge x_j=0$	a) $st_{ji}=c_{ij}$-tr_{ij}	---
		a) c_{ij}-tr_{ij}	b) c_{ji}+tr_{ij}	b) $x_i=0 \wedge x_j=1$	---	b) $st_{ij}=c_{ji}$+tr_{ij}

In the example of Figure 107, agent 1 has total costs of MU 21 (model A: K_1+tr_{12}=20+1=21). If, for instance, agents 2 and 3 do not standardize, the costs of agent 1 would remain unchanged (K_1+c_{12}+c_{13}-st_{21}-st_{31}=20G+10+15-9-15=21).

The five node network problem of Figure 8 that has also served as an example for the adapted Groves mechanism can also be solved by the bidding mechanism.

Table 68: "Bidding" using the example of Figure 8

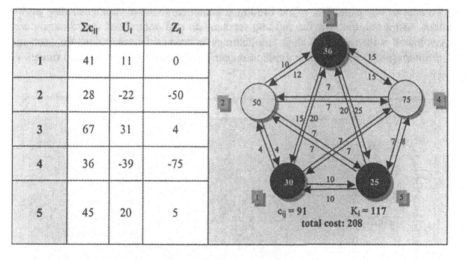

	Σc_{ij}	U_i	Z_i
1	41	11	0
2	28	-22	-50
3	67	31	4
4	36	-39	-75
5	45	20	5

$c_{ij}=91$ $K_i=117$
total cost: 208

The green shaded cells in Table 69 indicate positive, the red shading negative u-values. Those network nodes standardizing in the centralized solution (1, 3, 5) all mutually expect to standardize, the rest not to standardize; accordingly, there are no side payments necessary since in case of disharmonizing standardization preferences (no EXP (ij) value) positive u_{ij} are always smaller than negative u_{ij}.

Table 69: u_{ij} and standardization expectations for the example of Table 68

	u_{ij}	(u_{ji})	EXP (ij)	c		u_{ij}	(u_{ji})	EXP (ij)	c
u_{12}	1,073	-3,143	0	4	u_{41}	-7,581	1,878		7
u_{13}	5,366	6,945	1	20	u_{42}	-7,581	-5.502	0	7
u_{14}	1,878	-7,581	0	7	u_{43}	-16,245	6,945		15
u_{15}	2,683	4,444	1	10	u_{45}	-7,581	3,552		7
u_{21}	-3,143	1,073		4	u_{51}	4,444	2,683	1	17
u_{23}	-7,86	5,556		10	u_{52}	3,108	-5,502	0	7
u_{24}	-5,502	-7,581	0	7	u_{53}	8,888	11,575	1	20
u_{25}	-5,502	3,108		7	u_{54}	3,552	-7,581	0	9
u_{31}	6,945	5,366	1	15					
u_{32}	5,556	-7,86	0	12					
u_{34}	6,945	-16,245	0	15					
u_{35}	11,575	8,888	1	25					

5.5.2 A comparison between the bidding mechanism and centralized coordination

To analyze the capability of the bidding mechanism to solve standardization problems, using simulations the bidding mechanism and centralized coordination are compared with regard to their implications in terms of overcoming the start-up problem (i.e. closing the standardization gap) in the basic standardization model.

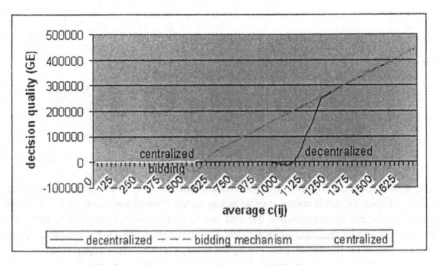

Figure 108: Centralized, decentralized, and "bidding" coordination

To make the influence of the bidding mechanism comparable to the efficiency discussions of section 4, simulations of 20-agents networks with different (increas-
ing) information costs (ND(c_{ij}| μ, 200^2) and K_i (ND(K_i| 10000, 1000^2) using cen-
tralized, decentralized and "bidding" coordination are shown in Figure 108.

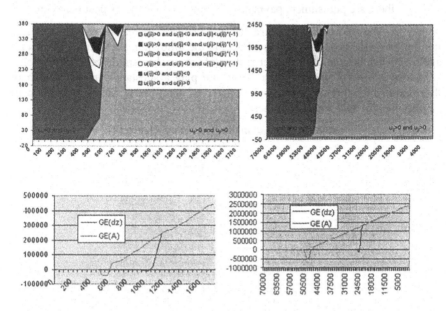

Figure 109: u_{ij} to u_{ji} relations (top) and total savings from bidding mechanism
(GE(A)) compared to decentralized coordination (bottom)
at increasing c (left) and decreasing K (right)

The overall pattern of the bidding graph is analogous to the decentralized graph,
including the initial negative lag, but on the whole using the bidding mechanism
agents standardize at lower information costs (which is equivalent (c.p.) to standardizing at higher standardization costs) and decision quality approximates much
better to centrally coordinated networks. For $\mu(c_{ij})$ between 425 and 575 total savings in the bidding case are negative as compared with the range between 875 and
1,050 in the decentralized model. And the errors in these constellations are worse
with overall cost increases of up to 36,685, compared with 14,824 in the decentralized case). The difference is explained by the fact that bidding agents standardize
earlier when standardization costs are simply relatively higher (see Figure 110). At
the same time, it makes no difference what method was used to determine the
transfer payments (model A or B).

Generally, the graph resulting from the bidding mechanism quite closely approximates to the centralized graph. The reasons compared to the basic model are:

228

- the individual information set is extended: agent i knows u_{ji} containing all (if aggregated) communication links of j. This effect is insignificant, though.

- there are side payments: "instant winners" can compensate "penguins"

- there are punishment payments aligning ex ante and ex post behavior.

At average deviation, only the third effect is relevant. Increasing deviation causes the first two effects to gain in importance. In the following, simulations using a 50 agent network help to get a clearer picture of the mechanism. In both simulations, situations 3-6 according to Table 70 do not play a substantial role although in these cases only, there are side payments agreed upon (those that are actually paid ex post are still only a subset of these).

Table 70: Simulation parameters for Figure 109

situation		Top of Figure 109: u_{ij} to u_{ji} relations			
1	right (blue)	$u_{ij}>0$ and $u_{ji}>0$			
2	left (dark red)	$u_{ij}<0$ and $u_{ji}<0$			
3		$u_{ij}>0$ und $u_{ji}<0$ and $u_{ij}>u_{ji}*(-1)$			
4		$u_{ij}>0$ and $u_{ji}<0$ and $u_{ij}<u_{ji}*(-1)$			
5		as 3 (i and j reversed)			
6		as 4 (i and j reversed)			
Bottom of Figure 109:					
Total savings from bidding mechanism compared to decentralized coordination					
left in Figure 109	n=50	myK=10,000	sK=1,000	myC= var	sC=200
right in Figure 109	n=50	myK=var	sK=1,000	myC=1,000	sC=200

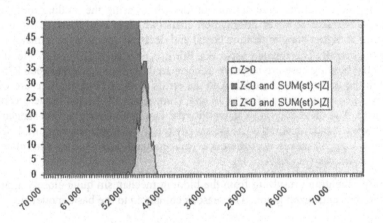

Figure 110: Rare side payments (total number of agents)

Long before any decentralized activities start the threat of punishment payments is sufficient for the network to (decentrally) decide efficiently. Ex post, standardization is efficient for every agent having adopted a standard. This is analogous to the findings in the box plots of section 4.2.4 with the difference that using the bidding mechanism agents are "convinced" ex ante. The proposition that ex post payments can be guaranteed, of course, is one of the major problems of the mechanism, although every agent is well aware that there won't be actual punishment payments for a deviating decision will simply make an agent worse off.

In the majority of cases (1 and 2) the bidding mechanism is reduced to: If $U_i>0$ then standardize! In these cases, mostly $Z_i=U_i$ since expectations are binary. The area in the middle of Figure 110 shows agents with expected savings (after transfers) below zero but that behave cooperatively anyway because of the threat of punishment payments. The large light shaded area on the right shows situations where punishment payments do not influence the decisions, and there are no side payments at all. The reason why agents standardize is that they weight their decision calculus using 1 instead of p_{ij} in the decentralized model. Strongly increasing the deviations will reduce the size of this area.

5.6 Managerial and policy implications

> "The distance between theory and practice
> is always smaller in theory than in practice."
> *Marshall T. Rose*

The relevance of an adequate coordination design in networks (such as enterprises, communities or countries) is as evident as its social implications. Incentive an control problems as well as network effects do not stop at national borders.

Important aspects of standardization decisions have been analyzed. When trying to derive managerial and policy guidelines one has to be very careful, however. The models could only consider very special cases and small parts of realistic standardization decisions. Part of the critique of the neoclassical paradigm in section 6.1 therefore focuses on the set of premises which cannot cope with the complexity of human behavior. That is why we cannot derive general decision support. Instead, the findings from the model and the contemplations above suggest a contingency theory of networks. The multitude of networks found in daily life makes it impossible, at this moment, to propose general patterns of behavior, and the lack of a general axiomatized theory of networks prohibits an easy specialization towards particular problem instances. Below, building on the findings of the simulations and experiences from the case studies with our industry partners, some frequently discussed matters will be discussed briefly.

5.6.1 Some general findings

When looking for ways of closing the standardization gap there are two principle cost/benefit situations when trying to achieve centralized solution quality in decentralized networks. Either the gap can be explained by agents wrongly anticipating their environments' actions or some agents that should standardize from a central perspective are individually worse off doing so. While in the second case in a decentralized network some form of redistribution needs to be established (like for example rebates on electronic orders or cost and benefit sharing), in the first case reducing uncertainty is in principal sufficient, i.e. designs aiming at enhancing the "information quality" concerning the respective standardization decision behavior. Accordingly, it has been shown that from the perspective of a principal responsible for information infrastructures and standardization in an enterprise or from a group of agents forming a committee to emulate centralized control the determination of the set of agents ideally participating in a solution mainly faces the data problem (section 5.2.2.1) and the complexity problem (section 5.2.2.2) while putting certain solutions into practice implies the implementation problem (section 5.2.2.3).

Often, these problems can be separated due to the particular decision situation as for example in an existing Intranet. Here, heuristically a (positive) standardization ROI (possibly for different sets of agents) can provide a valuable means of understanding and controlling particular standardization problems.

Generally, insurance solutions seem applicable to solving standardization problems, especially the implementation problem: Agents not only get a standard but also an exogenously enforceable promise to compensate for all costs exceeding the benefits. If the option issuer is convinced (and rightly so) that his chosen network of participants will pay off for everybody then this is an elegant way of overcoming the start-up problem (to get all penguins fishing). This assumes that the set of participants has already been determined. Additionally, there are the problems (and costs) of objectively determining cost and benefit data.

Moreover, if particular agents would suffer individually but contribute to aggregate efficiency a compensation plan needs to be established in that the option model would not per se solve the start-up problem by its pure existence but also some side payments would have to be made. But according to the simulations in sections 4.2.4 and 4.3.4 these cases are quite rare. One has to be aware of the fact that the model assumptions only consider positive network effects, though. If there were no side payments necessary, this mechanism would be equivalent to any information intermediation that offers all agents sufficient (complete) information to fully assess their partners' (and their partners'...) decision situation in such a way that every agent could emulate the centralized model and come up with identical results aiming at starting a bandwagon process.

One reason why the traditional theory cannot offer much help in solving standardization problems is the level of generalization. While there are many effects that might be considered to be network effects, it does not help much to aggregate them all or to search for one general overall effect. Rather, it is important to identify *relevant* network effects for a particular problem domain: While for a refrigerator there might be some network effects hidden somewhere, they won't play as prominent a role as with telephones [Wiese 1990, 3].

There has been discussion suggesting that agents standardize if they expect to be better off than otherwise. But due to the information asymmetries in decentralized standardization problems, some agents can be worse off ex post if others "make a mistake". A general procedure aimed at overcoming this problem is to offer each agent a choice between his status quo ante and his actual endowment at equilibrium state. The final allocation is only implemented if and only if all agents agree that they (weakly) prefer their current endowment and are therefore better off [Varian 1994]. If some agents object to the status quo, they could be excluded from a replay among the remaining agents. Thus a simple mechanism to overcome start-up problems could be giving out options to cover all possible net losses due to standardization.

5.6.2 Networks as a competitive advantage

> "Use a net. A net is more efficient
> than the other means discussed above (...):"
> *U.S. Army Survival Manual*

Using EDI as an example, benefits of integrating business processes with partners and the role of standards have been discussed and empirically validated. Analogous to the history of standards presented in section 2.1 the evolution of business process optimization started by focusing on internal processes. In the second half of the 20th century first approaches towards leaving the realms of individual companies could be witnessed when enterprises started to coordinate resources within their industry, in most cases around huge single firms. Over time flexibility and the ability to adapt to changing environments and global partners and customers became more and more important. Controlling entire supply chains with their interdependent elements became the focus of attention. The more coordination and cooperation was exerted outside particular firms and among various partners, the more these entities were called networks. At the same time, standardization problems became a primary topic of interest because standards are a necessary prerequisite for (coordination) networks, EDI being an important example.

In general, cooperation seems appropriate when common goals or interdependencies link otherwise independent agents. Analogously, coordination has been defined as the process of managing dependencies between activities [Malone/Crowston 1994]. Independent of the particular industry, Porter (1980) identifies general economic advantages of cooperation with regard to the competitive factors determining the competitive position of a firm:

▶ rivalry between existing competitors

> ▸ threat of new competitors (entrants)

> ▸ threat of substituting goods and services

> ▸ bargaining power of suppliers

> ▸ bargaining power of buyers

Cooperation can be interpreted as network participation (that requires coordination in terms of standardization) and hence offers both an improved competitive position for the entire network in contrast to other networks as well as a possible neutralization of competitive forces among network participants. Examples are economizing on costs (economies of scope and scale or as in the X500 example, see section 5.3.1), reducing uncertainty, improving service quality (e.g. code sharing among airlines) and developing new markets [Weitzel/König 2001a]. Focusing on communication or coordination quality, Powell (1990) calls information within a network "thicker" than outside the network.

5.6.3 Committees and consortia

There are many mechanisms found in real life aimed at reducing informational asymmetries concerning mutual goals and to coordinate individual decisions in a way that makes the participants better off. Especially for standardization problems between enterprises, one principal way of closing the standardization gap is agreeing on common standards in a committee. In fact, there is a cornucopia of organizations concerned with standards; some of them are governmental, some are privately organized. For instance, to overcome incompatibility problems between various EDI standards the United Nations and the global standardization organization ISO developed EDIFACT (EDI for Administration, Commerce and Transport, ISO 9735). There are almost 300 EDIFACT messages types (UNSMs) that are maintained by the Economic Commission for Europe (UN/ECE). Since 1997 the Center for Trade Facilitation and Electronic Business (CEFACT) of ECE has been host to the many EDIFACT working groups. Much work is done in the national EDIFACT boards, e.g. EBES (European board for EDIFACT Standardization) at CEN/ISSS in western Europe which is the European among four national entry points to CEFACT [Dedig 1998]. Recently, industry consortia such as W3C or OASIS seem to have produced standards faster than governmental organizations. If certain industries especially in the high-tech area require faster (technology life cycle) and more (existence of network effects) coordination than more traditional branches, the question arises what coordination form might be favorable. The simulations clearly showed a coordination demand in the form of the standardization gap that cannot be answered by pure market play if technologies are unsponsored due to network effects. Additionally, an analysis of the origin of inefficient decisions revealed that in many cases coordination requires informational agreements rather than subsidies. This makes consortia an attractive solution principle. One hypothesis why industry consortia might be favorable to legislative or governmental committees is not only that they are thought to be faster but they are also less binding, as Farrell and Saloner found to be of advantage: Farrell/Saloner (1988) model three coordination processes for agreeing on a standard. First, they model a committee: if agents can continuously meet to agree on a joint action this committee is faced with Battle of the Sexes situations each period (while the overall game is a war of attrition [Fudenberg/Tirole 1986]). Then the market solution ("bandwagon") is modeled as a grab-the-dollar game (the player who grabs first wins, but both lose when grabbing simultaneously) with basically the same structure. For both cases the mixed-strategy equilibrium shows the effectiveness of committee negotiation and market action respectively. Last, there is a hybrid between the former two coordination processes. In any period, committee members can also take market actions (e.g. adopt a standard on the market). It is shown that the committee dominates the market with the difference diminishing with the number of periods. "In a committee...nothing is likely to happen for a long time" while on the market early action is likely [Farrell/Saloner 1988, 239]. But pure market coordination in unsponsored networks - as in the simulations in the decentralized model in section 4 - often produces inefficient oligopolies. Even introducing time preferences by discounting payoffs does not change these findings. Most interestingly, the hybrid processes dominates the committee. Here, market and committee outcomes are possible. In fact, it is the fact that players have "two chances" that this system is advantageous. Additionally, in the words of the standardization model, the greater the standardization gap the more the hybrid system resembles the committee solution. Farrell/Saloner (1988, 250) find that committee and bandwagon (i.e. market) coordination are especially relevant if "neither tradition nor authority structure creates a decisive asymmetry".

The findings support the caveats of Farrell/Saloner (1988, 255) that "committees are always desirable". Intuitive reasons include the fact that commitment to a committee is hardly absolute, so eventually agents have two choices, so that costs are likely to be smaller than coordination benefits. Furthermore, committees often seem favorable when developing new standards. See also the references in section 2.2.1.2 for incentives concerning consortia participation.

5.6.4   Asymmetric network costs and gains

Among factors concerning the identification of the set of relevant network effects for particular standardization problems, the differentiation between hard and soft benefits may play an important role and partly determine the gravity of the conflict of interests: the more benefits from participating in a network are hard (i.e. increased revenue or cost reductions like, for instance, lower printing costs for directories, see section 5.3.1), the more agents are likely to enter the network. On the other hand, the more network benefits are future soft advantages, the more agents are likely to put their emphasis on harder costs. Another reason for this asymmetry is that basically all cost accounting systems are cost-based: inputs consist of hard historic cost (and revenue) data. As long as there have been no costs assigned to the duration of a process (like procurement, for example) it is difficult to quantify the benefits of improved processes. For example, empirical data about EDI as presented in section 5.1 often uses indicators like overstock etc. but often fails to deliver benefits from new customers, innovations due to better information etc. Hard costs and benefits regularly receive more attention than soft ones. In this context, problems of measuring alleged network effect benefits are also obvious: you can't control what you can't measure. Balanced Scorecards (BSCs) are aimed at offering a reasonable mix of soft and hard categories. They cannot offer help in measuring the underlying data but they try to make it controllable without reducing complex dependencies into singular measures such as an ROI. On the other hand, financial figures are sui generis scoring the past and are therefore problematic for a future that might be expected to exhibit e.g. increasing returns. The original intention of a BSC is to explicate dependencies between various activities within enterprises. Thus, its primary aim is analogous to trying to bridge the discrepancy between the centralized and the decentralized standardization model: the asymmetry of costs and benefits in terms of where they originate and where they become relevant. See also the further research proposals in section 7.2 for ways of approaching this problem.

5.6.5 Infrastructure subsidies and SME integration

Network effect theory owes much of its origin to anti-trust issues in ICT markets relying on standards and compatibility and therefore being subject to strong positive network effects. There is discussion whether markets subject to network effects fail, if traditional anti-trust policies fit ICT markets and if there should be high tech policies different from established industry policies. These issues are concerned with producer/vendor behavior. In this work, user adoption decisions in unsponsored networks have been analyzed. Thus no primary findings as to policy issues are within the framework of analysis. Yet the model might be used to focus on some particular public standardization discussions. Notably, in the EU, there have been substantial infrastructure subsidy programs that have recently shifted from building roads in rural areas of Europe to providing a common European information infrastructure as a global competitive advantage. In this context, the enormous potential SMEs could offer came to closer attention again and many programs trying to foster E-Commerce are particularly aimed at integrating them. Quite similar to Intranet planning, two questions are crucial: who, i.e. which SMEs should participate and how can they be integrated? This corresponds to the two steps proposed above: identify the optimal set of participating agents and develop mutually agreed upon coordination design. For the first question it is important to remember the drawbacks of SME integration in EDI networks described in section 5.1.6. The smaller the company the less likely they are to employ any automated material management system and have automizable processes and therefore *no unexploited network gains*. Thus, the more the "S" in SME and not just the "M" is considered, the greater the costs and the less probable a corresponding benefit increase: large companies' savings would have to accommodate for SMEs' expenses (given there are no additional goals to be achieved). And as could be seen in the EDI case, due to the asymmetric distribution of costs and benefits (according to size) large enterprises focus on benefits, SMEs on costs. But, given that overall standardization is desirable and that establishing an installed base is deemed an appropriate means of starting a domino effect, the find-ings of section 4.3.7 suggest building an installed base consisting of the smaller network participants. It might therefore be a an interesting application of the framework to analyze infrastructure development programs in the EU or develop-ing countries in this context.

In the next section, the theoretical requirements of a theory of networks are dis-cussed.

6 Theoretical implications: towards an interdisciplinary network theory

"An economic theory of norms and standards (…) is still lacking"
[Knieps/Müller/Weizsäcker 1982, 213]

The analysis has shown some important properties of systems subject to network effects that make standardization problems challenging for traditionally established scholarly systems, especially neo-classical analysis as one of the quite few fully axiomatized theoretical systems in economics. Beneath the externality property, there are other shortcomings of the neo-classical framework when information and communication systems (and their contents like for example information products) are the basic unit of analysis. Hence, after identifying these drawbacks, a requirements catalogue for an interdisciplinary theory of network effects and a possible methodological approach is proposed.

6.1 General drawbacks of the neo-classical paradigm

"I'd like to see a little less 'crash' and a little more 'program.'"
Wernher von Braun

Although individual utility maximization, as unanimously agreed upon throughout the neo-classical paradigm, should not be disputed here (the notion of network effects is a utility-theoretical construction) the "homo oeconomicus" comes with further premises, the economic literature on network effects quoted above implicitly assumes to fulfill. What these premises are and which one of them may default within an interdisciplinary context, will be discussed in the following.

However, if (and only if) all of these premises hold, then the validity of the following two so-called "fundamental theorems of welfare economics" (Hildenbrand 1976) can be proven:

- A competitive total *equilibrium* always represents a *Pareto-optimal allocation* of the total bundle of economic goods (a so-called Pareto optimum).

- For *each* realizable Pareto optimum a (positive) *price vector* exists, for which this Pareto optimum represents a competitive equilibrium.

The goal of an economy thus is to reach a Pareto-optimal allocation of goods. The ability of the market mechanism to accomplish this task (more or less strongly) depends on the following implicit assumptions summarized in sections 6.1.1 to 6.1.8:

6.1.1 Absence of externalities

In earlier definitions, an externality was considered to be present whenever the utility function $U_i(.)$ of some economic agent i includes real variables whose values are chosen by another economic agent j without particular attention to the welfare effect on i's utility. Three principal solutions to the problem of externalities have been proposed. Pigou (1920) suggests a tax imposed by a regulator. This Pigovian tax "corrects" the externality if the regulator knows its correct level (see the discussion about the data problem in section 5.2.2.1) (although then he could also just regulate the optimal level of the underlying problem). In the context of positive network effects this implies negative taxes, i.e. subsidies. A problem is that the Pigovian tax is only "right" in equilibrium and the theory does not say much about the optimal (intertemporal) price path [Wiese 1990, 5].

Another solution is shown by Coase (1960). He argues that the market mechanism may overcome some of these problems by adding well-defined "property rights" as tradable goods to the economy. Agents can then reach efficient outcomes by negotiation (given transaction costs are zero) the structure of which remains open, though. Accordingly, Arrow (1970) suggests setting up a market for the externality as the institution providing a negotiation structure. Therefore, nowadays an externality is said to be present whenever there is insufficient *incentive* for a potential market to be created for some good and the non-existence of this market leads to a *non-Pareto-optimal equilibrium*. So far, the absence of externalities is the only premise network effect literature – as discussed above – is trying to relax.

6.1.2 Complete rationality of the homo oeconomicus

Network effect literature often relies on the neo-classical assumption that all agents not only know their own action space and utility function but likewise have a complete and realistic model of all the other agents' current allocation, action spaces and utility functions as well. In a pure neo-classical "exchange economy" this assumption may be relaxed and even when we only bargain with our direct neighbors the decentralized exchange still leads to a unique and Pareto-optimal equilibrium, but unfortunately only if there are no network externalities or indivisibilities (see below). But for "real world" individuals, parametric and strategic (or strategic and statistical [Williamson 1985]) uncertainty [Hayek 1937] imposes constitutional bounds [Hayek 1994, 171] to the knowledge their decisions can be based upon. Additionally, heterogeneous institutional and structural environments influence the decisions of individual socio-economic agents. A frequent sociological argument for applying non-economic methodologies (i.e. surpassing the notion of a homo oeconomicus) is that "social patterns of human interaction transcend reductionist economic agendas" [Alstyne 1997]. The procedural setback is associated with the concept of a methodological individualism associated with a homo oeconomicus that is "a generic individual distinguished not by sex, ethnicity, religion, age, or any other social characteristic" [Biggart/Hamilton 1993, 480] while the "pursuit of economic goals is typically accompanied by [such] non-economic [goals] as sociability, approval, status, and power... Economic action is socially situated and cannot be explained by reference to individual motives alone" [Granovetter 1993, 25]. In this context, a market derived price seems to be not only too little dimensioned to capture network effects but also to be a simplification failing to capture the intricacies and complexity of human interaction [Powell 1990, 112]. See Alstyne (1997) and the literature cited there for an overview of a societal view of networks. See also Arthur (1994) on inductive reasoning.

Therefore, research in the area of *New Institutional Economics* (Hodgson 1993) rejects this concept of complete rationality in favor of a "learning" individual and search-theoretical models of evolutionary systems. Equilibrium analysis models are replaced by models of the evolution process of the examined multi-agent system, in which the optimal action of actor i at time t is modeled as function of his individual knowledge at this point in time. Implications of a methodological individualism and possible alternatives provided by institutionalistic theories are discussed in more detail later.

6.1.3   Exclusion principle

Prices only lead to Pareto-optimal collective action in a multi-agent system if the exclusion principle applies to the goods to be exchanged i.e. unique possession and ownership exists, permitting consumption only to a single individual. When common use or free duplication of products is possible (as is the case for information products like software), the equilibrium price is zero (if there were no copyrights artificially restricting this duplication as an incentive to the producer).

6.1.4   Consumption paradigm

Utility is drawn exclusively from consumption, i.e. the *destruction* of resources. The temporary possession of a good (like e.g. a piece of art or a game software), which is sold to some other individual after some periods, cannot be evaluated in the utility function. When extending the model to a multi-period economy, this inclusion becomes possible but immediately destroys the validity of price coordination. Especially for information products, the neo-classical notion of "consumption" (together with the exclusion principle mentioned above) poses a major obstacle to market coordination.

However, if not the consumption but the use of the resource comes to the center of attention, *property rights* lose their additional potential of generating utility compared to *usufruct rights*. The "Network Economics" of the Information Age has to migrate from a *consumer*-oriented to a *user*-oriented discipline, in which the efficient solution of scheduling problems (*which resources* are used *when* in *which process?*) will turn out to be a critical success factor for an efficient creation of social welfare.

6.1.5 Separation of consumers and producers

The classification of the economic actors into *consumers* and *producers* turns out to be problematic in a world replacing the classical notion of "work" more and more by freelance activities, thus "mixing" both concepts. In a "prosumer economics" we must not neglect the fact that human work does "flow out of the power plug socket" like energy but humans represent a discrete *renewable resource*, whose entire economic and "recovery process" must efficiently be synchronized with other individuals in the network.

6.1.6 Divisibility of resources

One of the most extensive restrictions is certainly the neo-classical assumption of arbitrary divisibility of all goods, i.e. each apple must be permitted to be cut into n pieces, sold separately. What may be acceptable for the apple, is impossible for screws or information. Interestingly enough, in defense of equilibrium theory it is argued, that the "rounding error" from unjustified acceptance of the divisibility assumption "washes out" for large quantities. While this may be true with screws, the argument breaks down at least for all goods, for which the optimal quantity of an individual's use is close to one (e.g. automobiles, nuclear power plants and all *information* goods).

6.1.7 Concave utility functions / no complementarities

The preference orders of the consumers over the bundles of goods must be representable by (strictly) concave, continuous utility functions. How far this assumption misses reality becomes clear if we realize that this does not allow for modeling complementary goods although complementarities can be found in all areas from recipes (if one ingredient is not available in sufficient quantity, the cake cannot be baked) and service industries (if I'd like to spend a three weeks vacation on an island, the flights without the hotel are as worthless as the hotel without being able to book the flights) to information (if we do not know the concept of Pareto optimality and there is no definition provided, the fundamental theorems stated above are of no value to the reader). This problem of complementarity is what renders the "market solution" of *scheduling* problems impossible: If a resource is needed for ten time slices in sequence and the process is not preemptive (as with the hotel stay), buying the ten time slices in separate auctions leaves me with too high a risk of ending up with some slices missing.

6.1.8 Absence of transaction costs

Neo-classical economics abstracts from transaction costs, i.e. from costs which are induced by the preparation or execution of the exchange process. In New Institutional Economics the effect of transaction costs is explicitly modeled and for example considered to be one reason for the emergence of companies economizing on transaction costs by being "islands of more centralized control" in a decentralized market.

6.2 Towards an interdisciplinary theory of network effects

"The story of the sciences in the 20th century
is one of a steady loss of certainty"
Brian Arthur

As could be shown in the previous sections, a general theory of networks or even just of network effects will have to consider several aspects that go beyond traditional analytical economic analysis. The implications of the network metaphor for many areas of economic, public, and social life as well as findings concerning social networks from other scientific disciplines make interdisciplinarity or, in other words, a tighter integration with other disciplines a promising way towards focusing on some of the problems outlined above. For example, network topology has, in different contexts, been an important object of research in sociology, geography and political sciences, to name but a few. An interdisciplinary theory of network effects will thus have to integrate and explain the social and economic interactions of human actors and automated agents (e.g. software agents trading on the stock exchange). Due to the deficiencies of the neo-classical paradigm the question of whether there are alternative theoretical foundations arises.

An extensive survey of the network metaphor ("network organization") comparing views and trying to identify commonalities from the points of understanding of network as a computer metaphor (coordinated problem solving), a rational agent metaphor (or economy metaphor; motivating self-interested parties to achieve mutually satisfactory Pareto-efficient outcomes) and a society metaphor (social patterns of human interaction) is presented by Alstyne (1997). In the field of institutional economics (or more general institutionalistic theories in the social sciences) the critique outlined above is widely supported. In general, "institutions" are considered to reduce uncertainty and thereby coordination costs between agents and can be, for example, property rights, contracts, or traditions. In economic theories of institutions, a commonality is the shared criticism concerning parts of the notion of the homo oeconomicus. In particular, the consideration of

▸ bounded rationality and

▸ opportunistic behaviour

is deemed crucial for explaining socio-economic systems. Some of these arguments have long been known from, for example, organization theory: deciding agents do not explicitly compare all possible alternative solutions, i.e. they do not decide based upon a perfect decision theory matrix of alternatives and states of the world due to the costs of doing so [Ewert/Wagenhofer 1993, 30-31] or they choose alternatives that satisfy certain quality levels [Simon 1981, 122-126]. In

Institutional economics, assumptions concerning agent behaviour are crucial: "Since institutional economics is behavioristic, and the behavior in question is none other than the behavior of individuals while participating in transactions, institutional economics must make an analysis of the economic behavior of individuals" [Commons 1931, 654]. The central assumptions about agent behavior are bounded rationality, opportunistic behavior, and utility maximization. Especially in the context of trying to find a theoretical foundation for the set of phenomena currently witnessed in the course of globally ubiquitous networks and the digitalisation of content and processes (sometimes called "the digital economy"), these branches of institutional economics are prevalent: transaction cost economics, property rights theory, principal agent theory, information economics, and network economics [Hummel 2000, 4; Picot 1991, 153; Adler 1996, 13]. Nevertheless, institutional economics as an extension to the neo-classical theory is based on a methodological individualism (social processes and institutions as pillars of the social world can, in principal, be explained by individual behaviour). Among others, new institution economics has faced criticism concerning the fact that, particularly due to path dependencies, agents with bounded rationality cannot possibly determine optimum institutions [North 1990].

In the social sciences, institutionalistic approaches have been successfully applied in the past 15 years when analysing questions like why different countries (or regions) react differently to technical and economic developments and why similar actions take different effects. For an overview of recent institutionalistic research approaches in the social sciences and disciplinary particularities see Esser (1999). In the context of network analysis, institution theories from disciplines like sociology focus on analogous important phenomena such as the importance of the socio-economic and institutional environment in that the social embeddedness of all deciding agents is a major determinant of system behavior (e.g. economic institutionalism [Williamson 1985; North 1990; Hodgson 1988; Dosi et al. 1988; Nelson 1993], political neo-institutionalism [Hall/Taylor 1996; Peters 1999] and institutional organization sociology [Granovetter 1985; Powell/DiMaggio 1991], see also Hall/Taylor (1996) for differentiating "historical institutionalism", "rational choice Institutionalism" (social phenomena are explained by individual decisions according to the methodological individualism), and "sociological institutionalism"). For the concept of social embeddedness see Veblen (1919), Polanyi (1944), Granovetter (1985); Granovetter /Swedberg (1992); Hodgson (1996). In contrast to the economic branch of institution theories, in sociology the complexity deriving from the social embeddedness of the agents and the impossibility of separating agents from their environments (among others due to path dependencies) has led many sociologists to neglect all micromodels of agent environments; from a theoretical point of view the notion of a homo oeconomicus and especially the associated methodological individualism is supposed to be inappropriate to describe a complex socio-economic reality.

Accordingly, in the research project "networks as a competitive advantage" researchers from the disciplines Computer Science, Economics, Geography, Information Systems, Labor Sciences, Law and Legal Sciences, Political Sciences and

242

Sociology agreed that for analyzing coordination in networks the consideration of these concepts is particularly crucial:

▸ bounded rationality
▸ uncertainty and incomplete information
▸ social embeddedness

Within this framework, as all agreed, the primary challenge is to overcome disciplinary differences concerning methodological individualism (homo oeconomicus) and a sociological macro perspective (homo sociologicus). Nevertheless, as elaborated above, no methodology has been developed that could help in answering the questions in focus. From an economist's perspective, the main reason is the refusal to explicitly model behavioral assumptions as needing to be used within models of social systems consisting of interacting agents. Naturally, game theory offers a rich ground for analyzing systems subject to interdependencies like network effects. Using game theory instead of decision theory is an important step leading away from a methodological individualism and into the direction of rather focusing on the interdependencies between particular decisions. Moreover, the differentiation between micromodels and macromodels vanishes in game theoretic models. Additionally, considering frictions resulting from incomplete contracts, asymmetric information etc. makes the models more realistic [SFB 2000, 14-15]. Unfortunately, most traditional game theory still strives for analytical solutions, which neglects the complexity deriving, among others, from network effects. An exception is parts of the evolutionary branch of game theory aimed at describing the evolutionary dynamics that are demanded by sociologists and political scientists [SFB 2000, 15].

These approaches together with recent contributions in the area of complex adaptive systems inspired a new research field which focuses on using computer-based models for understanding emergent system behavior. The paradigm of agent-based computational economics (ACE) rejects the complete rationality of the homo oeconomicus in favor of a learning individual [Vriend 1999; 1996]. "Agent-based computational economics is the computational study of economies modeled as evolving systems of autonomous interacting agents. ACE is thus a specialization to economics of the basic complex adaptive systems paradigm" [Tesfatsion 2002]. Although, as outlined above, in disciplines such as sociology, research approaches based on micromodels are often considered to be inappropriate for modeling complex social networks due to the proposed impossibility of modeling the social embeddedness of agents and the emergence of institutions, ACE might be a common way for conducting descriptive network analyses: "One principal concern of ACE researchers is to understand why certain global regularities have been observed to evolve and persist in decentralized market economies despite the absence of top-down planning and control (...). The challenge is to demonstrate *constructively* how these global regularities might arise from the bottom up, through the repeated local interactions of autonomous agents" [Tesfatsion 2002]. This methodological approach thus focuses on how structures (or institutions) *emerge* in decentralized networks (bottom-up) rather than being explicitly planned and rationally implemented (top-down).

For normative network analysis, which is the second principal concern of ACE researchers, we can use - as has been done in sections 4 and 5 - "computational laboratories within which alternative socioeconomic structures can be studied and tested with regard to their effects on individual behavior and social welfare" [Tesfatsion 2002]. Also, central to social network research, learning and the evolution of social norms are prevalent ACE research areas making this approach interesting for future research on various kinds of socioeconomic networks. Taking this into consideration, we can now formulate a requirements catalogue for an interdisciplinary theory of network effects.

6.3 Required modeling power of an interdisciplinary theory of network effects

After the critique of economic network effect theory and the neo-classical paradigm in general the question arises, which requirements have to be met by an *interdisciplinary* theory of network effects, allowing us to integrate and explain the *social* and *economic* interaction of *human* actors and *automated agents*.

6.3.1 Modeling of knowledge and uncertainty / bounded rationality

The network effect theory must allow for modeling knowledge of individual participants (human or automated) and uncertainty concerning this knowledge (in particular concerning the behavior and knowledge of other participants of the multi-agent system, we will call the "society" in the sequel).

6.3.2 Evolutionary system dynamics

However, since assuming bounded rationality usually implies the impossibility of determining analytical (ex ante) results for an aggregated entity - such as a whole network consisting of individually deciding agents - in terms of the existence and/or efficiency of equilibria, recourse to empirical and simulative approaches seems unavoidable.

While historic case arguments like the prominent QWERTY example (Liebowitz/Margolis 1990) or the battle for VCR standards (Liebowitz/Margolis 1994) proved to be at least ambiguous (section 2.3.7), numerical simulations based upon interacting software agents can help to get empirical evidence, since such complex systems giving up complete rationality renders the system of interactions "unsolvable" to an analytical determination of equilibria and proof of their uniqueness. Therefore we must rather rely on simulation of system dynamics and analysis of the observed behavior of the simulation model.

244

6.3.3   Emergence of system components and links

The approach should also be able to model the emergence of *new* participants and their "death" in the evolution process (to model for example the establishment or dissolution of institutional participants) as well as the emergence and dissolution of new links between existing actors, i.e. allow for an evolution of network structure.

6.3.4   Abolishment of convexity and divisibility assumptions

Since many of the decisions to be modeled will be *discrete* choices and exhibit interdependence with decisions made by other actors, convexity and divisibility assumptions are inadequate and thus have to be dropped (which is less problematic in a setting that has already given up all hope of analytical solvability).

6.3.5   Economics of intermediation

To overcome the lack of normative results from traditional models, a new approach to a theory of network effects should consider institutional designs for managing network related dependencies between individual network actors. In this context, the role of intermediaries needs to be emphasized. Generally speaking, intermediaries can compile and/or reallocate the information necessary for coordinating dependencies between actors. Considering the uncertainties inherent in novel technologies, intermediaries could contribute to solving the coordination problems associated with positive network effects. Quite contrary to the prominent hypothesis of disintermediation due to reduced transaction costs on markets, the benefits associated with IT such as decreasing communication and information processing costs appear to be available to intermediaries as well. Thus a new approach should integrate the analysis of intermediate coordination designs, essential data requirements and associated incentives problems for intermediaries to contribute to solving dependency issues problematic for markets.

7 Conclusions and further research

7.1 Summary of the findings

> "When I'm working on a problem, I never think about beauty.
> I think only how to solve the problem. But when I have finished,
> if the solution is not beautiful, I know it is wrong."
> *Buckminster Fuller*

Standardization problems are eminent in many areas. Especially in the context of information systems, the need for compatibility produces coordination problems. Network effect theory has emerged in recent years to explain the mechanisms behind standardization problems. Positive network effects as the underlying principle in communication networks describe interdependencies between agents in communication networks (e.g. intranet, electronic market place) as positive correlation between the utility derived from a good and the number of its users. Its general findings have been presented in section 2.2:

▸ In many cases, the existence of network effects leads to Pareto-inferior results in markets (i.e. unfavorable outcomes of decentralized standardization processes).

▸ Particularly, excess inertia can occur as no actor is willing to bear the overproportional risk of being the first adopter of a standard; thus, start-up problems prevent adoption even of superior products (lock-in, stranding). Also, excess momentum can occur, e.g. if a sponsoring firm uses low prices in early periods of diffusion to attract a critical mass of adopters.

▸ Positive network effects imply multiple equilibria and the (tippy) market will finally lock-in to a monopoly situation.

The externality property associated with network effects implies coordination problems that are not easily solvable by markets. Yet it is not clear if the "possession" of networks (i.e. sponsored networks) and the related possibility of sufficient individual incentives to develop and deploy internalization strategies (such as intertemporal pricing) can overcome the proposed market failure inefficiencies. In section 2.3 it was argued that traditional approaches addressing network effects offer great general insights to general problems concerning the diffusion of standards but they fail to explain the variety of diffusion courses in today's dynamic ICT markets, for example. The proposed rigor of the results from network effect literature is largely dependent upon assumptions not explicitly considered. Important determinants of network behavior and individual agents and networks such as agent size, decision sequence, network topology and individual heterogeneous network effects are responsible for weak explanatory powers and a lack of applicability to real world networks and standardization problems. The standardization framework developed in section 3 served as a first step towards incorporating some of these findings and offering decision support for practical standardization problems. Numerical simulations based on this allow a systematic analysis of network determinants. Two conceptual institutional settings (centralized and decentralized networks) were used to understand and disclose individual and aggregate mechanisms behind network agents' actions.

A fundamental finding in the game theoretical discussion of sections 3.2 and 3.3 as well as from the simulations in section 4 is the existence of a **standardization gap** quantifying the magnitude of the standardization problem (and at the same time determining the critical value for possible costs of coordination above which a centralized solution can no longer be advantageous). Overall, given decentralized coordination the frequency of standardization ceteris paribus increases with growing c_{ij} and decreases with rising K_i.

Using simulations, many of the phenomena identified in the literature on network effects could be supported. At the same time, though, it could be shown that these phenomena were often dependent on particular parameter constellations and can be described as special cases of the model at particular parameter constellations. Some forms of network instability could only be witnessed at comparatively high standardization costs; especially in a multi-standard scenario a significant influence of first movers showed the **path dependency** and **tippiness** property identified in sections 2.2.2 and 2.2.3, but that only accounted for rather high K. If agents can reconsider their decisions (reversible choice) a sudden decline in network efficiency could be seen for very low K. Five general diffusion patterns could be identified showing a possible dilemma: If standardization costs are (too) high, there is a start-up problem and if they are (too) low then there will be inefficient multi-standard equilibria.

Looking at the **individual consequences**, the kinds of wrong decisions made by agents in decentralized networks are quite promising with respect to possible solution strategies, since it appears that in many cases information intermediation can close a standardization gap without the necessity of heavy redistribution of costs and/or benefits which is regularly much more difficult. After all, the existence of externalities makes one expect exactly this: The implications of one's decision on those of the others cannot fully be considered. As in a neo-classical market with externalities, price has not enough dimensions to capture this information. Here, solution strategies such as the bidding mechanism proposed in section 5.5 try to improve the value of locally available information with respect to their connection to the entire system. Overall, initial deteriorations of the individual situation worsened with a growing number of alternative standards. At very low standardization costs, the increase of oligopolies imposed a negative influence on the standardization efficiency of a number of agents.

Building on the works of Wendt and Westarp an analysis of the influence of **network structure** showed a larger negative lag of the standardization gap in close topologies that is at the same time more gentle for high densities (agents start standardizing at lower V). While the overall findings of the basic model are the same, in multi-standard reversible choice scenarios we find a different distribution of the diffusion patterns at low K. While at high K closed and random topologies yield similar results, for low K monopoly rapidly replaces oligopoly in random topologies while oligopolies are more stable in closed topologies.

Looking at the prominent **installed base effects**, we found that an installed base can lessen the start-up problem but does not substantially shrivel the standardization gap. Accordingly, an installed base accelerates the equilibrium process: in monopoly ranges every 10% of a network pre-standardized reduce the process by 1 period. Still, almost no influence of an installed base on the distribution of the various equilibrium processes could be found. More precisely, especially with low standardization costs, the influence of installed base diminishes. It is interesting for discussing policy implications that the welfare effect is bigger when small agents are part of the installed base. Moreover, a monopoly standard does not have to have been part of the installed base, i.e. it is not always the first standard that wins the race.

One often unmentioned though important modeling aspect is the agents' **choice sequence**. Distinguishing different choice sequence scenarios network simulations showed these outcomes: with single choice, there are many oligopolies (low concentration) and a first mover can influence diffusion. Under reversible choice we mostly find efficient monopolies while „dynamic equilibria" and stable (individually disastrous) oligopolies can occur at very low standardization costs. In the special case of sequential choice as modeled in 4.2.3 and 4.3.3 we find high concentration regardless of standardization costs.

Empirical data (section 5.1) from various surveys showed that data needed for the standardization model is retrievable and helped in understanding real world standardization problems. **Solution designs** aimed at closing the standardization gap have been proposed (sections 5.3 - 5.6). In particular, a network ROI, an adapted Groves mechanism and the bidding mechanism have been developed and evaluated.

A **network ROI for a virtual principle** can provide valuable means of understanding and controlling particular standardization problems and propose a "fair" allocation of network costs and benefits. ROI-based compensations can establish a unique (Nash) standardization equilibrium that is Pareto-efficient as well as Kaldor-Hicks-efficient. Although fairness is a difficult concept, the model provides a rich ground for developing solutions suitable for particular standardization problems. Its practicability has already been shown using an elaborate case study.

A **Groves mechanism adapted to the standardization problem** has been developed in section 5.4 to ensure that agents tell the truth.

The **bidding mechanism** rests on the idea that agents use parts of their standardization gains to "bid" for others participating in a solution deemed favorable by the bidding agents. Although side payments might actually be executed, this mechanism works quite successfully due to its ability to reduce uncertainty because the bidding consists of communication between the agents concerning their standardization situation.

The systematic analysis of standardization problems and the underlying theory of network effects made possible the identification of determinants of network behavior and their interrelatedness in a way that should contribute to a limited extent to the explanation of networks.

7.2 Further research

> "The future is just as much a condition of the present as is the past.
> What shall be and must be is the ground of that which is"
> *Friedrich Nietzsche, Thus Spoke Zarathustra, 1883*

The standardization model has been developed and used to analyze fundamental phenomena in systems subject to network effects. Although it was possible to identify and explain many interesting phenomena in networks, the results highlight only a small fraction of all relevant phenomena. For further research, generalizations of the findings to explain general network behavior patterns that incorporate a wider variety of determinants appear to be valuable. Also, more empirical data is needed, among others to develop and evaluate strategies for corporate standardization decisions. Some areas of further research have already been discussed throughout the text. Generally, they include extensions and generalizations to the model, extending the framework to capture more aspects of real life standardization decisions and results from other disciplines, empirical research, and applications in terms of guiding managerial and policy decisions concerning standards or more generally networks. During the course of our research, the following research areas appeared to be of particular interest.

▸ *Further integration with the diffusion model and model extensions:* A first step towards broadening the scope of possible applications and the explanatory scope of the standardization model was the integration with the diffusion model. Extensions include the development of higher order anticipatory decision functions, among others incorporating more intertemporal aspects, additional information about the standards at choice, possibly hierarchical dependencies between standards or altering the anticipation of partner behavior according to their decision history. These aspects would allow the incorporation of the influence of vendor strategies (e.g. intertemporal pricing, marketing, bundling) and in turn the interplay with topology determinants such as centrality, group pressure or opinion leadership. An elaboration of the co-evolution of agents' expectations could be based on the interesting work on self-referential predictions about future choice of other network participants as presented in Arthur's (1995) model of an ecology of co-evolving expectations.

▸ *Negative and indirect network effects:* So far, only direct and positive network effects have been modeled. Strategically, this favors coordination games (section 3.2) and makes mutual coordination gains probable. Allowing negative effects would increase the probability of discoordination games. Besides snob effects, other reasons for negative network effects could be a loss of individuality [Thum 1995, 26] and an associated decline in relative competitive position. In their traditional understanding, indirect network effects could be modeled as a reduction of K determined by the total number of network participants: $K_i \rightarrow K_i - \alpha n$. Thum (1995, 26) notes a trade-off between heterogeneous consumer preferences favoring many different technologies and cost advantages of unification; see also Woeckener (1996).

▸ *Different technology qualities:* Although most contributions to the literature on network effects are concerned with worse quality standards being adopted, qualitywise the standardization model only considers substitutive standards: although they vary in price (distribution of K_{iq}) the quality is identical as standards always save information costs c_{ij}. The problems of evaluating quality aspects have been discussed and it is not yet clear if the internalization possibilities in sponsored networks are sufficient to avoid the proposed ubiquity of inefficiencies. Some empirical evidence has been presented by Liebowitz/Margolis (1999) that "there are good reasons to expect it to be very unusual for market participants knowingly to choose the wrong technology" (Liebowitz/Margolis 1999, 117]. Their analysis is based on hundreds of reviews of spreadsheets, word processors, desktop publishing programs, personal-finance software, browsers, and online services from leading computer and finance magazines. They find a strong positive correlation between market-share change and quality in all of the markets.

▸ *Physical and informational infrastructures:* Another important extension is the consideration of the relation between logical and physical network layers. In the context of the standardization model, this means that only those edges that coincide with a relation between two agents where there is an actual connection (e.g. a cable) available can take a positive value (i.e. have a cost savings potential). Or if there is none, agents could consider building one in order to reap more network benefits. Ultimately, this approach could extend the model to capture substitution relations between physical and informational infrastructures as well. Since informational logistics in contrast to physical goods logistics is considered to be characterized by the irrelevance of the costs of the reproduction of data, the question as to the optimum storage strategy and location of data arises. In computer science, the file allocation problem focuses on this aspect [Chu 1969; see Dowdy/Foster 1982 for an overview of approaches].

▸ *Solution strategies:* Better solution strategies can be developed and tested using and adapting the findings from larger parts of the literature on game theory, controlling and organization theory, option price theories, to name but a few. One approach could be using the model to analyze the influence of local coalitions in networks: similar to the network principal proposed in section 5.3, agents could make binding agreements with their most important (e.g. biggest c_{ij}) one, two, or more partners imitating centralized decision behavior within their individual clusters. If coordination costs increase with the number of partners forming the coalition, we can expect to find an optimum number of internalization partners. Empirical data concerning the cost development of the coordination costs compared to K_i, for example, could provide especially valuable assistance in evaluating coalitions as such. Standardization domains suitable for retrieving empirical data and for testing the results are, among others, EDI networks. In this context, "fair" mechanisms should be discussed again. No distribution or cost allocation is fair per se; rather they should meet certain requirements like those, for example, proposed by Shapley values. See Güth/Königstein/Kovács/Zala-Mező (2001, 100) for an experiment suggesting "that fairness concerns should be built into behavioral models of economic organizations". It appears a very promising area of further research to integrate and adapt findings from controlling theory to enhance network behavior. Among others, budgeting programs based upon residual earnings concepts to address agency problems under incomplete information as proposed by Ewert/Wagenhofer (1993, esp. 397-559) might offer particularly good starting points for designing mechanisms for networks.

▸ *Policies for network effect markets:* A question of predominant importance is the welfare implications associated with standards or IT infrastructures: do ICT markets need more regulation to help internalize network effects, and do they need antitrust policies different from those applied in more traditional industries? While many analytical models see a predominant danger of market failure (like excess inertia), others suggest that market inefficiencies provide sufficient incentives for producers. Accordingly Liebowitz/Margolis (1999, 228) "find no evidence of market inertia or tipping". Also, they find that monopolies might be efficient but not persistent thus an economy's efficient path can be from one monopoly to the next: *"Because bigger is better in increasing-returns industries, such industries tend to evolve into monopolies. Monopoly, however, does not lead inevitably to a bad economic outcome for society. [...] Sometimes an industry develops in such way, that monopoly is not only a likely outcome but also a desirable one. In such industries, what we are likely to witness is not conventional monopoly, but rather serial monopoly: one monopoly or near monopoly after another."* [Liebowitz/Margolis 1999, 10]. The standardization model served as a first step towards disclosing the influence of a variety of possible determinants that people have often failed to consider and which might be used to analyze equilibrium transitions with exogenous technology change by adding new and/or "better" technologies (lower K, higher c) to the simulations at different periods.

▸ *Empirical research*: Empirical data about information cost development over time and coordination costs of centralized coordination in particular are useful. Additionally, incorporating cost and benefit changes over time, for example resulting from vendor side pricing strategies, would enable the determination of the optimum standardization period and a better comparison with historic standardization cases.

▸ *Make network effects accountable*: Many corporate standardization problems result from an asymmetric distribution of costs and benefits between agents. In section 5, we have developed mechanisms to overcome this problem. Another approach is to change the underlying data: not only is there an asymmetry concerning the incentives available to the deciding agents but also an asymmetry between availability of cost and benefit data. Most internal and external accounting systems (which are used to model the "real" flow of financials) are cost-based and cannot comprise many benefit categories like network effects (or the associated opportunity costs when internalized) in particular. Thus, a rich area of research of high practical relevance is the adaptation and evaluation of cost accounting systems in order to enable the capture of network effects. This is also a way of developing mechanisms to control networks better. For example, introducing a fifth category "network effect" to a balanced scorecard could improve network clusters' controllability. Valuable findings could also be retrieved from the literature on managerial accounting or from modern controlling and capital markets theories that draw from agency theory or more generally from game theory [Ewert/Wagenhofer 1993, 2-6].

▸ *Endogenize information relations:* Eventually, an endogenization of the information relations between agents could help answer the question with what partners to have any relation at all. Thus, dynamic network infrastructures (changes of density, topology, participants, etc.) could be a research objective. An analysis of the influence of IT innovations on supplier relations has recently been presented by Weber (2000). Additionally, agents could consider building physical infrastructures to enable informational relations. This exchange relation between physical and informational infrastructures incorporating all relevant decision criteria on the level of an entire company and associated phenomena like the dynamic evolution of network topologies and the "birth" (e.g. new (intermediary) services) and "death" of participants and their relations has already been discussed as the underlying goal for a theory of networks.

Ultimately, a general theory of network effects (or a subsequent theory of networks) as proposed in section 6.2 will hopefully explain and guide theoretical, policy, and managerial considerations.

"For I am well aware that scarely a single point is discussed in this volume on which facts cannot be adduced, often apparently leading to conclusions directly opposite to those at which I have arrived. A fair result can be obtained only by fully stating and balancing the facts and arguments on both sides of each question; and this cannot possibly be here done."
Charles Darwin, "Introduction", Origin of Species (185)

Variables and symbols

$\mu(C)$	mean expected communication costs ($c\sim ND(c_{ij}\mid \mu, \sigma^2)$)
$\mu(K)$	mean expected standardization costs ($K\sim ND(K_i\mid \mu, \sigma^2)$)
$\sigma(C)$	deviation of communication costs ($c\sim ND(K_i\mid \mu, \sigma^2)$)
$\sigma(K)$	deviation of standardization costs ($K\sim ND(K_i\mid \mu, \sigma^2)$)
a_i	technology (or stand-alone) effect
A_{ij}	side payments paid by agent i to agent j
b_i	network effect in network effect literature ($\rightarrow b_i n$)
BG_i	bonus base of agent i in Groves mechanism; $BG_i=G_i-K_i$.
c_{ij}	communication costs of agent i's information relation to agent j that can be saved by bilateral standardization
$C_i^{X.500}$	short-term benefits of X.500 directory service (section 5.3.1)
$C_{User}^{X.500}$	time savings per user of X.500 directory service (section 5.3.1)
$C_{Admin}^{X.500}$	administration cost savings of X.500 directory service (section 5.3.1)
$C_{Print}^{X.500}$	printing cost savings of X.500 directory service (section 5.3.1)
$C_P^{X.500}$	product costs of X.500 directory service (section 5.3.1)
$C_{PS}^{X.500}$	costs of professional services of X.500 directory service (section 5.3.1)
e	edge of graph G ($e<ij>$ (directed) $e(ij)$ (not directed))
E_i	savings of agent i (individ. standardization benefits; *ex post* utility): $$E_i = \sum_{\substack{j=1 \\ j\neq i}}^{n} y_{ij}\cdot c_{ij} - \sum_{q=1}^{Q} x_{iq}\cdot K_{iq} \qquad s.t.: \sum_{q=1}^{Q} x_{iq} \leq 1$$
$E(s_{i\chi})$	expected value of agent i choosing strategy χ

E[U(i, q)]	expected utility from standardization *(ex ante* utility) $$E[U(i,q)] = \sum_{\substack{j=1 \\ j \neq i}}^{n} p_{ijq} \cdot c_{ij} - K_{iq} = \sum_{\substack{j=1 \\ j \neq i}}^{n} \left(\frac{c_{ji} \cdot n_j - K_{jq}}{c_{ji} \cdot n_j} \right) \cdot c_{ij} - K_{iq}$$
$E(G_i)$	expected benefits of agent i from resource in Groves mechanism
f	relative error occurrence (number of agents having made a wrong decision ex post relative to all agents; $f = f_{pos} + f_{neg}$)
f_i	bonus rate of agent i in Groves mechanism; $f_i > 0$ and $\sum_{i=1}^{n} f_i < 1$.
f_{neg}	relative error occurrence of agents standardizing and regretting afterwards
f_{pos}	relative error occurrence of agents not standardizing and regretting afterwards
G_i	benefits of agent i from using resource in Groves mechanism
GE	total network wide savings (i.e. the horizontal aggregation of all individuals' benefits): $GE = \sum_{i=1}^{n} E_i$
GE(dz)	total decentralized savings
GE(z)	total centralized savings
GEe	total savings in sequential choice model
GEi	total savings in simultaneous choice model
GK_i	Groves costs
HK	Herfindahl coefficient (concentration measure)
HKa	adapted Herfindahl coefficient
i	index of network agents; $i \in \{1,...,n\}$; $i \neq j$
j	index of agent's communication partner, $j \in \{1,...,n\}$; $i \neq j$
K_i, K_{iq}	standardization costs
K^H_i	agent with standardization costs higher than savings potentials
K^N_i	agent with cost savings exceeding standardization costs
m^A	matrix element in adjacency matrix
m^I	matrix element in incidency matrix

MU	monetary units
N	set N={1, .i, j, … , n} of nodes of graph
n	network size (number of network agents)
n_j	number of direct neighbors of j; $n_j \leq n-1$
$no\_stan(.)$	number of agents standardizing in centrally (z) or decentrally (dz) coordinated networks
p_{ij}, p_{ijq}	probability with which actor i believes that node j will standardize: $p_{ijq} = \dfrac{c_{ji} \cdot n_j - K_{jq}}{c_{ji} \cdot n_j}$ or for the 2nd degree neighborhood: $p_{ijq} = \dfrac{\sum_{k=1}^{n} x_{ijq} \cdot sign(c_{jk})}{n(j)}$
P_i	premium for agent in Groves mechanism; $P_i = f_i \cdot BG_i$
q	index of standards; $(q \in \{1,...,Q\})$
Q	total number of alternative standards
ROI_{DS}	return on investment (of directory services)
r(a,b)	Spearman's correlation coefficient between stochastic variables a and b
rc_{ij}	reported information cost saving in Groves mechanism
rG_i	reported benefits G_i
$rE(G_i)$	reported expected benefits G_i
s	number of standards of set Q with Q=(1, 2, …, q, … , s)
s(q)	number of agents having adopted standard q
$s_{i\chi}$	strategy χ of player i
size(i)	size of agent i (as his "communication weight"), $size(i) = \sum_{\substack{j=1 \\ j \neq i}}^{n} c_{ij}$
SPNE	subgame perfect Nash equilibrium
st_{ij}	punishment payments
T	total number of periods

t	index of period $t \in \{1,...,T\}$
$t_{stan}(i)$	period of agent i standardizing
t_{stat}	period of reaching stationary state
tr_{ij}	side payments
U_i	maximum possible benefit from standardization in bidding mechanism; utility of agent i derived from technology (or stand-alone) effect a_i and the network effect $b_i n$ in network effect literature
u_{ij}	edge utility in bidding mechanism (relative individual valuation of the communications relations to i)
V	network density ($0 < V \leq 1$)
$w(n)$	change frequency, measured as number of standards an agent has implemented (one after the other) until reaching t_{stat}
$w_i^{X.500}$	friction cost saving of X.500 directory services (section 5.3.1)
x_i, x_{iq}	binary action variable $\left\{ \begin{array}{l} \text{1 if agent i implements standard (q)} \\ \text{0 else} \end{array} \right.$
y_{ij}	binary variable $\left\{ \begin{array}{l} \text{0 if } x_i=1 \wedge x_j=1 \\ \text{1 else} \end{array} \right.$
Z_i	utility-based standardization rules in bidding mechanism

List of equations

258

List of figures

262

264

List of tables

266

References

Adler, J. (1996): Informationsökonomische Fundierung von Austauschprozessen, Wiesbaden 1996.

Agre, P. (1998): A graduate seminar on the economic, legal, and strategic aspects of technical compatibility standards, http://dlis.gseis.ucla.edu/people/pagre/standards.html.

Alstyne, M. van (1997): The state of network organization: a survey in three frameworks, in: Journal of Organizational Computing, 7(3) (1997).

Amann, E. (1999): Evolutionäre Spieltheorie: Grundlagen und neue Ansätze, Heidelberg 1999.

Arrow, K. (1970). The organization of economic activity: Issues pertinent to the choice of market versus non-market allocation, in: Haveman, R.H./Margolis, J. (eds.) (1970): Public Expenditures and Policy Analysis, Markham 1970, 59- 73.

Arthur, W.B. (1983): Competing technologies and lock-in by historical small events: the dynamics of allocation under increasing returns; International Institute for Applied Systems Analysis Paper WP-83-92, Laxenburg, Austria (Center for Economic Policy research, paper 43, Stanford).

Arthur, W.B. (1989): Competing technologies, increasing returns, and lock-in by historical events, in: The Economic Journal, 99 (March 1989), 116-131.

Arthur, W.B. (1994): Inductive reasoning and bounded rationality - the El Farol Problem, in: American Economic Review (papers and proceedings), 84, 406 (1994).

Arthur, W.B. (1995): Complexity in economic and financial markets, in: Complexity, 1 (1) (April 1995).

Arthur, W.B. (1996): Increasing returns and the new World of business, in: Harvard Business Review, 74 (July-August 1996), 100-109.

Aruka, Y. (2000): Avatamsaka Game Structure and It's Design of Experiment, in: Working Paper Series, The Institute of Business Research Chuo University, Tokyo 2000, http://arukalab.tamacc.chuo-u.ac.jp/Articles/Avatamsakarev.pdf.

Aumann, R. J/Hart. S. (eds.) (1994): Handbook of Game Theory, vol. 2, Amsterdam (Elsevier).

Bagnoli, M./Lipman, B. (1989): Provision of public goods: fully implementing the core through private contributions, in: Review of Economic Studies, 56, 583-602.

Bakos, Y./Brynjolfsson, E. (1999): Bundling Information Goods: Pricing, Profits and Efficiency, in: Management Science (December 1999), http://www.stern.nyu.edu/~bakos/big.pdf.

Balderston, F.E. (1958): Communication Networks in Intermediate Markets, in: Management Science, vol. 4, 154-171.

Baligh, H.H./Richartz, L.E. (1967): An Analysis of Vertical Market Structures, in: Management Science, vol. 10, 667-689.

Bashein, B.J./Markus, M.L./Riley, P. (1994): Preconditions for BPR Success, in: Information Systems Management 11(2), 1994, 7-13.

Beacon, M. (2000a): History of typing, http://www.mavisbeacon.com.

Beacon, M. (2000b): Seek and ye shall find, http://www.mavisbeacon.com/history_seek.html.

Beck, R./Weitzel, T./König, W. (2001): The Myth of WebEDI, in: Proceedings of IFIP I3E 2002, Lisbon, Kluwer 2002.

Beck, R./Weitzel, T./König, W. (2002): Promises and pitfalls of SME integration, in: Proceedings of 15th Bled Electronic Commerce Conference, e-Reality: Constructing the e-Economy; Bled, Slovenia.

Berg, S.V. (1989): The production of compatibility: Technical standards as collective goods, Kyklos 42, 1989, 361-383.

Berg, T./Kirwin, W./Redman, B. (1998): TCO: A Critical Tool for Managing IT, online: Gartner Group Inc., 12.10.1998.

270

Besen, S.M./Farrell, J. (1994): Choosing How to Compete: Strategies and Tactics in Standardization, in: Journal of Economic Perspectives, vol. 8 (1994), no. 2, 117-131.

Besen, S.M./Johnson, L.L. (1986): Compatibility Standards, Competition, and Innovation in the Broadcasting Industry, in: RAND Corporation R-3453-NSF, November 1986.

Biggart, N.W./Hamilton, G.G. (1993): On the Limits of a Firm-Based Theory to Explain Business Networks: The Western Bias of Neoclassical Economics, in: Nohria, N./Eccles, R.G. (eds.): Networks and Organizations, 1993, Harvard Business School Press: Boston, 471-491.

Bitsch, H./Martini, J./ Schmitt, H.J. (1995): Betriebswirtschaftliche Behandlung der Standardisierung und Normung, in: ZfbF vol. 47, 1995, 66-85.

Bosak, J. (2000): The Problem of Business Semantics, http://www-db.stanford.edu/dbseminar/speakers/jbosak/

Bossert, W./Stehling, F. (1990): Theorie kollektiver Entscheidungen, Berlin 1990.

Böventer, E.v./Illing, G. (1995): Einführung in die Mikroökonomie, 8. Auflage, München; Wien 1995.

Branscomb, L.M./Kahin, B. (1995): Standards processes and objectives for the National Information Infrastructure, in: Kahin, B./ Abbate, J. (eds.): Standards Policy for Information Infrastructure, Cambridge: MIT Press, 1995.

Braunstein, Y.M./White, L.J. (1985): Setting technical compatibility standards: An economic analysis, in: Antitrust Bulletin, vol. 30 (1985), 337-355.

Brownell, D. (1998): XML and Java Technology, An Interview with Dave Brownell, http://www.webpaulo.com/html/xml_and_java.html

Bundesumweltministerium (1998): Bundesumweltamt (Hrsg.): So geht's auch! Gasantrieb, Bonn 1998.

Butler Cox Foundation (1987): Elektronischer Datenaustausch – ein entscheidendes neues Anwendungsgebiet, Forschungsbericht 59, December 1987.

Buxmann, P. (1996): Standardisierung betrieblicher Informationssysteme, Wiesbaden 1996.

Buxmann, P./Weitzel, T./König, W. (1999): Auswirkung alternativer Koordinationsmechanismen auf die Auswahl von Kommunikationsstandards, in: ZfB (Zeitschrift für Betriebswirtschaft), Ergänzungsheft 02/99 Innovation und Absatz, 133-151.

Cabral, L.M. B./Leite, A.P.N. (1992): Network Consumption Externalities: The Case of Portugese Telex Service, in: Cristiano Antonelli (eds.): The Economics of Information Networks, Amsterdam 1992, 129-139.

Cabral, L.M.B. (1987): On the adoption of innovations with "network" externalities, Center for Economic Policy Research Technical Paper Number 97, Stanford University, May 1987.

Calaebresi, V.G.: (1968): Transaction costs, resource allocation and liability rules: a comment, in: Journal of Law and Economics 11, 67-74.

Callon, M. (1991): Techno-economic networks and irreversibility, in: Law, J. (ed.): A Sociology of Monsters: Essays on Power, Technology and Domination, London: Routledge, 1991.

Cargill, C. (1997): Open Systems Standardization: A business Approach, Prentice Hal, 1997.

Carlton, D.W./Klamer, J-M. (1983): The need for coordination among firms, with special reference to network industries, in: University of Chicago Law Review 50, 1983, 446-465.

Carrigan, R.A. (Jr.) (1978): Decimal time, in: American Scientist, vol. 66 (1978), no. 3, 305-313.

Ceci, S.J./Kain, E.L. (1982): Jumping on the bandwagon: The impact of attitude polls on polling behaviour, Public Opinion Quarterly, 46, 228-242.

Chou, D./Shy, O. (1990): Network Effects Without Network Externalities, in: International Journal of Industrial Organization, 8, 259-270.

Chu, W.W. (1969): Optimal file allocation in a minicomputer information system, in: IEEE Transactions on Computing, C-18 (1969), 885-889.

Church, J./Gandal, N. (1992): Network effects, software provision, and standardization, in: Journal of Industrial Economics 40, 85-103.

Clarke, E. (1971). Multipart pricing of public goods, in: Public Choice, 11, 17-33.

Coase, R. H. (1960). The problem of social cost, in: Journal of Law and Economics, 3, 1-44.

Coase, R.H. (1964): The regulated industries: discussion, in: American Economic Review 54, 194-197.

Coles, J.V. (1949): Standards and labels for consumers' goods, New York 1949.

Commons, J.R. (1931): Institutional Economics, in: American Economic Review, vol. 21 (1931), 648-657.

Cooper, R./DeJong, D.V./Forsythe, R./Ross, T.V. (1989): Communication in the battle of the sexes game: some empirical results, in: Rand Journal of Economics 20, 568-587.

Cooper, R./DeJong, D.V./Forsythe, R./Ross, T.V. (1992): Communication in co-ordination games, in: Quarterly Journal of Economics 107, 739-771.

Cowan, R. (1990): Nuclear Power Reactors: A study in technological lock-in, in: The Journal of Economic History, vol. L, no. 3 (Sept. 1990), 541-567.

Cowan, R. (1991): Tortoises and Hares: Choice Among Technologies of Unknown Merit, in: The Economic Journal, vol. 101, 801-814.

Crane, R. (1979): The Politics of International Standards, Norwood, N.J., 1979.

Curtis, C. (1996): EDI over the Internet: Let the games begin, in: Internetweek, Issue 627, September 9, 1996, http://www.techweb.com/se/directlink.cgi?CWK19960909S0076

Dahlman, C. (1979): The problem of externality, in: Journal of Law and Economics 22, 141-163.

David, P.A. (1985): Clio and the economics of QWERTY, American Economic Review, Papers and Proceedings, vol. 75, 332-337.

David, P.A. (1987): Some New Standards for the Economics of Standardization in the Information Age, in: Dasgupta, P./Stoneman, P. (eds.): Economic Policy and Technological Performance, Cambridge 1987.

David, P.A. (1995): Standardization policies for network technologies: The flux between freedom and order revisited, in: Hawkins, R./Mansell, R./Skea, J. (eds.): Standards, Innovation and Competitiveness: The Politics and

Economics of Standards in Natural and Technical Environments, Edward Elgar, 1995.

David, P.A../Bunn, J.A. (1988): The economics of gateway technologies and network evolution: Lessons from electricity supply history, in: Informational Economics and policy, vol. 3, no. 2, 165-202.

David, P.A./Greenstein, S. (1990): The economics of compatibility standards: An introduction to recent research, in: Economics of innovation and new technology, 1, 3-41, 1990.

David, P.A./Shurmer, M. (1996): Formal Standards Setting: Towards Institutional Renovation or Collapse, in: Telecommunications Policy, vol. 20 (10), 789-815.

David, P.A./Steinmueller, W.E. (1996): Standards, trade and competition in the emerging Global Information Infrastructure environment, in: Telecommunications Policy 20(10), 1996, 817-830.

Dedig (1998): Einstieg in den Elektronischen Geschäftsverkehr - Internet, EDI und UN/EDIFACT, DEDIG Deutsche EDI-Gesellschaft e. V., 1998.

Densmore, B. (1998): EDI vs. The new kids, in: Computerworld, April 6, 1998, http://www.computerworld.com/home/Emmerce.nsf/All/980406edi.

Deutsch, M. (1994): Unternehmenserfolg mit EDI: Strategie und Realisierung des elektronischen Datenaustausches, Braunschweig 1994.

Dhebar, A./Oren, S.S. (1985): Optimal dynamic pricing for expanding networks, in: Marketing Science 4 (4), 336-351.

Dhebar, A./Oren, S.S. (1986): Dynamic nonlinear pricing in networks with interdependent demand, in: Operations Research 34 (3), 384-394.

DIN (1991), En 45020: Allgemeine Fachausdrücke und deren Definitionen betreffend Normung und damit zusammenhängende Tätigkeiten, August 1991, 15.

Dixit, A./Nalebuff, B. J. (1995): Spieltheorie für Einsteiger (Thinking Strategically. The Competitive Edge in Business, Politics, and Everyday Life). Deutsche Übersetzung der 1. Auflage von Christian Schütte, Stuttgart, 1995.

274

Domschke, W./Mayer, G./Wagner, B. (2001): Effiziente Vorgehensweisen zur Lösung von Standardisierungsproblemen. Arbeitspapier Fachgebiet Operations Reserach, TU Darmstadt.

Domschke, W./Mayer, G./Wagner, B. (2002): Effiziente Modellierung von Entscheidungsproblemen: Das Beispiel des Standardisierungsproblems, forthcoming in: Zeitschrift für betriebswirtschaftliche Forschung, August 2002.

Dosi, G. et al. (ed.) 1988: Technical Change And Economic Theory, London 1988.

Dowdy, L.W./Foster, D.V. (1982): Comparative Models of the File Assignment Problem, in: Computing Surveys 14 (1982), 287-313.

Drake, W.J. (1993): The Internet religious war, in: Telecommunications Policy 17 (9), 1993, 643-649.

Dybvig, P.H./Spatt C.H. (1983): Adaption externalities as public goods, in: Journal of Public Economics, vol. 20 (1983), 231-247.

Eccles, R.G./Crane, D.B. (1987): Managing through networks in investment banking, in: California Management Review 1987, 30 (1), 176-195.

Economides, N. (2000): An interactive bibliography on the economics of networks and related subjects, http://www.stern.nyu.edu/networks/biblio.html.

Economides, N./Himmelberg, C. (1995): Critical Mass and Network Size with Application to the US FAX Market, Discussion Paper EC-95-11, Stern School of Business, New York University.

Economides, N./White, L. (1993): One-Way Networks, Two-Way Networks, Compatibility, and Antitrust, in: discussion paper EC-93-14, Stern School of Business, http://www.stern.nyu.edu/networks/93-14.pdf.

Eichler, B. (1998): Informations- und Vermittlungsdienste in offenen verteilten Systemen. Wien 1998.

Einhorn, M. (1992): Mix and match compatibility with vertical product dimensions, in: RAND Journal of Economics, Winter 1992, 23, 535-547.

Ellis H.S./Fellner, W. (1943): External economies and diseconomies, in: American Economic Review 33, 493-511.

Emigh, J. (2001): Total Cost of Ownership, online: Computerworld: http://www.computerworld.com/cwi/story/0,1199,NAV47_STO42717,00 .html.

Emmelhainz, M.A. (1993): EDI: A Total Management Guide, 2nd edition, New York 1993.

EMSS (1999): The Evolutionary Models in Social Science (EMSS) Web Bibliography, http://users.ox.ac.uk/~econec/economics.html.

Esser, J. (1999): Institutionalistische Forschungsansätze als mögliche Basis einer interdisziplinären theoretischen Vereinheitlichung des SFB "Vernetzung als Wettbewerbsfaktor am Beispiel der Region Rhein-Main", SFB Arbeitsbericht 99-43.

Ewert, R./Wagenhofer, A. (1993): Interne Unternehmensrechnung, Berlin 1993.

Farrell, J. (1987): Cheap Talk, Coordination and Entry, in: Rand Journal of Economics, 18 (1987), 34-39.

Farrell, J. (1989): Standardization and intellectual property, in: Jurimetrics Journal 30 (1), 1989, 35-50.

Farrell, J./Saloner, G. (1985): Standardization, Compatibility, and Innovation, in: Rand Journal of Economics 16, 1985, 70-83.

Farrell, J./Saloner, G. (1986): Installed Base and Compatibility: Innovation, Product Preannouncements, and Predation, in: The American Economic Review, vol. 76, no. 5 (December 1986), 940-955.

Farrell, J./Saloner, G. (1987): Competition, compatibility, and standards: The economics of horses, penguins, and lemmings, in: Gabel H. Landis (ed.): Product standardization and competitive strategy, Amsterdam 1987, 1-21.

Farrell, J./Saloner, G. (1988): Coordination through committees and markets, in: RAND Journal of Economics, Vol. 19, No. 2 (Summer 1988), 235-252.

Farrell, J./Saloner, G. (1992): Converters, Compatibility, and Control of Interfaces, in: Journal of Industrial Economics, 40 (1), 9-35.

Feess, E. (2000): Mikroökonomie - Eine spieltheoretisch- und anwendungsorientierte Einführung, 2. Auflage, Marburg 2000.

276

Ferguson, C./Morris, C. (1993): Computer wars, New York 1993.

Ferris (1998a): Enterprise Directory Case Studies. In: Ferris Research: Report ID 19981104RP, November 1998 – Governement of Canada.

Ferris (1998b): Enterprise Directory Case Studies, in: Ferris Research: Report ID 1998110 RP, November 1998.

Fisher, F.M./McGowan, J.J./Greenwood, J.E. (1993): Folded, Spindled, and Mutilated: Economic Analysis and U.S. Vs. IBM, 1993.

Franke, G./Hax, H. (1995): Finanzwirtschaft des Unternehmens und Kapitalmarkt, 3. Auflage, Berlin; Heidelberg; New York 1995.

Fronefield, L. (2000): B2B: The Bigger Wave, in: The Internet Stock Report, 21.02.2000,http://www.internetstockreport.com/reporter/article/0,1785,246631,00.html

Fudenberg, D./Tirole, J (1983): Learning by doing and market performance, in: Bell Journal of economics, vol. 14 (1983), 522-530.

Fudenberg, D./Tirole, J (1986): A Theory of Exit in Duopoly, in: Econometrica, vol. 54 (1986), 943-960.

Fudenberg, D./Tirole, J. (1995): Game Theory, 4. print., Cambridge, Massachusetts et al. 1995.

Fumy, W. (1995): Standards und Patente zur IT-Sicherheit, München 1995.

Gabel, H.L. (1987): Product Standardization and Competitive Strategy, Amsterdam 1987.

Gabel, H.L. (1991): Competitive Strategies for Product Standards, London 1991.

Gaillard, J. (1934): Industrial standardization - its principles and applications, New York 1934.

Gallaugher, J. M./Wang, Y. (1999): Network effects and the impact of free goods: an analysis of the web server market, in: International Journal of Eletronic Commerce 3 (4), 67-88.

Gandal, N. (1994): Hedonic price indexes for spreadsheets and empirical test for network-externalities, in: Rand Journal of Economics, vol. 25 (1994), no. 1, 160-170.

Gandal, N. (1995): A Selective Survey of the Literature on Indirect Network Externalities, in: Research in Law and Economics (17) 1995, 23-31.

Gartner (2000): GartnerGroup Says Business-to-Business E-Commerce Transactions Becoming More Global – GartnerGroup Forecasts Regional B2B Outlook through 2004, http://gartner5.gartnerweb.com/public/static/aboutgg/pressrel/pr021600.html

Gerwin, J./Höcherl, I. (1995): Video 2000: Strategische Produktpolitik bei internationalem Wettbewerb, in: Brockhoff, Klaus (Hrsg.): Management von Innovationen: Planung und Durchsetzung; Erfolge und Misserfolge, Wiesbaden 1995, 17-44, 217-244.

Giddens, A. (1988): Die Konstitution der Gesellschaft. Grundzüge einer Theorie der Strukturierung, Frankfurt a. M./New York 1988.

Glanz, A. (1993): Ökonomie von Standards: Wettbewerbsaspekte von Kompatibilitäts-Standards dargestellt am Beispiel der Computerindustrie, Frankfurt am Main 1993.

Gleick, J. (1987): Chaos: making a new science, New York 1987.

Glushko, R./Tenenbaum, J./Meltzer, B. (1999): An XML Framework for Agent-based E-commerce, in: Communications of the ACM, vol. 42, No. 3 (March 1999), 106-114.

Goldman, Sachs & Co (1999): B2B: 2B Or Not 2B?, in: InternetNews, September 17, 1999, http://www.internetnews.com/ec-news/article/0,1087,4_2071 21,00.html.

Gonyeau, J. (2000): Virtual Nuclear Tourist, http://www.cannon.net/~gonyeau/nuclear/index.htm.

Granovetter, M. (1985): Economic Action and Social Structure: The Problem of Embeddedness, in: American Journal of Sociology 91, 481-510.

Granovetter, M. (1993): Problems of Explanation in Economic Sociology, in: Nohria, N./Eccles, R.G. (eds.): Networks and Organizations, 1993, Harvard Business School Press: Boston, 471-491.

Granovetter, M./Swedberg, R. (1992) (eds.): The Sociology of Economic Life, Boulder, Colorado 1992.

Gröhn, A. (1999): Netzeffekte und Wettbewerbspolitik. Eine ökonomische Analyse des Softwaremarktes, Kieler Studien 296, Tübingen.

Groves, T. (1973): Incentives in teams, in: Econometria 1973, 617-631.

Groves, T. (1976). Information, incentives, and the internalization of production externalities, in: Lin, S. (ed.): Theory and Measurement of Economic Externalities, New York 1976.

Groves, T. (1979): Efficient collective choice when compensation is possible, in: Review of Economic Studies, 46, 227-241.

Groves, T./Ledyard, J. (1977): Optimal allocations of public goods: A solution to the 'free rider problem', in: Econometrica, 45, 783-809.

Groves, T./Loeb, M. (1979): Incentives in a divisionalized firm, in: Management Science 1979, 221-230.

Güth, W. (1999): Spieltheorie und ökonomische (Bei)Spiele, Berlin; Heidelberg; New York 1999.

Güth, W./Königstein, M./Kovács, J./Zala-Mezõ, E. (2001): Fairness within firms: The case of one principal and multiple agents, in: Schmalenbach Business review, vol. 53 (April 2001), 82-101.

Habermeier, K.F. (1989): Competing technologies, the learning curve, and rational expectations, in: European Economic Review 33 (1989), 1293-1311.

Haitz, U. (1994): Integration unternehmensinterner und –externer Informationsströme auf Basis einer Standardisierten Kommunikationsinfrastruktur, Inauguraldissertation, Mannheim 1994.

Hall, P./Taylor, R. (1996): Political Science and the three Institutionalisms, in: Political Studies, vol. 44, no. 5, Dec. 1996, 936-957.

Hanseth, O/Monteiro, E./Hatling, M. (1996): Developing information infrastructure: The tension between standardization and flexibility, in: Science, Technology, and Human Values 21(4) (1996), 407-426.

Hanson, W. (1985): Bandwagons and orphans: dynamic pricing of competing systems subject to decreasing costs, Ph. D. Dissertation, Stanford 1985.

Harsanyi, J.C. (1967-68): "Games with incomplete information played by 'Bayesian' Players, part I: The basic model, part II: Bayesian equilibrium points, parts III: The basic probability distribution of the game", in: Management Science, vol. 14, 159-182, 320-334, 486-502.

Hartmann, R.S./Teece, D.J. (1990): Product emulation strategies in the presence of reputation effects and network externalities: some evidence from the minicomputer industry, in: Economics of innovation and new technology, vol. 1-2, 157-182.

Hayashi, K. (1992): From network externalities to interconnection: the changing nature of networks and economy, in: Antonelli, C. (1992) (ed.): The economics of information networks, Amsterdam, 195-216.

Hayek, F.A. (1937): Economics and Knowledge, in: Economica, 4 (1937), 33-54.

Hayek, F.A. (1994): Rechtsordnung und Handelnsordnung, in: ders., Freiburger Studien, Tübingen 1994.

Hein, M. (1998): TCP/IP, 4. Auflage, Bonn 1998.

Heinzl, A. (1996): Die Evolution der betrieblichen DV-Abteilung, Berlin 1996.

Hemenway, D. (1975): Industry wide voluntary product standards, Massachusetts 1975.

Herges, S./ Wild, M. (2000): Total Cost of Ownership (TCO) – Ein Überblick, in: Arbeitspapiere WI, Nr. 1/2000, Lehrstuhl für Allg. BWL und Wirtschaftsinformatik, Johann Gutenberg-Universität Mainz 2000.

Hildenbrand, W./Kirman, A.P. (1976): Introduction to equilibrium analysis, North-Holland, Amsterdam, 1976.

Hodgson, G.M. (1988): Economics and Institutions, Cambridge 1988.

Hodgson, G.M. (1993) (ed.): The Economics of Institutions, Hants (Edward Elgar Publishing) 1993.

Hodgson, G.M. (1996): Varieties of Capitalism and Varieties of Economic Theory, in: Review of international political economy, vol. 3, no.3, Autumn 1996.

Holler, M./Illing, G. (2000): Einführung in die Spieltheorie, 4. Auflage, Berlin; Heidelberg; New York 2000.

Horvath, P. (1988).: Controlling und Informationsmanagement. In: HMD (1988) Heft 142, 36-45.

Hummel, J. (2000): Die Grundlagen der digitalen Ökonomie - eine Analyse aus Sicht der Neuen Institutionenökonomie, mcminstitute Report 2000-02.

Hurwicz, L. (1979): Outcome functions yielding Walrasian and Lindahl allocations at Nash equilibrium points, in: Review of Economic Studies, 46, 217-225.

ISO (1988): ISO/IEC 88 - International Standard Organization/International Electrotechn. Commission: Information processing systems – Open System Interconnection – The Directory, Draft International Standard ISO/IEC DIS 9594, 1988.

Jackson, M./Moulin, H. (1992): Implementing a public project and distributing its cost, in: Journal of Economic Theory, 57, 125-140.

Jakobs, K. (2000): Standardization Processes in IT – Impact, Problems and Benefits of User Participation, Lengerich 2000.

Jakobs, K./Procter, R./Williams, R. (1996): Users and standardization: Worlds apart? The example of electronic mail, in: StandardView 4(4), 1996, 183-191.

Jonas, C. (1992): Datenfernübertragung mit Personal-Computern, Würzburg 1992.

Kaplan, R.S. (1984): The evolution of management accounting, in: The accounting review 1984, 390-418.

Kargl, H. (2000): Management und Controlling von IV- Projekten, München 2000.

Katz, M. L./Shapiro, C. (1985): Network externalities, competition, and compatibility, in: The American Economic Review, vol. 75, no. 3 (June 1985), 424-440.

Katz, M. L./Shapiro, C. (1986): Technology adoption in the presence of network externalities. in: Journal of Political Economy, vol. 94 (1986), no. 4, 822-841.

Katz, M. L./Shapiro, C. (1992): Product Introduction with Network Externalities, in: Journal of Industrial Economics, 40 (1) (1992), 55-83.

Katz, M. L./Shapiro, C. (1994): Systems Competition and Network Effects, Journal of Economic Perspectives, Spring 1994, 8, 93-115.

Kelly, J. S. (1978): Arrow impossibility theorems, New York 1978.

Kettani, O./Oral, M. (1990): Equivalent Formulations of Nonlinear Integer Problems for Efficient Optimization, in: Management Science 36 (1), 115-119.

Kilian, W./Picot, A./Neuburger, R./Niggl, J./Scholtes, K.-L./Seiler, W. (1994): Electronic Data Interchange, Baden-Baden 1994.

Kimberley, P. (1991): Electronic Data Interchange, New York 1991.

Kindleberger, C. P. (1983): Standards as Public, Collective and Private Goods. Kyklos - International Review for Social Sciences, 36(3), 377-396.

Kleinaltenkamp, M. (1990): Der Einfluß der Normung und Standardisierung auf die Diffusion technischer Innovationen, working paper SFB 187, Ruhr-Universität Bochum, 1990.

Kleinaltenkamp, M. (1993): Standardisierung und Marktprozeß – Entwicklungen und Auswirkungen im CIM-Bereich, Wiesbaden 1993.

Kleinemeyer, J. (1998): Standardisierung zwischen Kooperation und Wettbewerb, Frankfurt 1998.

Knieps, G./Müller, J./Weizsäcker, C.C.v. (1982): Telecommunications policy in West Germany and challenges from technical and market development, in: Zeitschrift für Nationalökonomie (Supplement) 2, 205-222.

Knight, F.H. (1924): Some fallacies in the interpretation of social cost. Quarterly Journal of Economics 38: 582-606.

Konrad, K.A./Thum, M (1993): Fundamental standards and time consistency, in: KYKLOS, vol. 46 (1993), Fasc. 4, 545-568.

Konstroffer, M. (2001): Solving Planning Problems with Noisy Objective Functions - A Comparison of Genetic Algorithms, Simulated Annealing, and Tabu Search, and the Effect of Noise on their Performance, dissertation, Frankfurt 2001.

Krcmar, H. (ed.) (2000): IV-Controlling auf dem Prüfstand: Konzept - Benchmarking – Erfahrungsberichte, Wiesbaden 2000.

Krislov, S. (1997): How Nations Choose Product Standards and Standards Change Nations, Pittsburgh 1997.

Langlois, R.N./Robertson, P.L. (1992): Networks and innovation in a modular system: Lessons from the microcomputer and stereo component industries, in: Research Policy 21(4), 1992, 297-313.

Laux, H. (1995): Entscheidungstheorie 1, Grundlagen, 3. Auflage, Berlin 1995.

Lehr, W. (1995): Compatibility standards and interoperability: Lessons from the Internet, in: Kahin, B./Abbate, J. (eds.): Standards Policy for Information Infrastructure, Cambridge: MIT Press, 1995.

Leibenstein, H. (1950): Bandwagon, snob, and Veblen effects in the theory of consumers demand, in: Quarterly Journal of Economics, 64 (2), 183-207.

Lemley, M.A. (1996): Antitrust and the Internet standardization problem, in: Connecticut Law Review 28, 1996, 1041-1094.

Lewis, J./Blum, D./Rowe, G. (1999): The Enterprise Directory Value Proposition, in: The Burton Group: Network Strategy Overview, 23.02.1999.

Liebowitz, S.J./Margolis, S.E. (1990): The fable of the keys, Journal of Law and Economics, vol. 33, 1990, 1 - 25.

Liebowitz, S.J./Margolis, S.E. (1994): Network Externality: An Uncommon Tragedy, in: The Journal of Economic Perspectives, Spring 1994, 133-150.

Liebowitz, S.J./Margolis, S.E. (1995a): Are Network Externalities A New Source of Market Failure? In: Research in Law and Economics, 1995.

Liebowitz, S.J./Margolis, S.E. (1995b): Path Dependence, Lock-In, and History, in: Journal of Law, Economics and Organization, April 1995, 11, 205-226.

Liebowitz, S.J./Margolis, S.E. (1996): Should technology choice be a concern of antitrust policy?, in: Harvard Journal of Law and Technology 9(2), 1996, 283-318.

Liebowitz, S.J./Margolis, S.E. (1998): Path Dependence, in: The New Palgraves Dictionary of Economics and the Law, 1998, http://wwwpub.utdallas.edu/~liebowit/palgrave/palpd.html

Liebowitz, S.J./Margolis, S.E. (1999): Winners, Losers & Microsoft, Oakland 1999.

Lipsey, R.G. (1989): An introduction to positive economics, 7th ed., London 1989.

Luce, R.D./Raiffa, H. (1957): Games and Decicions, New York, 1957.

Malone, T.W./Crowston, K. (1994): The Interdisciplinary Study of Coordination, in: ACM Computing Surveys, 26 (1) (March 1994), 87-119.

Malone, T.W./Yates, J./Benjamin, R.I. (1987); Electronic Markets and Electronic Hierarchies, in: Communications of the ACM, vol. 30 no. 6 (June 1987) , 484-496.

Marcella, A.J./Chan, S. (1993): EDI Security, Control, and Audit, Norwood 1993.

Martin, S. (1994): Industrial Economics. Economic Analysis and Public Policy, 2nd edition, Englewood Cliffs 1994.

Matutes, C./Regibeau, P. (1988): Mix and Match: Product compatibility without network externalites, in: RAND Journal of Economics, 19 (Summer 1988), 221-234.

Matutes, C./Regibeau, P. (1996) A selective review of the economics of standardization, Europe, in: Journal of Political Economy, vol. 12, 1996, 183-209.

Mauboussin, M.J./Schay, A./Kawaja, S.G. (2000): Network to Net Worth, The Rising Rolke of the Replacement Cycle, Credit Suisse First Boston, Equity Research, Frontiers of Finance, vol. 5 (May 11, 2000), http://www.capatcolumbia.com/Articles/FoStrategy/Ni1924.pdf.

Mayer, E./Liessmann, K./Freidank (eds.): Controlling-Konzepte, Werkzeuge und Strategien für die Zukunft, 4. erw. Aufl., Wiesbaden 1999.

284

McKelvey, R.D. (1996): Computation of Equilibria in finite games, Minneapolist, Minnesota, 1996.

Meffert, J.P.H. (1994): Standards als Integrationsinstrument in der Computer- und Kommunikationsindustrie: wettbewerbsstrategische Bedeutung und Durchsetzung, Konstanz 1994.

Mertens, P./Knolmayer, G. (1998): Organisation der Informationsverarbeitung, 3rd edition, Wiesbaden 1998.

Meyer zu Nautrup, U. (1991): Aspekte des Datenschutzes im X.500-Verzeichnisdienst, Technischer Bericht 1991/4, TU Berlin 1991.

Mintzberg, H. (1979): The Structuring of Organizations, Englewood Cliffs 1979.

Mirchandani, P.B./Francis, R.L. (1990): Discrete location theory, New York 1990.

Moch, D. (1995): Ein hedonischer Preisindex für PC-Datenbanksoftware: Eine empirische Untersuchung, in: Harhoff, D./Müller, M. (Hrsg.): Preismessung und technischer Fortschritt, Baden Baden.

Mokyr, J. (1991): Evolutionary biology, technological change and economic history, in: Bulletin of Economic Research, 43, 127-147.

Müller-Merbach, H. (1973): Operations Research: Methoden und Modelle der Optimalplanung, 3. Auflage, München 1973.

Mycielsky. J. (1992): Games with Perfect Information, in: Aumann, R./Hart, S.: Handbook of Game Theory, Volume 1, Amsterdam 1992.

Nelson, R. (ed.) 1993: National Systems of Innovation, New York/Oxford 1993.

Neuburger, R. (1994): Electronic Data Interchange: Einsatzmöglichkeiten und ökonomische Auswirkungen, München 1994.

Neumann, J.v./Morgenstern, O. (1967): Spieltheorie und wirtschaftliches Verhalten (Theory of Games and Economic Behavior). Deutsche Übersetzung der 3. Auflage von M. Leppig, Würzburg 1967.

Neumann, K. (1991): Graphen und Netzwerke, in: Gal, Thomas (Hrsg.): Grundlagen des Operations Research, Bd. 2, 3. Auflage, Berlin, 1991, S. 3-164.

Neumann, K./Morlock, M. (1993): Operations Research, München, Wien 1993.

Niggl, J. (1994): Die Entstehung von Electronic Data Interchange Standards, Wiesbaden 1994.

North, D. (1990): Institutions, Institutional Change And Economic Performance, Cambridge 1990.

OAG (1999): White Paper – Plug and Play Business Software Integration, ftp://ftp.openapplications.org/openapplications.org/whtpaper.zip

Oren, S.S./Smith, S.A. (1981): Critical Mass and Tariff Structure in Electronic Communications Markets, Bell Journal of Economics, Autumn 1981, 12, 467-87.

Oren, S.S./Smith, S.A./Wilson, R. (1982): Nonlinear pricing in markets with interdependent demand., in: Marketing Science 1(3), 287-313.

Parfett, M. (1992): What is EDI? A guide to Electronic Data Interchange, 2nd Edition NCC Blackwell 1992.

Perine, L.A. (1995): In pursuit of an optimum: A conceptual model for examining public sector policy support of interoperability, http://nii.nist.gov/pubs/optimum.html.

Perry, J. (1955): Story of standards, New York 1955.

Peters, G. (1999): Institutional Theory in Political Science, London 1999.

Pfeiffer, G. (1989): Kompatibilität und Markt: Ansätze zu einer ökonomischen Theorie der Standardisierung, Baden-Baden 1989.

Picot, A. (1991): Ein neuer Ansatz zur Gestaltung der Leistungstiefe, in: ZfbF, 43 (4), 336-357.

Picot, A. (2000): "Die Bedeutung von Standards in der Internet-Ökonomie – Selbstorganisation ersetzt den hoheitlichen Akt", in: Frankfurter Allgemeine Zeitung (FAZ), 16.11.2000, 30.

Picot, A./Neuburger, R./Niggl, J. (1993): Electronic Data Interchange (EDI) und Lean Management, in: Zeitschrift für Führung und Organisation, Nr. 1/1993, S. 20-25.

Pietsch, T. (1999): Bewertung von Informations- und Kommunikationssystemen: Ein Vergleich betriebswirtschaftlicher Verfahren, Berlin 1999.

Pigou, A.C. (1920). The Economics of Welfare. Macmillan, London.

Plummer, A. (1937): New British Industries in the Twentieth Century, London 1937.

Polanyi, K. (1944): The Great Transformation, Boston 1944.

Poole, K.T. (1997): Entrepreneurs and Path Dependence, http://k7moa.gsia.cmu.edu/entrepd.htm.

Porter M.A. (1980): Competitive Strategy, New York 1980.

Powel, W./DiMaggio, P. (1991) (eds.): The New Institutionalism in Organizational Analysis, Chicago 1991.

Powell, W. (1990): Neither Market Nor Hierarchy: Network Forms of Organization, in: Research in Organizational Behavior, 1990. 12: p. 295-336.

Radicati, S. (1997): Directory Services – Measuring ROI, in: Radicati Report: vol. 6, no.9, September 1997.

Radner, R. (1992): Hierarchy: The economics of managing, in: Journal of economic literature, 30, 1382-1415.

Rajagopalachari, C. (1949): Inaugural address at Conference on standardization and quality control (February 1948 in Calcutta), in: ISI Bulletin, vol. 1 (1949), 8-14.

Reece, J.S./Cool, W.R. (1978): Measuring investment center performance, in: Harvard Business Review, 1978, also in: A. Rappaport (ed.): Information for decision making, Englewood Cliffs 1982, 264-277.

Regibeau, P. (1995): Defending the Concept of Network Externalities: A Discussion of Liebowitz andMargolis, in: Research in Law and Economics 33 (1995).

Rieck, C. (1993): Spieltheorie: Einführung für Wirtschafts- und Sozialwissenschaftler, Wiesbaden 1993.

Riepl, L. (1998): TCO versus ROI, in: Information Management, 2/1998.

Roever, Andreas (1996): Negative Netzwerkexternalitäten als Ursache ineffizienter Produktwahl, in: Jahrbuch für Nationalökonomie und Statistik, Nr. 251 (1996), 14-32.

Rohlfs, J. (1974): A theory of interdependent demand for a communications service, in: Bell Journal of Economics 5(1), 1974, 16-37.

Rosenberg, N. (1982): Technological interdependence in the American economy, in: Inside the Black Box: Technology and Economics, Cambridge: Cambridge University Press, 1982.

Rosenbloom, R.S./Cusumano, M.A. (1987): Technological pioneering and competitive advantage: the birth of the VCR industry", in: California Management Review 29, 51-76.

Sakurai, M. (1989): Target costing and how to use it, in: Journal of cost management, summer 1989, 39-50.

Saloner, G. (1990): Economic Issues in Computer Interface Standardization: the Case of UNIX, in: Economics of Innovation and New Technology, vol. 1, 135-156.

Schär, J. F. (1923): Allgemeine Handelsbetriebslehre, Leipzig 1923.

Schmidt, K. (1995): Globaler Verzeichnisdienst nach X.500, in: Connection, April 1995, no. 3.

Schmidt, R.H./Terberger, E. (1997): Grundzüge der Investitions- und Finanzierungstheorie, 4. Auflage, Wiesbaden 1997.

Schober, F. (1994): Modellgestützte Kapazitäts- und Konfigurationsplanung für ein Bürokommunikationssystem, in: Informatik Forschung und Entwicklung (1994) 9, 1-8.

Schrijver, A. (1986): Theory of Linear and Integer Programming, New York 1986.

Schumann, M. (1990): Abschätzung von Nutzeffekten zwischenbetrieblicher Informationsverarbeitung, in: Wirtschaftsinformatik 32 (1990), 307-319.

Segev, A./Porra, J./Roldan, M. (1997): Internet-Based EDI Strategy, working paper 97-WP-1021, Fisher Center of Management and Information Technology, University of California Berkeley, http://haas.berkeley.edu/~citm/wp-1021.pdf.

SFB (2000): Vernetzung als Wettbewerbsfaktor am Beispiel der region Rhein-Main: Finanzierungsantrag des Sonderforschungsbereiches 403.

Shapiro, C./Varian, H. R. (1998): Information rules: A strategic guide to network economy, Boston, Massachusetts.

Siemens (1999): Arbeitsplatz-basiertes Client/Server-Preismodell für DirX, DirXweb, DirXdiscover. In: Preisliste für DirX Produkte der Siemens AG, München, 1. 2. 1999.

Silver, M. (Gartner Group) (1997): Directory Services: Who needs them? Gartnerweb, 25.04.1997.

Simon, H.A. (1981): Entscheidungsverhalten in Organsiationen ("Administrative Behaviour"), Landsberg 1981.

Sirbu, M.A./Zwimpfer, L.E. (1985): Standards setting for computer communication: The case of X.25, in: IEEE Communications Magazine 23(3), 1985, 35-45.

Stigler, G. (1941): Production and Distribution Theories, New York, 1941.

Tassey, Gregory (1995): The roles of standards as technology infrastructure, in: Hawkins, R./Mansell, R./Skea, J. (eds.): Standards, Innovation and Competitiveness: The Politics and Economics of Standards in Natural and Technical Environments, Edward Elgar, 1995.

Taudes, A./Feurstein, M./Mild, A. (1999): How Option Thinking can Improve Software Platform Decisions. Working Paper Series Adaptive Informations Systems and Management in Economics and Management. Working Paper 38, May 1999.
http://www.wu-wien.ac.at/am/Download/wp38.ps.

Taudes, A./Feurstein, M./Mild, A. (2000): Options Analysis of Software Platform Decisions: A Case Study. In: MIS Quarterly, vol. 24/2, (June 2000).

Teece, D.J. (1987): Capturing value from technological innovation: Integration, strategic partnering, and licensing decisions, in: Guile, B.R./Brooks, H. (eds.): Technology and Global Industry: Companies and Nations in the World Economy, Washington, DC: National Academy Press, 1987.

Tesfatsion, L. (2002): Agent-based computational economics, http://www.econ.iastate.edu/tesfatsi/ace.htm.

Thum, M. (1995): Netzwerkeffekte, Standardisierung und staatlicher Regulierungsbedarf, Tübingen 1995.

Timmermans, S./Berg, M. (1997): Standardization in action: Achieving local universality through medical protocols, in: Social Studies of Science 27(2), 1997, 273-305.

Trebing, H.M. (1994): The networks as infrastructure: The reestablishment of market power, in: Journal of Economic Issues 28(2), 1994, 379-389.

Tucker, M. (1997): EDI and the Net: A profitable partnering; in: Datamation, April 1997, http://www.datamation.com/PlugIn/issues/1997/april/04e com.html.

Varian, H. (1989): What use is economic theory? Working Paper, School of Information Management and Systems, UCB 1989.

Varian, H. (1991): Grundzüge der Mikroökonomie (Intermediate Microeconomics). Deutsche Übersetzung der 2. Auflage von Reiner Buchegger, München; Wien; Oldenburg 1991.

Varian, H. (1994): A Solution to the Problem of Externalities When Agents are Well-Informed, in: American Economic Review, December 1994, 1278-93, also: Microeconomics/Economics Working Paper Archive at WUSTL, RePEc:wpa:wuwpmi:9401003.

Varian, H. (1997): Versioning information goods, working paper, March 1997, http://www.sims.berkeley.edu/~hal/Papers/version.pdf.

Varian, H. (1999): Market structure in the network age, working paper, April 1999, http://www.sims.berkeley.edu/~hal/Papers/doc/doc.html.

Varian, H. (2001): High-technology industries and market structure, working paper, July 2001, http://www.sims.berkeley.edu/~hal/Papers/structure.pdf.

Veblen, T.B. (1919): The Place of Science in Modern Civilisation and Other Essays, New York 1919.

Verman, L.C. (1973): Standardization - a new discipline, Hamden, Connecticut 1973.

Vriend, N. (1996): Rational Behavior and Economic Theory, Journal of Economic Behavior and Organization 29 (1996), 263-285.

290

Vriend, N. (1999): Was Hayek an ACE?, Working Paper 403, Queen Mary and Westfield College, University of London, UK, May 1999.

Waller, W.S./Bishop, R.A. (1990): An experimental study of incentive pay schemes, communication, and intrafirm resource allocation, in: The Accounting Review 1990, 812-836.

Walpuski, D. (1996): Die empirische Relevanz von Netzeffekten – eine industrieökonomische Analyse am Beispiel des Teletex-Dienstes, in: GfK Jahrbuch der Verbrauchsforschung, vol. 4/1996, 435-456.

Waltner, C. (1997): EDI Travels The Web - EDI over the Web offers companies cheaper E-commerce and messaging via browsers, in: Internetweek, Issue 668, June 16, 1997, http://www.techweb.com/se/directlink.cgi? CWK19970616S0066

Wärneryd, K. (1990): Economic conventions - essays in institutional evolution, dissertation, Stockholm 1990.

Warren, M.E./Warren, M. (1983): Baltimore - when she was what she used to be, 1850-1930, Baltimore: John Hopkins University Press.

Weber, S. (2000): Information technology in supplier networks: A theoretical approach to decisions about information technology and supplier relationships, Frankfurt 2000.

Weitzel, T./Buxmann, P./Kronenberg, R./Ladner, F. (1999): XML/EDI - the (r)evolution of EDI, Institute of Information Systems WP 99-10, http://www.wiwi.uni-frankfurt.de/~tweitzel/XMLEDI.doc.

Weitzel, T./Gellings, C./Beimborn, D./König, W. (2003): IS Valuation Methods - Insights from Capital Markets Theory and Practice, in: Proceedings of the Seventh Pacific-Asia Conference on Information Systems (PACIS'2003), Adelaide, Australia.

Weitzel, T./Harder, T./Buxmann, P. (2001): Electronic Business and EDI mit XML, Heidelberg 2001.

Weitzel, T./König, W. (2001a): Zwischenbetriebliche Kooperationen und elektronische Märkte, in: Frankfurter Allgemeine Zeitung (FAZ), 26.03.2001, 36.

Weitzel, T./König, W. (2001b): Strategien im M-Business: Kooperation oder Alleingang?, in: Frankfurter Allgemeine Zeitung (FAZ), 28.03.2001.

Weitzel, T./Wendt, O./Westarp, F.v. (2000): Reconsidering Network Effect Theory, in: Proceedings of the 8th European Conference on Information Systems (ECIS 2000), 484-491, http://www.wiwi.uni-frankfurt.de/~tweitzel/paper/reconsidering.pdf.

Weitzel, T./Wendt, O./Westarp, F.v. (2002): Modeling diffusion processes in networks, in: Geis/Koenig/Westarp (ed.): Networks - Standardization, Infrastructure, and Applications, Springer 2002, 3-31.

Wendt, O. (1995): Tourenplanung durch Einsatz naturanaloger Verfahren, Wiesbaden 1995.

Wendt, O./Westarp, F.v. (2000): Determinants of Diffusion in Network Effect Markets, SFB 403 Research Report, Frankfurt University, http://www.vernetzung.de/eng/b3.

Wendt, O./Westarp, F.v./König, W. (2000): Diffusionsprozesse in Märkten mit Netzeffekten, in: WIRTSCHAFTSINFORMATIK, 5/2000.

Westarp, F.v. (2003): Modeling Software Markets - Empirical Analysis, Network Simulations, and Marketing Implications, Dissertation, Frankfurt, Springer 2001.

Westarp, F.v./Buxmann, P./Weitzel, T./König, W. (1999): The Management of Software Standards in Enterprises - Results of an Empirical Study in Germany and the US, SFB 403 Working Paper, Frankfurt University, Jan. 1999, http://www.vernetzung.de/eng/b3.

Westarp, F.v./Weitzel, T./Buxmann, P./König, W. (1999): Innovationen im Bereich der B2B-Kommunikation - Fallstudien und technische Lösungen zu WebEDI, in: Steiner, M./Dittmar T./Willinsky, C.: Elektronische Dienstleistungsgesellschaft und Financial Engineering, 1999, 263-285.

Westarp, F.v./Weitzel, T./Buxmann, P./König, W. (1999): The Status Quo and the Future of EDI, in: Proceedings of the 1999 European Conference on Information Systems (ECIS'99).

Westarp, F.v./Weitzel, T./Buxmann, P./König, W. (2000): The Standardization Problem in Networks - A General Framework, in: Jakobs, K. (Hrsg.): Information Technology Standards and Standardization: A Global Perspective, 168-185.

292

Westarp, F.v./Weitzel, T./Klug, M./Buxmann, P./König, W. (2000): Einsatz betrieblicher Standardsoftware - Fallstudien in fünf deutschen Unternehmen, working paper SFB 403 AB-00-06.

Westarp, F.v./Weitzel, T./Putzke, D./Buxmann, P./König, W. (2000): EDI-Systeme bei der Lufthansa AG, SFB 403 AB-00-07.

Westarp, F.v./Wendt, O. (2000): Diffusion Follows Structure - A Network Model of the Software Market, in: Proceedings of the 33nd Hawaii International Conference on System Sciences (HICSS-33), 2000.

Wey, C. (1999): Marktorganisation durch Standardisierung: ein Beitrag zur Neuen Institutionenökonomik des Marktes, Berlin 1999.

Wiese, H. (1990): Netzeffekte und Kompatibilität, Stuttgart 1990.

Wiese, J. (2000): Implementierung der Balanced Scorecard. Grundlagen und IT-Fachkonzept. Dissertation, Wiesbaden 2000.

Williamson, O.E. (1985): The Economic Institutions of Capitalism, New York et al. 1985.

Williamson. O.E. (1993): Transaction cost economics and organization theory, in: Industrial and Corporate Change (2), 107-156.

Windfuhr, M. (1993): Fusion – Neuorganisation der Unternehmen und der Informationsverarbeitung bei der Fried. Krupp AG Hoesch Krupp, in: Wirtschaftsinformatik 35 (1993), 516-521.

WITSA (1998): Digital Planet, in: The Global Information Economy, Vol. 1, World Information Technology and Services Alliance (WITSA), http://www.witsa.org, Vienna.

Woeckener, B. (1996): Standardisierungspolitik für die Informationsgesellschaft, Jahrbücher für Nationalökonomik und Statistik vol. 215, 1996, 257-273.

Yang, Y. (1997): Essays on network effects, Dissertation, Department of Economics, Utah State University, Logan, Utah.

Young, A.A. (1913): Pigou's Wealth and Welfare. Quarterly Journal of Economics 27, 672-86.